D1457389

Merchant Mariners at War

New Perspectives on Maritime History and Nautical Archaeology

UNIVERSITY PRESS OF FLORIDA

Florida A&M University, Tallahassee
Florida Atlantic University, Boca Raton
Florida Gulf Coast University, Ft. Myers
Florida International University, Miami
Florida State University, Tallahassee
New College of Florida, Sarasota
University of Central Florida, Orlando
University of Florida, Gainesville
University of North Florida, Jacksonville
University of South Florida, Tampa
University of West Florida, Pensacola

SS Cape Cod—*First Convoy to Pass through Suez Canal When Re-opened, 1943,*
by Robert Glenn Smith. By permission of Robert Glenn Smith.

MERCHANT MARINERS AT WAR

AN ORAL HISTORY OF WORLD WAR II

George J. Billy and Christine M. Billy

Foreword by James C. Bradford and Gene Allen Smith

University Press of Florida

Gainesville/Tallahassee/Tampa/Boca Raton

Pensacola/Orlando/Miami/Jacksonville/Ft. Myers/Sarasota

Copyright 2008 by George J. Billy and Christine M. Billy
Printed in the United States of America. This book is printed on
Glatfelter Natures Book, a paper certified under the standards of the
Forestry Stewardship Council (FSC). It is a recycled stock that contains
30 percent post-consumer waste and is acid-free.

13 12 11 10 09 08   6 5 4 3 2 1

Library of Congress Cataloging-in-Publication Data
Merchant mariners at war : an oral history of World War II / [interviews
and editing] by George J. Billy and Christine M. Billy; foreword by
James C. Bradford and Gene Allen Smith.
p. cm.—(New perspectives on maritime history and nautical
archaeology)
Includes bibliographical references and index.
ISBN 978-0-8130-3246-7 (alk. paper)
1. World War, 1939-1945—Transportation—United States. 2. World
War, 1939-1945—Naval operations, American. 3. World War, 1939-
1945—Personal narratives, American. 4. Merchant marine—United
States—History—20th century. 5. Merchant mariners—United States—
Interviews. I. Billy, George J., 1940- II. Billy, Christine M.
D810.T8M395 2008
940.54'59730922—dc22   2008008250

The University Press of Florida is the scholarly publishing agency
for the State University System of Florida, comprising Florida A&M
University, Florida Atlantic University, Florida Gulf Coast University,
Florida International University, Florida State University, New College
of Florida, University of Central Florida, University of Florida,
University of North Florida, University of South Florida, and
University of West Florida.

University Press of Florida
15 Northwest 15th Street
Gainesville, FL 32611-2079
http://www.upf.com

CONTENTS

FOREWORD

Water is unquestionably the most important natural feature on earth. By volume, the world's oceans compose 99 percent of the planet's living space; in fact, the surface of the Pacific Ocean alone is larger than that of the total land bodies. Water is as vital to life as air. Indeed, to test whether the moon or other planets can sustain life, NASA looks for signs of water. The story of human development is inextricably linked to the oceans, seas, lakes, and rivers that dominate the earth's surface. The University Press of Florida's series New Perspectives on Maritime History and Nautical Archaeology is devoted to exploring the significance of the earth's water while providing lively and important books that cover the spectrum of maritime history and nautical archaeology broadly defined. The series includes works that focus on the role of canals, rivers, lakes, and oceans in history; on the economic, military, and political use of those waters; and upon the people, communities, and industries that support maritime endeavors. Limited by neither geography nor time, volumes in the series contribute to the overall understanding of maritime history and can be read with profit by both general readers and specialists.

Waterborne transport was never more vital than during World War II, and men serving in the merchant marine suffered a higher rate of casualties, one in twenty-six, than in any other service during that global conflict. Despite these facts, few Americans know of the service and sacrifice of the merchant mariners who transported vital supplies from the United States, the "Arsenal of Democracy," to Allied forces around the world. The immense increase in shipping that began with the introduction of Lend-Lease in March 1941 led to the establishment of the United States Merchant Marine Academy to train officers for the merchant service. *Merchant Mariners at War* provides a window through which to view the lives of these officers by making available edited transcripts of fifty-nine graduates from the U.S. Merchant Marine Academy classes 1940–46. When George J. Billy conducted the interviews, he asked each man three questions: (1) What recollections do you have of your days as a cadet? (2) What were your most memorable wartime experiences? and (3) What significance did the American merchant marine play during World War II?

The responses from those interviewed reveal the harsh shipboard conditions that men endured while transporting desperately needed food, weapons, and supplies to North Africa, Europe, and the South and Central Pacific. The experiences related by the men interviewed, both in the merchant marine and the U.S. Navy, also offer a startling view of the young cadet-midshipmen and officers who sailed in all theaters of military action: the Battle of the Atlantic, the Murmansk run, the vast Pacific, as well as in the Indian Ocean and Mediterranean Sea carrying all types of cargo. They all suffered the constant threat of sinking ships and death at sea. Some merchant mariners suffered inhumane conditions in Japanese prisoner of war camps. Others survived harrowing ordeals only to realize that they had been the lucky ones—they had returned home.

In 1990, George Billy began conducting audio and video interviews of World War II–era alumni of the U.S. Merchant Marine Academy. Along with Christine Billy, he selected and edited the contributions for this volume. Not all of the interviews conducted for the project are included in the volume, but those selected clearly convey a sense of the substantial contributions made by those unsung veterans during the conflict. At its basic level, this book is a collection of firsthand accounts of merchant mariners during World War II. It is also a story of introspective growth and maturation, memory, and an account of survival against the enemy and the elements of nature. This is the story of modest, too often forgotten, veterans who braved hostile elements and an unforgiving enemy, believing throughout that they were simply doing their job, doing what was expected of them. In effect, this book provides another important perspective on the contributions of the men who truly delivered the equipment and supplies that made it possible for the "greatest generation" to succeed.

James C. Bradford and Gene Allen Smith
Series Editors

INTRODUCTION

During World War II, the U.S. Merchant Marine Academy at Kings Point was a beehive of activity. Through its federal training program, Kings Point graduated more than six thousand students in a feverish effort to provide badly needed officers for merchant ships.[1] Yet, few Kings Pointers have told their story. The present volume seeks to redress this omission by providing the oral histories of wartime graduates. The result is a vivid picture of vulnerable ships and dedicated merchant mariners facing the perils of the open sea and of armed conflict. However, before the Kings Pointers relate their experiences, some background information is useful.

Under normal conditions, the U.S. merchant marine could be defined as the privately owned and run merchant fleet of working ships, which carried cargoes to and from the United States and throughout the world. Although U.S. statutes and regulations governed commercial activities, for the most part American merchant ships plied the seas relatively unfettered, and tramp steamers, for example, would travel wherever profits could be made. Similarly, seamen's unions usually filled the merchant ship crews, again relatively unhindered by regulations. Men could sign on to whatever ships were available, and could go wherever the sea lanes led. The hard times of the Great Depression of the 1930s proved to be the most formidable barrier to pursuing a livelihood at sea. As war clouds gathered on the horizon during the last half of the 1930s, this image of merchant shipping changed with new regulations, and President Franklin Roosevelt signed into existence two major neutrality laws in 1935 and 1937. The laws were the first steps that the United States took in response to the growing possibility of widespread conflict, and the initial concern was to keep America out of war. When U.S. involvement became a distinct possibility, Roosevelt attempted to modify the laws in order to facilitate trade with probable allies, particularly Britain. However, the end result was that no longer could American merchant ships go anywhere unharmed. A total of six U.S. flagships were sunk due to war-related causes between September 1, 1939, when war broke out in Europe, and America's entry into the world war on December 7, 1941.[2]

The plunge into war that occurred with the Japanese attack on Pearl Harbor drastically transformed the merchant marine. Total war called for a massive logistical program the likes of which the world had not seen previously. The U.S. merchant marine was shaped into an integral part of a grand strategy of fighting a war on several fronts and, at the same time, supplying America's allies throughout the world. No longer solely private-sector undertakings, American merchant ship operation, construction, and manning now reflected cooperation among federal regulators, naval strategists, and the traditional private-sector components. That is, although overall control of the merchant marine was ceded to the U.S. Maritime Commission and, later, the War Shipping Administration, the advantages and incentives inherent in a system of free enterprise were retained. As agents of the federal government, ship operators were provided with contracts and incentives to operate the ships in combat zones. Shipyards retained their personnel while contracting with the government to build an expanded fleet of ships, and, instead of being absorbed into the Navy, the labor unions were allowed to retain their identities as the major suppliers of merchant marine crews. This unique blend of general government supervision and private enterprise had telling effects in the massive expansion of the U.S. merchant marine and in the ultimate Allied victory in World War II.[3]

Even before America's entry into the conflict, American military planners had chosen a British design for constructing a new cargo vessel, the Liberty ship. At the outset of the war, German U-boats sank American merchant ships at an alarming rate, and the federal government embarked on a crash program to build more Liberty ships than the enemy could sink. American shipyards responded with the rapid construction of prefabricated Liberty ships, many completed in forty days. The rapid construction of a wartime fleet of Liberty ships is now legendary. Over 2,700 Liberty ships were built during the war, and they became the workhorses of the American merchant marine in World War II. A total of two hundred Liberty ships were lost while delivering war supplies, including fifty Liberty ships sunk on their maiden voyages.[4] Numerous Kings Pointers sailed aboard these sturdy vessels, and many describe their experiences in this volume.

Along with the need for more ships was the need for many more merchant marine officers. Fortunately, the concept of a federal training program for merchant marine officers was contemplated well before the outbreak of hostilities. When fire gutted the cruise ship *Morro Castle* in 1934, just six miles off the New Jersey coast, with a major loss of lives, the U.S. Congress was prompted to draw up legislation aimed at instituting better safety measures aboard ship, and for establishing a formal government-supervised program for training ships' officers. The result was the Merchant Marine Act of 1936, the basis for the training.

Originally conceived as a four-year program, the federal training was initially aboard merchant ships, and the students were inducted into the U.S. Merchant Marine Cadet Corps, established in 1938. Correspondence courses and shipboard instruction prepared the cadets to undergo a comprehensive U.S. Coast Guard test for ship's officer. Upon passing the test, the cadet was issued a license as third mate or third assistant engineer. The third mate's duties as "deck officer" involved the navigation, steering, and berthing of a vessel. On the other hand, the third assistant engineer helped in operating the ship's propulsion and other power systems.[5]

The entry of the United States into World War II served as a catalyst for establishing land-based training centers for merchant marine officers. By the end of 1942, the government had designated Kings Point, New York, as the ultimate central site for training prior to sitting for the merchant marine license. The school was formally dedicated as the United States Merchant Marine Academy on September 30, 1943, but instruction was under way at Kings Point as of January 1942. Two additional "feeder" schools for initial training were founded at Pass Christian, Mississippi, and at San Mateo, California. Kings Point, Pass Christian, and San Mateo would be entry points for the training, but the final instruction was at Kings Point. Subsequently, all the members enrolled in the federal Cadet Corps since 1938 have taken on the designation of Kings Pointers.[6]

With the United States in the war, the originally envisioned four-year training program was compressed into sixteen months, and was subject to modifications in detail throughout the war. There was a three-part program of instruction. The first phase was basic training, which usually lasted ten to twelve weeks. In this first phase, students received instruction in fundamental seamanship, basic navigation or mechanical engineering, naval training (including gunnery), and lifeboat training. The cadet program was centered on regimental life, which included military bearing and marching in military formation (drill). At Kings Point, the more colorful aspects of training were the vessels used for instruction, which included the *Emery Rice*, a three-masted bark that was originally a naval ship, the USS *Ranger*. Several subjects included in the prewar plan of instruction, such as English and history, were discarded as a matter of necessity in the push to man the Liberty ships with officers.[7]

Many of the experiences related in this volume occurred during the second phase of training, the sea year. After undergoing preliminary training at Kings Point, Pass Christian, or San Mateo, the cadet was assigned to a merchant ship for hands-on training at sea. Here was the dangerous part. Often sent out in pairs (deck and engine), the students usually trained aboard a Liberty ship, where they were an integral part of the crew and, in hostilities, the defense of the ship. Many civilian ships had military personnel aboard, known as the Naval Armed Guard, and trainees were expected to assist them. Students traveled into war zones, and the risks of encounters with the enemy were often present. Indeed, the dual status of trainees as both merchant marine cadets and Naval Reserve officers was defined in a War Shipping Administration circular dated November 1, 1942. Approved by Acting Secretary of the Navy James Forrestal, and signed by the judge advocate general of the Navy, the term "cadet-midshipmen" was applied to all members of the U.S. Merchant Marine Cadet Corps. They were declared part of the Merchant Marine Reserve, which, according to the circular, was part of the U.S. Naval Reserve.[8] This was a significant document. It clearly designated the cadet-midshipmen as part of the naval personnel aboard civilian merchant ships. The present volume of interviews includes those of cadet-midshipmen who actively defended their ships. Cadet-midshipmen would bring ammunition to the Naval Armed Guardsmen and, at times, operate weapons. Their gunnery training before going to sea was more than a mere formality.

Sea-year training was officially set for six months, but the requirements of war frequently kept them ocean borne for longer periods of time, some for more than a year before returning to Kings Point. Along with the hands-on training, the trainees were ordered to fulfill sea-project assignments, which were major written reports reflecting what had been learned either on deck or in the engine room. Today, Kings Point undergraduates still go to sea, even in war zones, and they still must complete sea projects. In fact, Kings Point is the only federal academy permitted to fly a battle standard in recognition of the sea-year training, which can include actual military operations.[9]

When cadet-midshipmen returned to the United States Merchant Marine Academy at Kings Point, they embarked on a rigorous period of final instruction, which usually lasted approximately thirty weeks. They steeped themselves in advanced courses concerning deck or engine operations. The expectation was that, upon graduation, they were qualified to be ships' officers and were deemed ready to take the U.S. Coast Guard license for either third mate or third assistant engineer. For this final period of training, as well as for the entire process, variations in time frame occurred. Much depended upon a student's training and sea experience prior to enrolling in the federal program. In addition, extra time at sea during the sea year could alter the training period. Another factor also came into play. As the need for more merchant marine officers became apparent, the courses took a pragmatic turn and were stripped to their essentials to accommodate the swelled ranks of cadet-midshipmen at Kings Point, Pass Christian, San Mateo, and at sea. During its most accelerated period, total enrollment jumped from 4,658 on January 1, 1943, to 7,338 as of July 1, 1943.[10] By this time, Kings Point had become the major supplier of merchant marine officers.

In the interviews, a number of Kings Pointers spoke of cramped conditions and the expedient nature of training. In addition, as cadet-midshipmen returned from the sea year with tales of U-boat attacks and aircraft bombings, the seriousness of the training took hold. Upon passing the license, the Kings Pointer was considered a finished officer and ready to go back to sea. Most of them did. They joined the ranks of new merchant marine officers trained at other centers, such as the state maritime academy at Fort Schuyler, New York, and those seamen who, while at sea, rose through the "hawespipe" (the various grade levels of sea service). In addition, federal training sites, such as at Hoffman Island, New York, turned out personnel for other positions aboard ship, such as radio operator.[11] The maritime unions retained their role as providers of seamen.

Wherever the U.S. military forces went, so did the civilian merchant marine, bringing the necessary supplies that tipped the balance in favor of Allied success. In the Battle of the Atlantic, the U.S. merchant marine held center stage. German military strategists recognized that they had to isolate and starve Britain into submission if the war was to be won. Even before the U.S. entry into the war, the commander of Germany's U-boat fleet, Admiral Karl Doenitz, authorized attacks on American merchantmen in a *guerre de course* (commerce war). Franklin Roosevelt and Winston Churchill realized the threat. They agreed that the highest priority would be to secure the freedom of Europe. Maintaining the merchant marine supply line to Britain was deemed vital as a first step toward wresting the Continent from German occupation. Toward this end, Allied planners believed that they would succeed if they could build and send to Britain more merchant ships than the U-boats could sink. Hence, a major impetus for the rapid expansion in Liberty ship construction and the training of merchant marine personnel, including at Kings Point, emanated from the objective of overwhelming the U-boats with a continuous stream of merchant ships traversing the Atlantic. The lines of conflict were drawn.[12] Numerous interviews in this volume describe the tensions inherent in the Atlantic passage of the Liberty ships.

During the early years of the war, the German U-boat commanders had a relatively easy pick of targets. Patrolling off the east coast, German submarines torpedoed American merchantmen. At this early stage in the war, the merchant ships were often unescorted, and the convoy system had not reached its full potential. At night, silhouettes of American ships stood out in bold relief as the hapless vessels passed before well-lighted eastern coastal cities. Curfews were not in practice. The U-boats seized the opportunity to sink ships up and down the coast and in the Gulf of Mexico. This early period was a happy time for the German submarine commanders.[13] They were impeding Allied plans for saving Britain and winning back Europe.

By 1943, however, the tide was changing. The U.S. Navy, along with British and Canadian warships, escorted American and Allied ships across the Atlantic. In addition to sheer determination, a number of developments accelerated the successful passage to Britain. In particular, American airplanes flying off the decks of "jeep carriers," small Navy aircraft carriers, hunted down the U-boats. The interview with Richard Kelahan demonstrates the operations of the hunter aircraft carriers. Even at night, the aircraft could employ strong searchlights to spot the U-boats and bomb those caught on the surface. The gap midway across the Atlantic, normally beyond the range of land-based planes, was no longer a safe haven for the German submarines. In addition, the capture of German codebooks enabled Allied military personnel to decipher enemy orders sent to the German submarines. Armed with notification of impending wolf pack attacks, defensive measures were taken. By 1943, as discussed in chapter 4, merchant marine and Navy tacticians had developed a convoy system that protected most ships in the moving fleet of merchantmen. Nevertheless, Admiral Doenitz's U-boats continued to sink American ships until the war's end. The merchant mariner was never completely out of harm's way.[14]

In peacetime, Mediterranean ports of call, such as Casablanca and Oran, would conjure up exotic images for the merchant mariner. However, during the Second World War, the ports were fraught with danger. Trips to the Mediterranean involved not only the possibility of U-boat attacks on the way, but, when berthed, the risk of strafing and bombing from the Luftwaffe. German aircraft stationed in Italy would make daring runs across the water in a desperate attempt to check the advance of U.S. and Allied forces in North Africa. Kings Pointers relate in this volume the terrors of aircraft attacks. In North Africa, and later in Italy, the merchant ships were key providers of tanks and other wheeled vehicles, as well as the aircraft, which pushed back German and Italian forces. The Mediterranean campaign was originally conceived as a means of opening up a second front, thus relieving the Russians in the East. It turned into an unforeseen ordeal for the merchant mariners, as well as the military personnel.[15]

For Kings Pointers who sailed on the Murmansk run, their trips will be forever planted in their memories. Their interviews form a special chapter of wartime hell. Frigid waters and foul weather, coupled with the dangers of German attacks from both air- and seacraft, challenged these men of the sea with an unrivaled severity. Yet, the materiel delivered was essential. The trucks, locomotives, and other equipment, brought to the ports of Murmansk and Archangel, were shipped to the Russians in order to keep open the Eastern Front.

The irony of the Murmansk run was that the merchant ships were, themselves, the object of battle. As in the Atlantic, German strategists recognized that the Russian war effort was substantially aided by the ships traveling to North Russia. The losses of Convoy PQ-17 illustrate the dangers under which American and allied crews labored. Of the thirty-three ships that embarked for Russia, a total of twenty-four were sunk. As a trainee aboard the Liberty ship *John Witherspoon* in Convoy PQ-17, Arthur Erb relates how, as a cadet-midshipman on his sea year, he had to twice abandon ship on the same voyage. Other Kings Pointers also describe their Russian ordeals.[16]

The cataclysmic event of the D-Day invasion of June 6, 1944, provides an apt example of the close association between the Navy and the merchant marine that the circumstances of war dictated. Among the ships of the Allied armada were Liberty ships with officers trained at Kings Point, including Walter Botto and Edwin Kaminski, who relate their D-Day experiences in this book. The Normandy beachhead and the push inland from the French coast were greatly aided by the troops and materiel ferried over by the merchant marine.

Wartime conditions for the merchant marine in the Pacific Ocean differed from the Atlantic. Although the risk of going into harm's way was substantial, the vastness of the Pacific Ocean allowed American merchant ships to, so to speak, "get lost." It was possible to avoid most Japanese submarines and airplanes by taking southerly routes to Australia and the war fronts. Except for approaching battle areas, naval escorts were deemed unnecessary. Also, unlike the German submarine command, Japanese naval strategists never fully recognized the need to stem the flow of supplies to the various areas of conflict. Whereas German submarines eagerly hunted merchant ships, Japanese submarine commanders preferred to attack U.S. Navy ships. In contrast to the Atlantic, in the Pacific it was American submarines that preyed upon Japanese merchant ships. The Japanese were tardy in developing convoys. American submarines ultimately sank 55 percent of Japanese merchant fleet tonnage.[17]

As the merchant ships entered the immediate areas of combat, the possibility of Japanese aircraft bombing and strafing increased significantly. As the interviews reveal, Kings Pointers and their fellow mariners found themselves in the thick of action. They would operate anti-aircraft weapons and struggle to douse fires aboard the ships. In addition, several interviews given by Kings Pointers in the U.S. Navy describe the unnerving kamikaze attacks that greeted U.S. Navy forces as they advanced toward the Japanese home islands. In particular, Rear Admiral Carl Seiberlich related the tenacity with which Japanese fliers attempted to defend Japan.[18]

Ports in the Indian Ocean offered a unique advantage. They were supply points for combating both Germany and Japan. Because Russia's need for equipment was so acute, and the Murmansk run so perilous, a second portal to Russia was opened at Khorramshahr, Iran. Materiel off-loaded at Khorramshahr was sent north into the Soviet Union, for the Eastern Front. In contrast to North Russia, the warm-water Iranian port permitted commerce year-round. Similarly, British and American forces drew upon supplies delivered to Indian ports for use in the Burma campaign. Japanese attempts to sink merchant ship traffic in the Indian Ocean marked trouble for the mariner. As Peter Van der Linde describes, Japanese submarines would torpedo merchant ships that crossed their paths. Unpredictable weather conditions added to the strain of possible attack.[19]

The basis for this volume has been the Academy library's Mariners at War Project at Kings Point. Since 1990, numerous Kings Pointers have related their wartime stories on audio- and videotapes. They are maintained at the Academy library. The experiences that the mariners have described constitute a basic part of the record of the Second World War. The method of the interviews was designed to allow the Kings Pointers to tell their own stories. Three main questions were asked: what recollections do you have of your days as a cadet, what were your most memorable wartime experiences, and what thoughts do you have concerning the significance of the U.S. Merchant Marine in the Second World War? As the Kings Pointers replied, other questions arose, and the information flowed freely.

Whether in the merchant marine or the Navy, certain general features characterized the experiences of the Kings Point veterans interviewed. No matter how unique or dangerous their wartime assignments, Kings Pointers did not regard their travails as worthy of special attention. Time after time, the veterans expressed the feeling that they were simply doing what was expected. Many mariners braved extraordinary dangers with little or no protection. Yet, they consistently stated that they were only doing their duty. As with most veterans from World War II, Kings Pointers sincerely believed they were doing their part to defend their country and, indeed, the free world.

Another characteristic evident from the interviews was that as youths, usually eighteen to twenty-one years of age, they were quite willing to sail into risky situations, even after seeing military action and witnessing the loss of close friends. A total of 142 cadet-midshipmen died in action before graduating. One mariner summed up the feelings of many Kings Pointers when he said those being interviewed believed they were the lucky ones; they had returned home. Altogether, over two hundred thousand men served in the U.S. merchant marine during the war, and an estimated seven thousand were killed.[20]

It was the firm conviction of all the veterans interviewed that the U.S. merchant marine was vital to victory in World War II. Several mariners described their participation in huge convoys of fifty to one hundred ships, bringing desperately needed materiel to American and Allied forces. Kings Pointers were involved in all theaters of military operation. Unfortunately, two factors have militated against the revelation of the achievements of these veterans: their own modesty and a historic prejudice against merchant marine veterans. At the time, the fundamental nature of their contribution—mainly conveying vital supplies for the combat forces—had been largely taken for granted. Looking back at history, one shudders to think what would have happened if American merchant mariners had not delivered their cargoes. Thankfully, as the following interviews vividly recount, Kings Point veterans did not fail to make their contribution to the war effort. They delivered!

AROUND THE WORLD

Whether they were cadet-midshipmen or graduates, many Kings Pointers traveled to more than one theater of military operations. Their ships went wherever men and materials were needed, and by war's end it was not unusual for a Kings Point mariner to have sailed all over the world. The following interviews convey a sense of the assignments that drove Kings Pointers over the seven seas.

Captain Edwin C. Kaminski, Class of 1940

Captain Kaminski maintains he had a lucky career in World War II, even though circumstances put him in harm's way on several occasions. His luck in historical situations continued after the war. He was skipper of a ship that ferried some of the first French troops to Indochina (Vietnam), and he was a captain in training on the maiden voyage of the NS *Savannah*, America's first commercial nuclear ship. He has also sailed on container ships.

Please describe your maritime training and experiences during World War II.

On December 7, 1941, I was on a ship called SS *Exceller*. The ship was manned by a merchant crew. We had ninety-nine Coast Guardsmen on board to handle the cargo operations and run the landing craft ashore. We also had a full gun crew. I had been promoted to deck officer, third mate, with American Export Lines. We had been loaded with full cargo for the Far East to ports in Calcutta and Rangoon. On arrival in Rangoon, we found the country had been pretty well taken over by the Japanese. We managed to evade some of the Japanese submarines and their warships, but there was no point in discharging our cargo. We had the choice of either trying to run the blockade at the mouth of the Rangoon River or going overland with General Stilwell. The captain had a fast ship. The *Exceller* could make 25 knots. He was quite sure we were going to be fortunate. We managed to get out to the mouth of the Rangoon River and outrun the submarines.

Then we went to Calcutta. Meanwhile, we picked up about twelve American civilians from Rangoon. It was supposed to be in support of General Stilwell's operation, but at that time he was retreating overland from Rangoon along the Burma Road. We discharged all our cargo in Madras and Calcutta, then returned home to take on another load.

At that point, we were assigned to the convoy going into Algiers, North Africa. We fitted out the ship for five or six hundred troops, but we had to take a few more because the emergency of the situation required it. We landed our troops east of Cape Matifou, which is just at the eastern side of Algiers, on the North African coast.

There the Germans had a battery of guns that could have easily knocked us out of the water. Thankfully, the forces ashore managed to still those guns. They were operational, but they were in the hands of our friendly forces, the French. They called them Partisans. After we landed, all our troops were there, and we were discharging our cargo. The bombers came in and hit quite a few ships. Two bombs straddled our ship, picked it up out of the water, and broke the stern frame. But we didn't sink, and we didn't sustain any injuries. We were fortunate. That was November 8 or 9, 1942. We also had a torpedo plane drop a torpedo, which was directed right at the side of the ship where we had about three hundred tons of ammunition. I watched that torpedo come right at the ship and break at the surface. A wave just managed to turn it a little bit, so it clanged along the side of the ship, and went over and hit another ship and sank it. So I was lucky.

Then we came back to Gibraltar. We had repaired enough on the ship so that we could continue to Glasgow, Scotland. We got further repaired in Glasgow and then came back to New York. It was very unpleasant weather, but we managed to make it. Because we were damaged, it took us twenty-one days to cross. We couldn't go at full speed. We had to go at "not in excess of two-thirds speed." We laid in a New York shipyard to have things put together on the ship, so we could operate again. Next, the ship was assigned to take troops to Bombay. We made one more trip.

See chapter 8, for Ed Kaminski's role in the D-Day operation.

John K. (Jack) Sweeney, Class of 1944

Growing up near Lake Michigan, Jack Sweeney was drawn from an early age to ships and the sea. Joining the merchant marine was a natural for Sweeney. Mr. Sweeney states, "When I moved to Chicago in 1937, I had joined a boat club, and Lake Michigan had a very good influence on my love of water and possibly thinking of being on the ship in any capacity, preferably deck, of course." After the war, he worked as a chief engineer for the Keller Crescent Company; he is now retired.

After preliminary training, did you go on a sea training trip prior to sitting for your license?

Oh, yes, we had a manual that we had to take with us on the ship. And I was out for not a very long time, probably five or six months. I was assigned to the *Fairland*, which belonged to the Waterman Steamship Line. It was a C2, and it had a turbine. Because it had a turbine, there were four engine cadets, and one deck cadet.

It was quite an experience. Hoboken [New Jersey] was about the spookiest place I've ever been. And that's where the ship was. I just expected anything to spring out at me, and I said: "Well gee, wouldn't Chicago be nice right now? How did I ever get into this?"

There's a funny story. Back in Hoboken somebody approached me, not really approached me, but he saw me coming and he said, "You going on that ship over there?" And I took one look at him and I said, "Yes." And he said, "You'll be in Avonmouth in twenty-two days." And I said, "My God." We saw all these films, you know, the captain swallows the orders, and it's just something that is unheard of. This guy can't be right. And when we hit Avonmouth in twenty-two days, it was almost too much for me. I couldn't believe it. I wished I bet some money on it. It's not to make fun of, but it shows don't ever underestimate a person by his clothes or his status. He may know a lot more than you, that's for sure. The trip back we ran light, and it wasn't too bad. The length of time was almost the same. I don't think we had the same ships, but we had some slow ones.

We went on our first trip across the North Atlantic in a convoy. It was a very slow convoy. I think it took twenty-two days to get over there. We docked at Avonmouth, which was near Bristol [England]. We were carrying troops in between decks—not too many, but they were there. From what I could gather, there were some shells. I don't think that we could be classified as an ammunition ship with the troops being in there. I think that the danger wasn't that great because of the troops being in there. I don't know exactly. I think they had some tanks in the bottom, the larger hold. We had five holds altogether, three fore and two aft. It was one of the designs that came out in 1936 in the Maritime Commission. It was a beautiful ship. It could travel 17 knots, but in convoy, 8 or 9 knots.

I'd say about eighty ships in the convoy, if I'm not mistaken. This was 1943. We were escorted by Canadian corvettes. The only thing we ever saw where there might have been trouble, the corvette was right out there with a searchlight and everything. We thought the iceberg was more of a threat than anything else.

The convoy broke up one time in fog. They had a unique system. If you were third ship in the first column, you'd blow your whistle once a minute, one blast, then the second ship would blow one blast and then two blasts. And you'd hear these whistles all around you.

The corvettes were like mother hens; they were just going around. These corvettes, by the way, I don't know how people ever lived on them. I think that if you had wet grass out there, they would roll in it. They just plowed on. They were steamships to begin with. I went aboard one after we got to Avonmouth, and these guys had all their bedding out, everything. They just lived in misery. I mean water was just slopping around the gangways and everything. I give them a lot of credit. There were a lot of people out there I give a lot of credit to.

Did you use a zigzag pattern at all or were you traveling across?

Not in the convoy, no.

The second trip took us around the world. Because of the conditions up at Murmansk [North Russia], they were starting to send ships down to the Persian Gulf and up to Iran, where we ended up in Khorramshahr on that trip. We had the deck cargo of planes there and crates. And they had oil. They had some mechanized equipment that I never really saw. They loaded it in the dark and at night. It was just combat equipment, pretty heavy stuff. They used a fifty-ton boom, and then they even came over and had a heavier crane to get some of the equipment off. It was the same ship, *Fairland*. From there we left for Philadelphia. We went from New York to Philadelphia. And from there, we went through the Panama Canal and we went across the South Pacific. Then we came to Fremantle, Western Australia, which is near Perth.

Did you go very far south on that trip to Fremantle?

Yes, we went down in what they called the "roaring forties."[1] We were down there to avoid hostilities. We didn't see a ship or a plane in I think it was around thirty-two days. We zigzagged a little on that one. Again, planes were on the deck. There was about eleven thousand tons of cargo. We had troops again. I'm sure that time we had shells down there. Now they must have been taken apart when they shipped them because they didn't seem to consider the cargo dangerous. The only time we were in convoy on that trip was after we left Australia.

We went off to the Persian Gulf, and we were in a convoy there. And we went up the Shattal al Arab River to Khorramshahr. We were there about ten to fourteen days, I imagine. They had these Iranians unloading with troops from an American quartermaster company. They would warehouse the stuff, and then when the truck convoy was ready, they'd take it over the Ural Mountains into Russia. Probably into the Ukraine, I don't know what countries.

It was very dangerous. The Iranians told us not to go ashore alone. It wasn't a matter of money; it was a matter of your shoes or whatever you had on. They even were so bold as to attack the convoy one time. They found the Army driver, minus his shoes, killed. Local residents, so many of them were nomadic. They were merely down there for the money. They moved around according to the season, if it got too hot, which I considered very hot 135 [degrees] in the shade. You could take a T-shirt and wash it and in ten minutes it was dry. And you'd burn your hands going down to the engine room on the rails. That's a nice trick; try doing that sometime. There were physical hardships, but we could still take showers. We weren't like the Army over there, especially infantry. I still have respect for the people that fought in the infantry because of their harsh conditions. We had showers. We had a lot of things. We had danger. I don't want to understate that.

Did you have any alerts for aircraft or any alerts for submarines that might have been sighted?

There was supposed to have been an incident down in the Caribbean; I don't know who saw it, but there was a sub on the surface. They were probably charging their batteries, but they dove. And somebody said we might have hit it. But if we had hit a submarine, I think we would have had a badly damaged bow. I don't think we could have continued.

After the sea duty of about five months, we were here [Kings Point] I imagine at least nine months. The sea project had to be in. It had to be done. And they gave us an immediate leave. On the ship, I was under a—I'll say the polite word—British master. It wasn't a lot of things, come to think of it. I guess I was on there to be like the old cabin boy of the sailing ships. That's the feeling I had. He was sort of an intimidating person, and he'd yell "k-deck" and you'd jump almost out of your shoes. We didn't mop the slop room right.

He had a cuspidor I had to clean, and I got rid of that thing in New York Harbor when we returned. That was a ceremony. I just heaved the thing. I never heaved a thing so far in my life. It was the most disgusting job I ever had to do in my life, but I guess that's all par for the course at that time. I heard all about the British Army and how he came up through all this hawsepipe and didn't have any of that darn book learning. I listened to a lot. I wouldn't listen to it today. I'd get up and walk out, but that's the privilege of old age and wisdom.

After sitting for your license, was the war still on?

Oh yes, it was '44, June of '44.

After graduation from Kings Point in 1944, Jack Sweeney continued to sail.

Captain George M. Marshall, Class of 1942

George Marshall's grandfather was an American shipmaster, and during World War II young George Marshall, at age twenty-four, achieved his goal of emulating his grandfather's achievement. With the end of the war and a subsequent marriage, he remarks, "I commenced a twenty-nine-year career with the Atlantic Mutual Insurance, which is a notable maritime insurance company."

I served as a deck cadet on ships operated by three shipping companies from August 1938 until January 3, 1942.

What was life as a cadet like at that time?

My first voyage, right after Pearl Harbor, was on the SS *Exchange*. We were very unprepared for this. The only armaments we had on the *Exchange* were two Browning machine guns mounted on the boat deck, left over from World War I. That was the only armament we had. And this was a very, very modern ship in comparative terms. It was one of the fastest single-screw steam-turbine ships in any merchant marine at that time. So we could travel alone and didn't have to be in convoy. We had a zigzag course to follow. We didn't have any problem proceeding alone during those early years of war, even though most of the sinkings that occurred at that time were torpedoings off of the east coast of the United States. During that period, because of our speed, we were safer than most ships. The ships that were being torpedoed were mostly the old tonnage and those ships that were not in convoy.

We didn't really have gun crews at that time. Merchant crews were trained on how to operate these old Browning machine guns. Subsequently, the ships were armed with a 5-inch on the stern and a 3-inch gun on the forward deck. They had four, what they called 20mm Oerlikons, rapid-fire guns. Then they started to train gun crews. They had to put quarters on to accommodate them under the command of a U.S. naval officer.

There were some early problems. When they began the program, some of the naval officers felt they were in command of the ship. So there was conflict between the master of the ship and merchant crews and the gun crews. But then the Navy, I think, saw through the problem and started to assign officers who were more people-oriented and who could accommodate themselves to the merchant ship situation. When I was master, I made an effort to cultivate a relationship with the gunnery officers so that the men below would see that we got along together, and we had a very cooperative arrangement. The merchant crews were getting bonuses, and the gun crews were all serving on very low pay scales. At the end of a voyage, the merchant crew would "pass the hat," drop money in the hat and then distribute it amongst the men serving in the gun crew.

The whole thing bothered me because we had in a very small confined area two standards of discipline. We had the merchant marine standard of discipline, controlled by the Coast Guard, and we had the U.S. Navy standard of discipline. That always bothered me, and I said, "That's no way to run a war." I think the problem was that the merchant marine was expanding so rapidly at that time, it was hard to find civilian crews. They were pulling men off the street that hadn't gone to sea for years. I had a second officer who was a man in his late fifties, who was a graduate of the naval academy in Russia. He was what they call a White Russian, who had escaped through China and had come to the United States. He was given a license, and I had him on my ship, SS *Charles Carroll*, as a second mate.

James H. Ackerman, Class of 1944

Hailing from Long Beach, California, Jim Ackerman displayed a fondness for the sea at a very early age. As a youngster he frequently sailed small boats back and forth to Catalina, California. In the postwar years, he pursued a very successful career as a West Coast attorney. During the Korean War, Jim Ackerman again sailed for fourteen months in the merchant marine in supply runs between Japan and Korea. Cordial in manner, throughout his career Ackerman never forgot his early Kings Point education, and he has been a generous benefactor of the Academy.

I'm from the Los Angeles, California, area and Long Beach specifically, a port town. I've sailed out of there a lot on small boats and yachts, back and forth to Catalina and that, so that sort of created a desire in me for the sea. This was sometime before the war. My formal training was at Kings Point, the Academy. This was during the war, and the total time had been practically cut in half. This was in the early days of the Academy, so we took our training at basics school first and then went to sea. Because the war was on they couldn't govern the time you were at sea; you didn't know. I had an extraordinarily long time at sea. I left Los Angeles on a Liberty ship just out of the Kaiser yards and ended up in New York in a one-way around-the-world voyage sixteen months later.

The name of the ship was the *Rachel Jackson*. She was President Andrew Jackson's wife. The first port was Sydney, Australia, and one of the cargoes was beer. I guess that's a necessary requirement in a war. The blockbuster bombs weighed anywhere around five to seven hundred pounds, and they were a pretty devastating weapon in those days. Those were the main cargoes and then some general cargoes. The main precaution taken that I was aware of was in shoring them up so they wouldn't roll around in there. Remember this was my first ship as a cadet that had never been anywhere more than a few hundred miles away from home.

We sailed as a single vessel, but we joined three vessels in formal convoy without any protection, no Navy or Coast Guard vessels with us. We had a prescribed course that took us on the way to Sydney, Australia. Instead of going the normal way, we went south of New Zealand. Our captain, an old ex-German gentleman named Captain Bartmann, even went further south than the other two ships. We were running about eight hours apart in a single line. The other two ships were sunk, and we picked up the survivors of one.

Were they sunk by submarines?

Submarine action. And there wasn't that much submarine action in the South Pacific. We always thought that old German captain knew something we didn't know, because he did go away from the course line that he was given, and we were down almost into the Antarctic Circle. That's how far south we went. But it turned out to be a good choice.

I remember pulling in survivors, most of them made their lifeboats, and some had been picked up by other ships. There was a regular "train" of activity going to Sydney in those days.

How long did you stay in Sydney?

Well, from the time we arrived there, the first time we were there, thirty-five days. It struck me: in the war effort and everybody gung-ho and we're taking supplies to Australia so they could defend themselves, and after we got there the longshoremen went on strike and wouldn't unload the ship. This was during the war. Then after they ended the strike, after about ten days or two weeks, if the slightest rain would come up, or mist, the longshoremen would leave and wouldn't work. An example, this was a pretty discouraging thing for a young man or any of the American crew on our ship to see all this. If any kind of moisture came up, they would quit and go into the warehouse. Then, for instance, if there was moisture from eight to ten o'clock, they're in the warehouse, and then it would clear up, they'd say: "No. It's [what they called] smoke-o time," and they'd knock off for twenty minutes to a half hour for their routine smoke time. Very discouraging, this wasn't a very good testimony for the Australian longshoremen, but that was it.

Then we went back and forth from Australia to New Guinea, because I'm telling you, this was a sixteen-month trip around the world, and it was a long time to be away from home for a young boy who had never been away from home. So we ran back and forth to New Guinea. We'd come back and get supplies in Sydney or Brisbane or some of the little towns there and then go up to a place called Milne Bay. At that time, New Guinea was still held, or two-thirds, in the hands of the Japanese, and we were on the eastern end of New Guinea. Why this all took so long, in addition to the five-week delay in Sydney, was when we got to New Guinea they said, "Well, you're going to unload at the docks." We said, "Well, there is no dock." And they said, "That's right, but we're going to build it with the lumber you brought." So that was another five weeks. The Army did a fast job and put it in pretty good, the Corps of Engineers and the [Navy] Seabees. They put in the dock, and then we discharged our five-hundred-pound bombs. At night we would have air raids now and then, just would be single planes. Almost always at night.

Did you take precautions to blacken out the lights at night?

Oh, well, there were never lights going over or when you're under way or in port. Because of our cargo, they wouldn't put us where other ships were. We were out by ourselves. That, then, was sort of an indication to the enemy, when you're out by yourself, that you were out there for some reason. So that sort of targeted us. As a matter of fact, I had just been there with my first trip up there when I got a piece of shrapnel in my ankle that has been bothersome for the rest of my life. It was just one bomb that had dropped and missed, but threw a little shrapnel around. I took my blackout out of the porthole. I had the lights out, sort of sticking my head out, wanting to see what was going on with the bombing. I then went back to my bunk to sleep, but I left that porthole blackout out, because the lights were out, so I could look out. A piece of shrapnel came in through that porthole, just a small piece that I still have. It just hit the walls and went zinging around off all the walls, three or four walls that it hit. It was a slight wound, not enough to disable you, but up in that bad weather, hot humidity, it didn't heal up and it ulcerated. Not painful, but just stayed with me until I got back to the States and got it cleared up.

One of the interesting things, when we got this dock built, we were discharging our cargo. When it was finished, General MacArthur came down on the dock and came aboard our ship. It was the first ship at the dock, and he looked around. That was my one and only dealing with the general.

During this trip, were there any Naval Armed Guard personnel aboard your ship?

Oh, yes. When we left we had a Navy gun crew with a Lieutenant Hickory from Alabama. I'm talking now, this is some fifty-two years ago, but he became a good friend, when you're out that long. We had good relations with the armed forces.

We made three trips between Australia and New Guinea and then one time ran up the coast of New Guinea, up near the enemy area. Then at that time it was so busy with small ships in there and other American ships getting ready for action on the other end of New Guinea that this struck me as a most unusual thing. We were then told, because we'd been blacked out ever since we left Los Angeles, to put on our running lights when we're up in this enemy area because there was more hazard from running into another ship than there was from enemy action. So we ran with our running lights on, the only time during the war that I ever saw that done. All on board the *Rachel Jackson*.

Then we'd been so long in going back to Sydney that we had fellows in the crew getting engaged, and then it had been so long the engagement broke up. They had the wedding date; we were all going to go to the wedding. This was after about five months of back and forth, just before we were leaving there.

We thought, well, here we've been out a long time now, we're going back to the States. We went in; we got orders to go to Melbourne, Australia, and there we picked up the First Marine Division. They're the ones who had originally landed at Guadalcanal and had been pretty much shot up and beaten up. They were sent down there for R & R and their recuperation and had been down there several months. We took them. They were living on deck or in the holds of the vessel. We took them up north of New Guinea to New Britain, where we landed them in the invasion of New Britain at the Gasmata Airport, which the Japanese had held but had been so bombed out, when we got there, there was no action. There wasn't a shot fired, a plane didn't come from the airport, and so the Marines had a very easy go of it. We let the Marines over the side.

They had their own little huts they built on our deck for cooking. Meals weren't that much. One of the personal things that bothered us all is we would be sitting in the dining room and the mess hall, and the Marines would be looking through the portholes at us eating much better food with white tablecloths on the table, and they were out there eating Spam. They only had two meals a day in their little tin dishes, sometimes in the rain, standing in the rain eating or looking through the portholes at us as we sat there having dessert or cake or that type of thing. Very uneasy feeling and not one that was good for your appetite, that's for sure.

An interesting little story or vignette: on leaving Los Angeles, we were tied up I guess aboard the ship about a week. This was the first trip for the ship, just out of the yards, and they sent down a cook, sent down the whole crew. But the meal was pretty bad, and the captain called the cook in and he said to him: "You know, this meal's bad. Where did you learn to cook?" He said he had gone to three weeks training school. And the captain said: "Well, what did you do before you went to school? What was your experience in cooking?" And he said: "Oh, no. I was a bricklayer." And so the captain says: "You're off. We've got to get somebody else." That was after two days.

So the third day a new cook was aboard. We had the meal, and the meal wasn't very good. The third engineer was a guy named Brady. I don't know how these names are coming back, but this was such an impressive thing to a young fellow, and we had spaghetti and meatballs. You really couldn't eat the meatballs or cut the spaghetti. There was an engine cadet on the ship with me. And we sat at a little table to the side, not with the officers, just like we were second-class citizens, which I guess we were. Brady got up, and he says: "Cadets, come with me. I'll show you how to improve the meals." We followed him down the narrow pathway back to the quarters where the steward's department was, and he went in the cook's room and he pulled back the sheets and dumped the spaghetti and meatballs in the cook's bed and pulled the sheets back up and left. We were just gaping to see that done, had never seen anything like that done.

The captain then called the cook in when we got back. I guess he was asking the cook, "Well, where did you learn to cook?" And it was the same story. "What experience did you have before?" The fellow said: "Well, none. I was a professional wrestler." So the captain says, "Well, you're fired." Anyway, we're getting down near leaving time, close to sailing, and I saw the new cook coming up the passageway. It was just in the morning, and we all hoped for the best. In fact, we were sailing that afternoon. We did sail, and the food was horrible. Captain called the cook in. The captain was a tough old German with a German accent. "Listen," he said. "This meal's terrible.

What did you do before you went to that school? Did you have some cooking experience?" "No," he said. "Well, what were you?" So he said, "I was an embalmer." And that's the fellow we sailed with for the sixteen months.

Well, you know, in those days they were just looking for warm bodies aboard the ship—anybody they could get. I remember we had three or four ex-convicts, and the chief mate on there was an old gentleman that hadn't sailed in years. He'd been a night watchman in a warehouse, and I remember going to meet him.

I was a deck cadet, you know, and looking forward to it. I remember the first night I stayed up all night just to stand on the bridge. Never been on a bridge before. It was an exciting thing to me. The next morning the chief mate called me in to his quarters, and he didn't know what a cadet was. He sort of thought they were the equivalent of cabin boys or deck boys. He said: "I saw you up on the bridge. I never want to see you on that bridge again. You turn to with the bosun." And that's what I did. The next morning I was assigned the cleaning of the crew's head. That was my permanent assignment that I did every morning from eight 'til twelve, which was again a little bit discouraging for a deck cadet. But that was it.

Fortunately, just to make a poor story a little better, that chief mate was completely incompetent. He couldn't take a sight, he couldn't take a bearing, he couldn't take an azimuth, couldn't do anything. I didn't get to help him because I never got near the bridge. He got ill with dental problems, fortunately for me. In Sydney, Australia, they took him off, and here came a new chief mate. He was in maritime uniform, and he knew what cadets were. He found out I hadn't had a very good time on there. Some of the other mates were sympathetic to my cause but couldn't do anything. So he said, "Well, you're going to stand watch with me four to eight."

That turned out to be unbelievable. It was almost worth the bad times to get this good mate who said: "Now, only time you won't stand watch is when we're in port. I don't want to see you aboard ship when we're in port. You have to get ashore and see things," which I did. When we would sail out of port sometimes, he'd tell the AB [able-bodied seaman], when it was time to call at three thirty in the morning: "Well, don't call the cadet this morning, let him sleep in. He had a busy time ashore." So it was almost unbelievable, a 180-degree change.

I wanted to make one commentary on war and being at sea that was interesting to me, which was the effect the war had on some people, particularly in the emergencies. The lights were out, we slept with our life jackets on and maybe a little "ditty bag" with just essentials, wallet and passport and sea papers in it, and when that alarm went off at four in the morning to go to your gun stations, it was a pretty scary thing. What I remembered was the difference in emotional effect it had on people. Some guys just panicked. To me, I don't know if it's true, but the heavy drinkers on that vessel, the guys who did the most drinking ashore, were the ones who panicked the most in emergency. Some of the fellows that you thought were a little soft were very cool. I don't know if there's any psychological backing or precedent for that, but on that ship I observed that because it was very prominent.

After this experience and extensive time at sea, you were supposed to come back to Kings Point for training again. This was considered your sea year.

Right. But not before finishing in New Britain, going back to Sydney, and getting orders to go to India. We thought for sure we'd go home. Spent New Year's Eve in Hobart, Tasmania, then it was like a thirty-day run from there to India. And we ran the coast of India from Bombay, Calcutta, and that sort of thing, up the Hooghly River to Calcutta. I remember the British pilot coming aboard there with, naturally, a heavy British accent and an aide, an Indian boy carrying the pilot's golf clubs. And I remember the pilot wanting to change his socks, so he sat there while the Indian boy took off his socks, put clean socks on the pilot, and tied up his shoes. That was kind of impressive. That was my experience in India. We'd had some piloting in Australia, but never with this classic old English pilot. Then we went down to Suez and through the Suez Canal.

Jim Ackerman's first voyage continued to the Mediterranean.

I remember being tied up in Port Said. In those days, the world was divided in pay zones. You could get one-third pay in some zones, two-thirds in another, and 100 percent in another. We were dropping anchor in Port Said, and cadets were making $65 a month pay on the ship. The difference between the two-thirds area and the 100 percent war bonus area was a marker buoy out in Port Said Harbor. And we were told that. So everybody was out on deck, the pilot was taking us to anchor, to see if we were going to drop anchor before the buoy or just past the buoy. Fortunately for us we went on past the buoy, and everybody cheered and dropped the anchor with just a hundred-yard difference between the two-thirds bonus and the 100 percent bonus.

At that time our boilers went out. Still on the *Rachel Jackson*.

And knowing that Liberty ships are driven by steam.

Right. And our boilers were in such bad condition—in fact they had some blowouts on the tubes—that we had to go into the yard there and have them repaired. That was a thirty-day job. Naturally it didn't take that long, but with the waiting and the war, warships were priority, that gave us a chance to see Cairo. I remember the chief mate sent the third mate and second mate up to Cairo, and he and I stayed and stood watches on the ship, nothing doing, just waiting for the yard. When they came back, he and I went to Cairo and got a hotel room up there. We saw Egypt on the way up and then spent some days in Cairo and had some interesting experiences there. This was the "good" mate who made up for the seven bad months I had, so I remember that.

Then we left Port Said with orders to proceed down to Italy. This was at the time of the landing at Sicily, the American troops in Sicily, and we had to pick up some troops there, which we did. It turned out it was a very short experience there in Sicily because there was fighting, and they thought it was not a safe area, and it wasn't that important, what we were going to do, so they had us go on.

That was my first experience with balloons. When we left Egypt, they gave us these balloons on cables that we'd put up to discourage the torpedo planes and that. Barrage balloons. One of my duties as a cadet was to run the balloons up and down on the winch. Planes would not want to get near the cable. We never had it tested so we went on through there.

We had our orders; we were going right through Gibraltar, the Straits there, and head for New York. A big convoy formed there just after we got through the Straits. Our bottom was so fouled because of these many months, that we couldn't keep the speed. We could only do about 7.5 knots, and you had to do 10 to stay in this convoy. We were right about smack in the middle. I remember the instructions were, even for wartime, cruel to hear: that if we saw a ship, any of our fellow ships that got torpedoed, you did not stop, did not pick up any survivors, just kept going. Those were standard orders.

Did you have any carrier escorts or any other ships?

Yes. Not carriers, but DEs [destroyer escorts] and one larger Navy vessel that was the commodore of our fleet. I wasn't very long there in that convoy, so I don't know too much about it. It was obvious that we couldn't maintain speed. We just got kicked out the first day. We weren't that far out. We were hoping one of the DEs would escort us back, but they didn't. They didn't want to leave the convoy, and if they'd taken us clear back, they didn't think they could catch up. It was more efficient for them to stay and protect the other ships. So they just said, "You're on your own."

So the *Jackson* went in what direction now?

Well, it would have been going back in a southerly, southwesterly direction back to Casablanca.

Casablanca at this time was now Free French? It was already liberated by the Americans?

It was liberated, yes. One night we were out, and the shore patrol came. Of course, we were naturally in civilian clothes, and an American shore patrol came around. We were in an area that was forbidden to Americans, and I was with the chief mate in some bar. He said, "Don't say anything," and he started talking to me in French. The Americans of course passed us by, inspecting the bar personnel to see who didn't belong there. That was my first experience, intrigue, of that sort. That's when we went into the shipyards. We were there a month. Then we got out, got into another convoy where we could maintain 9, 10 knots. That was of no consequence to us, but several times we heard explosions and felt explosions. You couldn't tell sometimes whether it was our own DEs and escort vessels dropping depth bombs as precaution or whether a ship was going down. I know in one case it was a ship because we saw the heavy black smoke. I'll never forget that as we went on and it went under the horizon behind us. We didn't know what ship it was, never got any details on it. Don't know any more today than I did when it happened.

Did the *Jackson* get safely back to the United States?

It got safely back.

And then did you start training at Kings Point?

Oh, no. I'd had my four months. I was a cadet, and in those days we did sea projects and got credit for them, particularly if you were out over six months. They then sent you on advanced sea projects. You had to send this stuff in by mail.

So while this is all going on, all this war experience, you're also working on your sea project?

Oh, every day. It was a gigantic project of drawing sketches of all the rigging and lining up where the cargo was in the vessel, doing navigational problems.

Did you come back at all to Kings Point?

Yes, I came back. I brought back my sea projects, and they were in pretty good shape. I had a lot of time to work on them. Got my third mate's exam in San Francisco and then got married.

After sitting for your license, did you ship out again?

Went right out. During the war, I never made a trip that lasted less than nine months, just caught long trips down to South Pacific or whatnot. I went and got my third, second, and chief mate, sailing both in the Atlantic and the Pacific.

Eugene Harrower, Class of 1942

Eugene Harrower's long-term goal was to become a ship captain, and by age twenty-four (1945) he achieved his objective. He commanded a ship with a crew of forty-eight mariners and an Armed Guard unit of thirteen Navy personnel. After the war, Harrower stayed in maritime-related work. When the Korean War started, he volunteered for active duty in the Military Sea Transportation Service, eventually achieving the rank of captain in the Navy. Later, he became an occupational safety director for the State of Oregon.

My most memorable experience was an eleven-month voyage I made on the motor ship *Cape Alava* as a third mate. She was the first C1B type ship in the Maritime Shipbuilding Program. We started in San Francisco in May of 1942 and ended in April of 1943 in New York, during which time we went around the world. The *Cape Alava* was a 14-knot ship, and we traveled independently the entire voyage, except from the Panama Canal to Charleston.

We carried a full cargo of military supplies to Brisbane, Australia. We discharged it all out on one big pier. It's seldom that you see a full ship's cargo sitting in one spot, and I was amazed at how much we had packed in our hull. We picked up a load of coal and took it up to Noumea for the nickel smelter there. Then we went to Chile and loaded nitrate for Charleston. We were thinking the nitrate was probably going to be used for explosives, but it turned out to be fertilizer. Then we loaded the military cargo. Not knowing where we were going, we were nervous about going to Murmansk. Fortunately, when we left Charleston, we turned right, went south, and headed for India, via the Panama Canal. We sailed around Cape Horn to Cape Town [South Africa]. Leaving Cape Town for Karachi, we blew a generator and had to go into Durban for repairs.

The morning before our arrival into Durban, we picked up survivors from a British ship, the SS *Mendoza*, which had been sunk the night before by a submarine. The chief mate was very badly burned when the second torpedo hit. He was directing the lowering of the boats. We picked up one boatload and took them into Durban, and alerted the authorities to go out and pick up the rest.

When we left Durban, we went in a convoy of about twenty ships and were escorted by British Navy ships. We were due east from Durban for about a day and a half or two days, at which time the convoy dispersed, and all the ships went to their separate destinations. They ordered a dispersal because some of the ships were going out to the Persian Gulf, some to the Red Sea. We were going to Karachi.

Were any extra precautions taken as a result of being in waters that were known to have U-boats in them and submarines?

Well, there were some. There was not much we could do, except go like hell, and zigzag. In my case, not having access to a zigzag plan book, I would draw up my own at first. We would change course maybe 20 degrees after six minutes, steaming on our base course, and then 20 degrees to the left for another six minutes. You could vary the number of degrees that you changed course, but you didn't want to change too much, because you did want to make some progress along your base line. The intervals at which you changed the courses could also vary, of course, but the main thing was that at the end of your one-hour, or two-hour, or four-hour period of zigzagging, you wanted to be somewhere on your base course. Later, the captain let us use the standard zigzagging plans in a book developed by the Navy.

There was really nothing else we could do to avoid detection from submarine or aircraft. We had no choice. We had to go from one place to another on a course that was laid out by the port director of the port of departure. Radio silence was maintained. We never used our radio, unless we were actually attacked, at which time we would send out a message. We darkened the ship every night. Kept a sharp lookout. We had no other way. We had no detection devices of any kind.

The *Cape Alava* had a 4-inch gun on the stern, and a 3-inch gun at the bow, and it had eight 20-millimeters for anti-aircraft. When we started our voyage, we didn't have all of those. We started out with Lewis machine guns, which wouldn't do anything to anybody at any time, but at least they reassured some of the people that didn't know better. And then as guns were available, we acquired some during the voyage. For example, while we were in Charleston, they put the 3-inch gun on the bow. So, we were able to upgrade our defensive capability, but at no time did we have an opportunity to utilize them. We carried a U.S. Navy Armed Guard crew of one officer, and generally twelve or twenty-four enlisted men, depending on what part of the world you were going near. Their primary function was the firing, maintenance, and preparation of the gun and the ammunition. The merchant crew was trained to operate the guns, as well as to assist the gunners. The gunners had the best skills, but if they weren't available, somebody had to do the job.

While the ship was in Ceylon, the entire crew went to a British two-day defense course. One day was spent in a classroom, where we studied aircraft recognition and the types of guns that were on the ship. The second day we went out to a firing range and actually fired some of the guns. We weren't able to fire the 20-millimeters because they didn't have enough ammunition at the time to do it, but everybody in the crew got a chance to fire a machine gun. The British also had a number of other exotic devices that they utilized to discourage dive bombers.

One device I recall used air pressure to fire a device up into the air. It streamed a wire from this device, and if a dive bomber came in, it would cut his wing off. Any type of strafing attack would be hindered by the wire across the plane's path. We'd fire this thing, which looked like a soup can, actually, and it pulled this wire behind it. Then another soup can came out of the thing, and one was higher than the other, and the wire was between them. It would stay in the air as long as gravity would permit, which wasn't very long. But the idea was that if the thing was fired, and the pilot of a plane knew it, he might decide he wants to change course, and thus might miss his target. Basically, it discouraged a pilot's aggressiveness.

The British warship, HMS *Asturias,* captured the *Mendoza,* and she was converted to a troopship for Britain. Subsequently, the German submarine *U-178* sank the *Mendoza* on January 11, 1942.[2]

Carroll J. O'Brien, Class of 1944

Popularly called "O.B.," Carroll O'Brien states that Kings Point helped him achieve "everything I've ever wanted, every hope, every desire. Every place I've ever wanted to go, I've been." During the war, O'Brien traveled in the Atlantic, Mediterranean, and Pacific theaters of operations and in the Indian Ocean. After the war, O.B. worked for a number of engineering companies and was a systems engineer. Today he does maritime-related consultant's tasks and ship survey work. He has a ready sense of humor.

At Kings Point, they gave us as much as you could give anybody in less than three months. When I arrived on January 19, 1943, I didn't know an engine from a condenser, a bullgear from a stern tube, a propeller from the bow, or anything else. The beautiful part of it is, every cadet that goes to sea has a sea project that's homework. You learn because the homework asks a lot of questions. You fill that in every day, and by the time you get done, you are pretty knowledgeable about the ship you're on.

By April, I was assigned to a ship that was going to make a run on the North Atlantic. They needed bodies. The North Atlantic was possibly the most dangerous body of water at that time, with the U-boats. Actually, every ship that left the east coast that was going to run the North Atlantic was written off before it even left port. In those days, we were just assigned to a ship where they needed a body, and you went where you were told to go. And where they needed a body, that's where you went.

That's how I ended up on the *Steel Traveler* going north. It was twenty-six years old, and it was also the twenty-sixth ship built of a fleet of twenty-five ships. When Isthmian Steamship Company, which was part of U.S. Steel, finished the twenty-fifth ship, they had enough left over to build another ship. So they built this monster. She had Parsons reaction turbines, and gears that whined. Whenever you have a turbine that travels so fast, the speed of the unit has got to be reduced to the point where it can be utilized. So you have reduction gears, and those reduction gears bring the speed down to the point where you can turn a ship's shaft, which in turn is going to turn a propeller, which in turn is going to propel the ship. That is how it went backwards and forwards. She also had Scotch boilers. That just means that instead of water going through boiler tubes, you have fire.

We had all kinds of general cargo. We carried 114-ton locomotives on deck as cargo, plus all kinds of supplies for the British, who were in dire need. Here you went on the North Atlantic in April. The further north you got, the worse the waves got. In those days, some of us went up above Iceland. We picked up the submarine packs. Those whining gears were like a homing pigeon to a submarine. They could pick up that convoy just from those gears whining. We ended up with a submarine right underneath us. These DEs and destroyers would circle us, dropping bombs. The bombs would go off, and the floor plates would jump. Everybody was a nervous wreck. I think we started out with fifty-two ships, and by the time we got to Boodle, Liverpool, there were twenty-six of us left. The other ships were sunk. One night, four of us fell behind the rest of the convoy. In the morning, the other three were gone, and we were the only one left.

The waves and the seas were so bad. We "kissed" an iceberg, and the fantail and steering-engine room had water running through it. The water would hit the up-and-down steering engine, and hiss and whine. All the doors above the weather deck were smashed, and all the lifeboats. There was only one raft left on board the ship. The passageways had water running up and down them. During that time, one of those locomotives broke loose. Well, you didn't want to see 114 tons on a pitching ship like that. Then a miracle happened. A second mate by the name of Willy got a shackle and secured that 114-ton locomotive. Unbelievable. How he did it without getting killed, I'll never know. And in those days if you got sunk, it was very interesting, because if you didn't blow up, you froze to death in the water. Maybe it was 35 degrees, maybe it was 28.

Off-loading the cargo in Britain took about two weeks, but it took us twenty-five days to get there. Here's this little boy from Nassau County, wants to see the world. He hears there's a war and goes to Kings Point, gets on a ship, never realizing that when that ship got that far from the dock he was seasick. And for the next twenty-five days, that kid didn't hold one meal, and he walked around with a bucket so that he could upchuck without messing the decks. Very interesting.

I made four crossings on that ship. I got back to New York, where Paddy Brennan, our famous chief engineer for US Lines, was our district inspector.[3] He takes a look at O'Brien, and he says "My God." I was down to 126 pounds. So he put me on *Cape Spencer*, a C1A out of Beaumont, Texas. It was loading up in Philadelphia and going to, of all places, Persia. She'd do 14 knots. Big deal, 14 knots, but we ran alone. There weren't any convoys.

So, lo and behold, we shipped out of Philadelphia, went down through the Panama Canal, down between Tasmania and Australia, all the way around to the port of Perth, and up to a place in Persia, seventy-five miles from Baghdad. We were down between New Zealand and Australia, and a guy pops his head in the engine room and says, "There's three ships burning out there!" Oh, fine. Here you are, thirty feet below the water line [with cargo]. So what are you going to do? I'm down the engine room. He might have been telling me lies, for all I know, just to scare the hell out of me. (*Laughter*) You got to stay in the engine room.

We had to run the Pacific, and then up the east coast of Africa. Then we headed to the Gulf of Oman and then into the Persian Gulf. At the very top of the Persian Gulf, they had a big army contingent of mostly colored troops. They were up there in all that heat, unloading those ships, and they did a terrific job. When the tide would come in, it would become an island, and fish would come up and walk on the dock. Don't ask me what kind. I don't know.

We were now empty, so we got to Kuwait and loaded up with fuel. Nobody had ever heard of Kuwait before then. There was a Polish refugee camp there. Then we headed down the gulf. When you are heading down the gulf, if the current is letting out, you are doing about 4 to 6 knots. You are really making time. Then we headed back down to Perth. Primarily, we carried general cargo and about eight thousand tons of ammunition.

We get back up to Los Angeles, New Year's Eve, 1944. Oh boy. No one can go ashore because we picked up a passenger in Perth. He was a displaced type of person, who had been digging for emeralds and rubies in Burma. I don't know the whole story. Being in the engine room, you don't know all the requirements of topsides. But once you have a passenger on a ship, until that passenger gets cleared, nobody is allowed ashore. And here we've just gone six months, thirty-six thousand miles, and we can't go ashore. (*Laughter*)

From there, we headed up to San Francisco. I've put in my sea time from April all the way up to February. I was only supposed to be at sea six months. Now I had already been at sea ten months. So now it was time to get back to the Academy. I call our district inspector in New York, and he keeps yelling, "Ship out! Ship out!" And I keeping flicking the phone, saying, "Sir, Sir, what sir?" Click, click, click. I am saying, "Uh-Uh, I am going to get an education come hell or high water."

I get back to school, and they say to me, "What are you doing here?" I said, "Well, I'm here." And that's how our classes started. I found out about ship construction, thermodynamics, and what a BTU was. Much to my utter amazement, I graduated. It was November of 1944.

TRAINING FOR WAR

During the Second World War, the course of instruction at the U.S. Merchant Marine Academy was rigorous and often danger-ous. The curriculum changed and adapted to the growing need for trained merchant marine officers, which was the mission of the Academy. The process of education was composed of three parts: basic training, sea training, and advanced training. All the train-ing was in preparation for an examination to become a ship's offi-cer, either third mate or third assistant engineer. The total training period could be as short as sixteen months, but the period would vary greatly according to individual qualifications or the cir-cumstances of war. Basic training was normally for ten to twelve weeks, either at Kings Point or one of two other, regional schools at Pass Christian, Mississippi, or San Mateo, California. When a cadet-midshipman was deemed ready for sea training, he was as-signed to a ship for hands-on instruction. Here was the dangerous aspect of the curriculum. While still an undergraduate, the cadet went aboard civilian merchant ships that invariably sailed into war zones. The threat of enemy submarine and aircraft attacks was especially acute. Sea training would often last nine or ten months and, if the exigencies of war required, sometimes over a year. Students returning to Kings Point for their advanced training frequently related reports of U-boats and, at times, of torpedoed ships. After passing the license for ship's officer, the Kings Pointer usually returned to sea duty. Before the war's end, several Kings Pointers achieved the rank of shipmaster or chief engineer.[1]

Ralph J. Weir, Class of 1945

Ralph Weir came to the Academy at Kings Point for his initial training and was at sea when the official dedication occurred in 1943. He stopped sailing after the war, "but," as he relates, "I'll tell you, that experience made a man out of you quick." He went into the advertising business and later became president of a midwestern firm, Preferred Security Plans, Inc.

I had absolutely no knowledge about the merchant marine. Yearly, they'd come through with the recruiting in Chicago, and I thought I'd be interested in a sort of adventure. At the tail end of '42, I enrolled as a cadet. I was at sea when they dedicated the Academy.

When we came to the Academy, they had the Quonset huts. They had just finished Cleveland Hall, and we spent the last two weeks of our "prelim" at Cleveland Hall before we shipped out. As far as the classes, it was really a refresher course. I remember the circle of trade. I was an art major in high school, so I was really not that attuned to it. But it was primarily just so that you felt comfortable at sea, and so the Academy felt that you had the brain power to achieve their objectives for training officers. So that when you did go aboard a ship in your cadet period, that you knew "fore" from "aft," and didn't call something a "floor" when it was a "deck." It was just kind of a general indoctrination to what seagoing and seafaring was. The whole course was just being developed. We were among the first. They didn't have a curriculum. They didn't have the faculty. They were trying to put it all together. It was three months as a prelim, nine months or so at sea, and then you came back for nine months.

There was a training area where Jones Beach is now, where we fired 20-millimeters at the sleeves pulled by aircraft. We had drills on the 5-inch 50 gun at Kings Point. Then they took us into small arms, field stripping .45s. It was fairly extensive when you consider that we weren't considered military or ground troop types.

I was assigned to the *John Carroll*, a Liberty ship. I took her out of Oakland. I just watched her on a daily basis, nine to five, going through the completion of the rigging and all of that.

We sailed alone, unescorted, to Sydney. We were pretty well up to our Plimsoll mark,[2] which was what you're supposed to run. Then they decided that they had to get some other cargo, and they loaded our deck. I don't

Cadet-midshipmen marching at the United States Merchant Marine Academy, Kings Point, New York, during World War II. By permission of the United States Merchant Marine Academy.

Regimental formation for the official dedication of the United States Merchant Marine Academy, Kings Point, New York, September 30, 1943. By permission of the United States Merchant Marine Academy.

know if it was crated airplane parts or jeeps or what have you, but we were low in the water.

We were assigned, along with four or five other merchant ships, to start moving everything from Australia up to New Guinea. We crossed the Coral Sea unescorted, without a convoy. We carried the Guadalcanal boys back from Sydney to the battle area in New Guinea. They had been off for quite some time after Guadalcanal. It was a matter of months. They had to refurbish and build up their strength, and then we took them back. You can always tell what's going to happen when you start putting the outhouses on the side of a Liberty. All of a sudden you're not a cargo ship, you're a troop transport. We could hold about one thousand troops. They would live in 'tween-decks.

I was a deck cadet, and I was just fortunate that I had a good skipper who didn't just use me as a cabin boy, or worse, as a lot of us were used. Other than the fact we had Tokyo Rose on our case a couple of times, we knew exactly where we were at.

We had a couple attacks up on the northern tip of New Guinea. It was one or two planes at the most, probably Zeros. The Japanese would just come in, make a run at it, do whatever damage they could, and then go on. They were probably more interested in the coastal area. If they were interested in us, they didn't get that close, although it was a pretty confined area. We had 20-millimeters on board and one 3-inch. That's just about all the guns we had. They were considering dropping the hook, by which I mean letting all the chain out just to get out of the harbor.

We weren't escorted, with one exception, if you can call that a convoy. I mean it was probably only four or five ships. We were pulling an Australian coal barge and two PT boats across the corals. We were to take them up to Milne Bay, New Guinea. You'd have some Australian corvettes as escorts. They were very small little things. I think they were less armed than we were. There was also a French vessel that the Aussies had either taken over or inherited. It was probably the size of one of our full-size destroyers. It wasn't a major ship. We would only run up to New Guinea, discharge, and load up, constantly transferring supplies from Australia to New Guinea. The trip itself was maybe four or five days.

The *John Carroll* was the only ship I was assigned, and I stayed on it almost eleven months, which was over the time you were supposed to. The government, or the powers that be, had said: "We got all this material in Australia, and we've got to get it up to New Guinea or the nearby islands.

You don't leave until the job is done." (*Laughter*) I was about twenty-one at the time.

One time we got caught in a typhoon, went through the eye of it, in fact. We lost some of the deck. The major boom broke loose. We had to just turn and run, and the thing was, we were within the coral reef so our margin of maneuvering area was pretty limited.

I came back to the Academy in '44, and the Quonset huts were gone. The Academy was in pretty good shape at that time. I was there nine months. Because I had stayed out longer than was expected, I didn't finish my advanced training with my fellow cadets from my prelim, except for one cadet who was also out at sea. With my new section, it was immediate bonding. We'd all been out at sea. Some of them sat in lifeboats and had some harrowing experiences. Some were in the Atlantic. Some of them sailed around the world. I was only in the Pacific.

The Academy was quite a challenge. You've got to realize that they were not only trying to give us the education but also the experience to fulfill our duties in a merchant marine capacity. For funding, we were required to take a lot of Navy courses because we were midshipmen.

I can just remember the signal for a deck officer. For navigation for convoys, you'd have all your signals and whistles and flags. They wanted you to learn all the Navy squadron maneuvers. There's "round the buoy" and what course and speed you have to sail to meet your rendezvous point.

For a kid that's only twenty or twenty-one, you're trying to learn about four sets of signaling, plus the Rules of the Road and all those other good things. So it was quite a challenge. I think there was something like sixty-four hours of concentrated learning per week, and more if you were on a drill team. We had "Sarge." He was a short little officer, and he was tough. By comparison to what you get in the regular service, there was probably not that much drilling. But considering it was something that was really foreign to us, it seemed like a heck of a lot of time. But we were pretty good. (*Laughter*)

I don't know if you'd call them nightmares, but I still have a heck of a lot of dreams about the Academy, like not being able to find my room or I'm out of uniform. So it must have been a very memorable thing in my lifetime. I got my license in January of '45, and then I went to sea again. I sailed tankers the rest of the war.

I'll tell you, that experience made a man out of you quick. You went in a nineteen-year-old, snotty kid and you came out a man at twenty-three. It was invaluable. But it was a huge responsibility, and on that first trip coming through the Windward Passage, I would have gladly given my ticket away. You know, here you're in control of God knows how many millions of dollars worth of cargo, and the ship, and all the people aboard. That's a pretty good load to put on a twenty-some-year-old kid. But we've done it, and I'm sure there's a lot of kids today doing it.

Karl J. Aarseth, Class of 1943

Modest and quiet in manner, Karl Aarseth is the son of a Norwegian shipmaster. He has maintained his connection to the sea all his life. In his twenties, he sailed as a cadet-midshipman during the war and as an officer upon graduation in June 1943. After receiving his third mate's license, he worked his way up the ranks so that by age twenty-four he had his unlimited shipmaster's license. Later he participated in logistical support for American forces in Vietnam and witnessed the Tet Offensive. In the year 2000, he was issued his twelfth license as master and first-class pilot.

Please describe your experiences during World War II and during the genesis of the Academy.

On December 7, 1941, Hirohito gave me a permanent job which I was proud to do. They took twelve people here in New York, six engine and six deck, and we went to a place called Bayou St. John, where we berthed on Lake Pontchartrain, Louisiana. That was on a houseboat called the *North Star*, which had been donated to the cause. We were being indoctrinated into what was called the U.S. Maritime Commission Training Corps.

The twelve of us did not have the highest expectations for this craft, but we had a bunk to sleep in, with sheets, and we ate well. Unfortunately we had to go into the city YMCA once a week to clean ourselves. We spent about two months there in basic training, and also with the U.S. Naval Reserve.

We didn't really have a place to drill, so we did close order drills in a parking lot. Once we made a short voyage out to the international lock center in New Orleans, to the river. That was about the limit of our training. It was a diesel vessel, and we had no uniforms.

Then, finally, the great day came when we were assigned. I got my letter of assignment to a ship called the SS *James McKay*, a C1 coming in from South Africa to Baltimore. I never did see any of my close friends after that. Within two weeks to a month after they had left, two of my classmates were dead.

Well, I got into Baltimore and saw this vessel. She was painted black and white like all our vessels, with a big American flag on the side. They sent her to the shipyard in Sparrow's Point where she was built and started to prepare for war. They painted her all gray with armor plating on the overhead of the bridge and the wheelhouse and the wheelhouse windows, and they put gun mounts on the bridge. In those days, we had eight .50-caliber machine guns. We also had an old 5-inch, a relic of World War I, that stood on the stern. That was it.

After about a month in the shipyard, we sailed for New York on the SS *James McKay*. We'd go behind the torpedo nets. We stopped once in Delaware Bay, and then we finally got into New York Harbor. There they commenced to load the vessel at the Army base in Brooklyn, chartered to the Army transport command. It didn't take too long before they loaded it to full capacity. You just didn't go home that night. We anchored in the lower bay and loaded the other cargo on deck, including various cylinders.

When we had departed, I noticed that there were people coming from the U.S. Army aboard wearing these plastic boots. I talked to them, and our dialogue went something like this:

What are you people doing here?
We're in chemical warfare.
What do you mean?
Well, do you see those tanks on the hatch over there? Mustard gas.
Where's my equipment?
Gee, I don't know.[3]

Then we went to Halifax. Before we got out, they were going to have target practice. They used to throw an empty oil barrel overboard. But this time, when they went to fire the gun it wouldn't fire. They had a solenoid trigger, which is supposed to fire. Then they had a lanyard to pull it manually, and it did not work either. It could have been a misfire or a hangfire. When we got to Halifax, the Canadian Navy came aboard and said, "We're not going to have anything to do with this, but when you get out to sea, get some brave soul to open up the breech and pull the shell out and throw it overboard." I don't know who volunteered, but they did it. Then we shaped up our convoy at sea. They got rid of the shell, and maybe they fixed the gun.

We set sail for Iceland, where the Army had just taken over a base up there. I went to convoy school for a week. I had never realized how comprehensive and orderly it would be. I just thought we would sail like a bunch of geese. But there were all kinds of instructions and flags and signals and maneuvers.

The first thing I was told was to stay closed up. They told us: "If you lag behind, you might get picked off, and we can't guarantee your safety. So try to stay in the convoy." We sailed through fog, sleet, and stormy weather. As we got near Iceland, we heard a lot of rumors, but nothing officially. Apparently the submarines had located us. We sent the last depth charge over, and the whole convoy got safely into Reykjavik.

Ireland was a neutral country, and they would not allow British aircraft to be stationed there. So the furthest they could cover us was from Newfoundland to a little bit south of Iceland. Then they would pick us up again near Ireland. That was called a black hole. When we were in it, we had no air protection, and we were at the mercy of the U-boats. Nothing happened to us.

We discharged all our cargo there in Iceland with the Army. Next, we departed for a place called Barry, Wales, near Cardiff. We docked there for about a month or so while they were loading a ship chartered to the British Army. Then we set out for Chittagong, India (now Bangladesh).

One day, two GIs came down and hauled a 20mm gun onto our ship, which I thought was fantastic. I'd never even seen a 20-millimeter. I said, "Why do you suppose they're putting them on our ship?" One of the men said that all the ships that were going to Malta were going to get them. I said, "Is that true?" He said, "If I were going to Malta I'd jump overboard right now." I told the captain what he said, and the captain said, "You know, they're sailing in a 16-knot convoy. I'm not sure we can maintain a 16-knot convoy." So that was the end of the Malta gambit.

We left there with a regiment called the Red Hand of Ulster. There were three British officers and a few "noncoms." Going down with the convoy, I saw them pick up the first survivors off Casablanca. It was not a pleasant sight, and I felt I was too close to it. When we got near the equator, the convoy broke up, and we sailed independently to Capetown and then to Dhahran.

We didn't get to our next port, Chittagong, because the Japanese had captured all Bangladesh ports north of Singapore. We ended up in Bombay. This was all the country of India at the time. We discharged all the British there. There, at least I knew I was safe, and I didn't have to worry. We could open the portholes and get fresh air.

At that time, there was a famine there. I remember a woman I saw one night, sitting on a mat and feeding her three kids a little curried rice in bits of newspaper. Now I'm a twenty-year-old kid, and this British officer came down to check the equipment. I say, "I understand there's a famine here." He says: "Yes, they never have enough food, and now they have nothing. Every once in a while we take a three-ton truck full of grain, and we broadcast all over that people can come in and get emergency rations." I say: "Three tons of grain? They have a half a billion people!" He says, "Yeah, but they all rush to the center of the town, and the weak ones all die in one place, and we can dispose of them easily." I never forgot that.

As we got off the Brazilian coast, we got orders to zigzag. We had a clock that they gave us with a little electric signal. We went twenty degrees right, then left, and so forth. This was a great help to us, because any submarine would then have to spend much more time to get our true course and speed. We got to New York, safe and sound.

I was down on the SS *James McKay* for eight months and never got a letter from home. It wasn't until the Armed Guards complained that the Navy finally decided to send mail out of Brooklyn, and delivered it to the Armed Guards, and then to us.

Next, I reported to Kings Point. When I arrived, they said we had no place to sleep. Our berthing officer said to come back in a week or so. So I came back in a week, and he said that all they had was a place in top of the Marchant house, in the attic. So I slept up there on a mattress in the dark. I thought I was going to freeze that first night. I put on all my blues, and my cravenette, and I slept. That's where I slept more or less till I got a room down in the building.

Eventually we ended up in something called Juniper Barracks. It was a wooden structure, worse than a Quonset hut. It was built as a CCC on cinder blocks. At that time, it was starting to sag, and sections cracked open. The wind whistled through the cracks, so we put our bridge coats up there to keep the wind out. The oil furnace never worked, so it would get very cold. Every morning we had to get up and swab the decks. As we ran to the shower and back, all the decks were frozen into an ice-skating rink. To prevent sliding, we took sand out of the fire buckets and spread it on the deck. One day an off-duty officer came in and said, "Gee, this is a dirty barracks," and we were all put on report.

Needless to say, we were all very pleased to go over to [newly built] Murphy Hall. Things were generally good there, with the exception of the eating problem. We had 2,400 cadets, and we had twenty minutes to feed them on each shift, in and out. Those guys would just come running out with food. If you didn't get the food, you went hungry. A lot of times the plebes, the "boots," didn't get anything to eat. And the food wasn't even good.

Napoleon said the greatest characteristic of a soldier is valor, and the next is to endure suffering. No one enjoys it, but if you can get through the suffering, you can still live. I learned that people had it much worse than we did.

I graduated from the U.S. Merchant Marine Academy in June 1943. I received the third mate's license and gradually worked my way up. At the age of twenty-four, I had an unlimited master's license.

Karl Aarseth's next assignments took him to the Mediterranean and Middle East and later to Russia on the Murmansk run.

Note: A German U-boat torpedoed Aarseth's former ship, the *James McKay*, on December 7, 1942, resulting in the loss of the ship and all her crew, including the Naval Armed Guard aboard.[4]

Rear Admiral Thomas A. King, Class of 1942

When Tom King graduated in 1942, little did he realize he would one day return to Kings Point as superintendent. Indeed, the building in which he slept as a student, Wiley Hall, included what would later be his office as superintendent. After graduation he assumed positions of authority throughout the war and became a shipmaster before the war's end. He was at the U.S. embassy in Seoul when hostilities commenced in Korea in 1950 and was involved in the conflict. Prior to returning to Kings Point, he worked for many years for the U.S. Maritime Administration. Now retired, he's still active in alumni affairs.

I was competitively selected as a cadet-midshipman in the U.S. Merchant Marine Cadet Corps in late 1940 and reported in February 1941 to Fort Schuyler, New York. There, we were organized separately as "Federal Cadets" and were distinct in every way possible from the regular State of New York students. We were assigned our own barracks, classrooms, and workspaces. We ate separately and even had our own "monomoy," [small] pulling boat. When we had been indoctrinated, had demonstrated proficiency in signaling (Morse code, signal flags, blinker light), and had sewn a seabag, we were assigned to a merchant ship as a cadet. The goal was to become qualified for that shipboard training in four to six weeks. Some took longer.

I signed my first Shipping Articles on March 22, 1941, sailing with Moore-McCormack Lines on their C2, the SS *Mormacswan*. I made two foreign voyages to the east coast of South America and one domestic, coastwise voyage. In mid-July of 1941, I was transferred to one of that company's three passenger ships, the SS *Argentina*.

I had just completed my third voyage in November 1941 when I was ordered back to the USMMCC unit at Fort Schuyler for Naval Science and gunnery training. Within a few weeks after the attack on Pearl Harbor, December 7, all of the cadet-midshipmen were assembled one evening, and volunteers were sought to sail on a World War I, Hog Island–built freighter, the SS *Hoosier*. Since most of us had plans for New Year's Eve, only a few days ahead, no hands were raised, and our officer in charge arbitrarily chose Norman Brubaker and myself.

The SS *Hoosier* sailed New Year's Day, 1942, unarmed and unescorted, from the port of New York and bound, as we subsequently learned, for West Africa. We had cargo for Freetown in Sierra Leone and Monrovia, the capital of Liberia, but our primary cargo consisted of construction material destined for Robertsport, Liberia. Military aircraft were to be flown from the United States to British forces fighting in North Africa, and Robertsport was to be a refueling station.

At that time, the German submarine fleet had not yet organized itself to wage war off the east coast of America, so we proceeded safely across the Atlantic to the African west coast and British-controlled Freetown. We spent a few days there discharging at anchor, with the only excitement being the departure of a large convoy of Allied troopships with bands playing, cheering soldiers on deck, and an escort led by an impressively threatening British battleship.

Our turn came shortly after, but we departed with only a very small British escort which, while limited to speed less than that of the *Hoosier*, we were assured had a then highly secret, underwater detection device. This device was critical because a relatively short distance to the north of Freetown was Dakar, and that port was under German control. We were to proceed south along the African coast to Robertsport, where a German consul served, and we were to anchor in the open sea while discharging into large "Accra" [dugout] canoes.

Shortly after dropping anchor, our radio operator reported that the German consul had gone on the air and presumably reported to Dakar our arrival. The small British escort was to stay with us both during the sea passage and cargo discharge, patrolling to seaward while constantly listening. Fortunately, no enemy submarine came hunting for us.

The only incident that seriously threatened our safety arose when a crew member managed to set afire his wood-lined stateroom. That room happened to be adjacent to an open cargo hatch loaded with drums of high-octane gasoline. This was at nighttime when all discharging had ceased and we were anchored offshore with only some of the crew on board. All who were on board turned out. We covered the hatch and successfully fought the fire after some touch-and-go desperate moments.

As we continued, without challenge by the enemy, we concluded that the enemy must have higher priorities than our single ship. Several days later, we were free of the landing-strip cargo and proceeded with the escort to Monrovia and another discharge. When that discharge was accomplished, we proceeded independently further south to the port of Takoradi/Secondi [Ghana]. There we loaded a full cargo of manganese ore and departed, sailing independently and still unarmed, for the Delaware Capes and Philadelphia.

It was then the spring of 1942, and the German submarine forces were in the process of devastating shipping along the American east coast. The enemy's "Operation Drumbeat" had been triggered off in mid-January of 1942, and the following several months witnessed what has accurately been described as a second Pearl Harbor disaster for America. Without escort or a convoy system, many still unarmed merchant ships were being torpedoed, almost at will. Some were sunk in sight of spectators on the beaches.

Unfortunately, the local civil authorities were either without the higher authority they needed to black out their coastal communities or had succumbed to the often prevailing reluctance in the early months of 1942 to recognize that America was at war. Whatever the cause, ships approaching the well-illuminated Atlantic coast in the nighttime found themselves starkly outlined by shore lights and thus easy targets for offshore enemy submarines.

Steaming independently and blacked-out, the *Hoosier*, once past mid-Atlantic, proceeded like a broken field runner, mostly in the direction of the Delaware Capes. As the latest sinkings were received by radio and plotted, a decision was made by the captain and officers on which course to follow around the newly plotted position of a torpedoing. Time and again that process was followed.

Fortunately, the decisions were correct, or perhaps there were richer targets upon which to expend a torpedo. In any event, the *Hoosier* safely made its landfall at the Delaware Capes. Ironically, when land was well in sight, we were flown over by a Navy blimp. The next day, the Philadelphia paper had a story, with photographs, detailing how the Navy blimp patrols were making the coastal sea lanes safe for shipping.

After discharging the ore cargo and signing off the crew from foreign Articles of Shipping, the *Hoosier* moved to Sun Shipyard in Chester, Pennsylvania. There she was armed, degaussed,[5] and her steam deck-lines were re-lagged. Obviously the ship was heading into northern waters. There was an almost complete turnover of crew and officers occurring as we moved to a loading berth in Philadelphia. While still a deck cadet, I soon found myself pressed into duty as a cargo mate, loading our outbound cargo.

When personnel shortages had finally been overcome and sailing day was close at hand, I was rewarded with an afternoon off. Dressed in my freshly pressed blue uniform, I set out on shore leave in Philadelphia. Admiring the statue of William Penn atop the landmark public building, I heard a voice call out, "Cadet." Turning, I was face to face with a U.S. Maritime Service officer. After a few questions as to my name and "what ship," as well as letting me know that I should have "reported in," I was ordered back to the *Hoosier* to await the officer's arrival. First, he had to return to his nearby office and check lists of names. Once aboard, I sought out the captain, related my encounter, and stated in my own defense that I had never before had to "call in" or look for a training representative.

Shortly, the USMS officer arrived on board with the news that I was promptly being relieved and should report to the training representative in New York. I was told that I would probably go to our new facility at Kings

Point. I faintly remember having heard, when last at Fort Schuyler, talk of a permanent home for the Cadet Corps. I proceeded to New York and then Kings Point thinking that I would rather have made the voyage on the *Hoosier* as I considered it a good ship with a good skipper.

Actually I was fortunate as the *Hoosier* joined the infamous Convoy PQ-17 with other ships bound for Murmansk and Archangel. That convoy, abandoned by its escort, scattered just short of its Russian destination, suffering terrible casualties as enemy planes and submarines took their toll. The *Hoosier* did not make it.

In April of 1942, I reported to the "new training base" at Kings Point with the expectation of intensive but shortened courses followed by a return to sea as a cadet. At Kings Point, however, I found construction in progress and much disorganization and uncertainty. When I was here, the present campus buildings were being constructed. We lived in such places as Wiley Hall.[6] I lived upstairs, with a lot of other cadets I might add, double bunks inside and out on the porch there.

We were on a construction site, walking over wood walkways, over mud. The mud was memorable! It was certainly memorable. We had no organized activity. There was no gymnasium; there were no athletic facilities outside. We did have a pool that went with the Marchant family estate that became the Marshall pool. We did have the monomoys; we would get into the pulling boats, that type of thing. There was always marching. But there were no intramurals. There wasn't a great deal. No, not a great deal. It was in the terrible state of transition, with, really, hundreds of new cadets coming on board. While new cadet-midshipmen were arriving in large numbers and seemed to be reasonably organized, there was uncertainty for those of us returning from sea duty. We were not all equally experienced, some having had more than two years on board ship and others not much more than one year. The courses which had been planned to require four years, with a mix of shore- and sea-based training, were sure to be cut back to meet the rapidly expanding wartime ship construction and the resulting manpower needs.

Training and licensing requirements were also under review, and adjustments were anticipated shortly. Successive changes in the length of the course and clearly the structure of the program itself followed, one reduction after another. This undoubtedly reflected the developing urgency of the situation. For us cadets, however, it was simply a confusing start and stop, then start all over again.

Within a very short period of time, the training program had gone from the original four years to eighteen months. At each level, those cadet-midshipmen who qualified, dropped out of regular classes and commenced a crash effort of preparation for their license exam. Sometime in May or June of 1942, the impact of a massive shipbuilding program and the horrific losses due to enemy sinkings were reflected in a final and brief course reduction to sixteen months.

In that time frame and together with others, I was ordered to drop out of classes and prepare to take my third mate's license exam. Along with other cadet-midshipmen, I found myself spending long days learning by rote the Rules of the Road and studying the necessary other subjects.[7] In July 1942, I traveled to the federal license examination room in New York City and passed a long week of examination.

Tom King was superintendent at Kings Point from 1980 to 1987.

German aircraft bombed the SS *Hoosier* on July 10, 1942, approximately sixty miles off the coast of Russia. An escort from Convoy PQ-17 sank the crippled *Hoosier* when the ship had to be abandoned in order to escape the danger of an approaching German submarine, *U-255*. All hands were rescued.[8]

John K. (Jack) Sweeney, Class of 1944

When I moved back to Chicago in 1937, I had joined a boat club, and Lake Michigan had a very good influence on my love of water and possibly thinking of being on the ship in any capacity, preferably on deck of course. That just was my interest; I was interested in anything that was on the water, to tell you the truth. I went to boat shows and was very enthusiastic about the lake, of course. I studied the history of a lot of lake ships, and I had joined the Sea Scouts. It was sponsored by the Chicago Yacht Club. So I had every opportunity to go out on yachts and everything. My dad wanted me to be a doctor or a lawyer. Those were two professions that he didn't do, and he wanted me to do obviously. Well, it didn't work out too well in high school. Study periods I spent in the library studying ships and navigation.

So then World War II came along. And of all things, I found an ad in the *Popular Mechanics* magazine about the Merchant Marine Academy. I said I wanted to do that. My dad had other plans as he always did, but I prevailed on that one. I said, "I'm going to sign up, and I'm going to go to that academy." It worked out. I came and I reported on December 7, 1942. It was a very significant date. I reported on Broadway and was brought out here [Kings Point]. We stayed in Army barracks in a preliminary section. It was over by one of the caretaker's houses, I believe. We were in a regular single-story Army barracks, wooden structure. I remember that. I think a lot of the buildings were temporary at that time. In the preliminary section they tried to get us ready for seaboard duty. And it was very important because there was an awful lot to learn. They even had us jump in the swimming pool with fire on the surface. And they showed us how to breathe, to come up to the surface and spread the water around so we could get a breath of air. We did it.

I imagine any ship, a tanker mainly, had that as a problem, but I hesitated at first to jump. I don't know whether somebody pushed me or whether I went in, but in I went and I had no problem with it. It was a lot safer than I ever imagined.

We had signal cards. We were learning all the rudiments of seamanship. I was in a fortunate position having been in the Sea Scouts in high school. When it came to rowing a lifeboat, being the coxswain, I pulled up to the dock. We just braked on one side, and the person that was the instructor said: "No need asking you any more questions. We'll just let it go at that." He said, "You obviously know what you're doing." Well, it was just like going into the Air Force and knowing how to fly already. The interest didn't wane. There were some hardships but very few. It was mostly just freezing your butt off in one of those buildings, if you could call that hardship.

Eliot H. Lumbard, Class of 1945

Eliot Lumbard's ancestral roots were planted in America before the Revolution. Subsequent to his World War II career as a cadet-midshipman and ship officer, he had a very successful practice in maritime law. Most recently he has been a benefactor of the Academy library and head of several writing projects in maritime and Academy history. For these endeavors, Lumbard was awarded an honorary doctorate in June 2005 at Kings Point.

I remember sitting around a radio in the 1930s, with my father, listening to Hitler rant. The buildup began, I would say, in our house around the mid-1930s, as he came into power. Often, we heard him.

I remember hearing Churchill on the radio. My father was interested in news. This was of course before television. I actually was listening to the radio December 7, 1941, and the first flash came of the attack on Pearl Harbor. I'll never forget the moment. I was sitting with my father, and it was electric in its consequences. I began thinking then, even though I was only a kid in school, about being drafted or going to war or where was this going—confusion. No one really knew up from down.

I graduated from high school in 1942, shortly after Pearl Harbor, and I immediately got involved in "would I be drafted or not." At that time, the draft age was eighteen, and in this maritime town, where I grew up, you were disgraced if you allowed yourself to be caught by the Army. Everyone went into the Navy or Coast Guard or to the merchant marine. I had a hard time with my mother and father about that, especially my mother. She just couldn't imagine me volunteering or getting involved in all of this.

And thus, the issue came up of what to do. I thought, at that time, that I might make a career of the merchant marine if I went in, and so I joined. I went to the Sheepshead Bay Maritime Training Facility, out in Brooklyn. There were thousands of seamen there. A lot happened to me there, including the fact that one day I was assigned to cleaning the head, and there were like one hundred white, china urinals in a row. Some fellow came and told me I could get out of this if I'd go down and take a test to go to this officers' place in Kings Point. It was about the only thing that would get me out of there. So I went and took the test.

A few weeks later, I got the announcement that I'd been accepted, just on the basis of the test. I really didn't know much about it, and shortly thereafter I was hustled onto a bus and I came to Kings Point, and I was part of a section. By now we're in the winter of '43.

It was a very intensive three-month course. I remember very well the construction that was going on here. At one point, we moved into some green barracks. They were wooden. They were sort of like what we used to call old CCC, Civilian Conservation Corps, barracks that were lined up. There was a bunch of them, and the place was one gigantic construction camp. In fact, our physical education never was physical education, other than to go down to the obstacle course, outside the gate a little bit. We'd run down there, go through the course a couple of times, and run back. We didn't do that much. Mostly what we did was chop trees and pull out bramble bushes and poison ivy on what are now the athletic fields. We were clearing the land. It was just dense work.

It was just packed with people, to capacity. You'd have to stand in line to get to eat, and this and that. There was a whole air of crisis and of need about everything. There was almost nobody, that I remember, just sort of faking it, or whatever. There were some who did, and they threw them out promptly. I thought that was good, because it kept everybody shaped up, and the sense among the preliminary people was of a real anxiety, because we knew we were going out, shortly, into a very difficult situation.

There were at this time, of course, a lot of returning cadets who had gathered together and formed the basis of the sections for the advanced course, and they were full of tales of torpedoed ships, of this and that, and so everybody tended to be extremely serious. The most important things were how to be a seaman. They didn't make any pretense of having academic subjects at that time. The only thing that came close to it was some mathematics.

So these were practical courses in actual seamanship.

I was a deck cadet: navigation, seamanship, a lot of practical seamanship, some elementary naval architecture. They had a longer course when I came back as an advanced student, and that sort of made you comfortable. There also were a lot of courses in how to function, like signaling, semaphore, flags, and a lot of lifeboat drill. We used to row almost every day. Everybody rowed, and companies used to have intercompany races with them. The whole point, of course, was that having the complete ease of facility with the lifeboats was crucial to maybe saving your life. It was heavy, hard work, especially in bad weather. Whatever, off you'd go.

We had one famous sort of weekend, in which you had the survival training. Got in the lifeboat with one meal, and we had to go down, out near Little Neck Bay, no matter what the weather. You got it for that weekend, and stayed overnight out there, in the boat, just to function. It was a "bad day."

In any event, sometime in the summer of '43, my section finished its work, at least to some extent. We were all packed up, ready to go. They marched us down in full uniform to have what we used to call a "before you get shot" picture, which was where they had a big 5-inch cannon down in front of Wiley Hall, where it is now. The photographer would set up, and the people were standing in line. You'd get up, with your gloves and your dress uniform, and have this picture taken, when you were looking very military. Right from there you'd go out to the buses. You'd go home for a week's leave; then you'd go back to New York and were assigned to ships.

There was no doubt it would be a war zone. There was no other thought. They'd send a copy of the photo home to your parents, too, in case something happened, I guess, and try to get a morale-building kind of thing.

3

THE BATTLE OF THE ATLANTIC

The Battle of the Atlantic determined the fate of Europe. The American delivery of war supplies and military personnel was the lifeblood of the Allied effort to win back Europe from the Nazis. From the onset of war in 1939, ships sailed from America for Britain, and after the U.S. entry into the conflict in 1941, the Atlantic sea routes swelled with ships delivering material to Allied ports. The German naval command knew they had to stop the flow of supplies or lose the war. In single patrols and in wolf packs, German U-boats doggedly tracked the Atlantic convoys in missions of annihilation. German submarine commanders called the early years of the Atlantic war the "Happy Time" because they were able to patrol the American coastline relatively unmolested, sinking ships along the way. By mid-1943, the Allies had increased the number of convoy escorts, and they had broken the communications code that the German high command used to direct submarine attacks. From then on, the U-boats became more vulnerable to counterattack, but there was no sudden cessation of danger, and for Kings Pointers, as well as their brethren on the high seas, the Atlantic continued to be a graveyard for the unlucky merchant ship that was caught in the sights of an enemy periscope. A total of 278 American merchant ships were lost in North Atlantic and Arctic waters.[1]

Captain Douglas F. Ponischil, Class of 1940

After devoting ten years to the sea (including World War II), Douglas Ponischil expected to go on to a shoreside career. However, he was recalled to active Navy duty during the Korean War and worked as a public

An Atlantic convoy during World War II, including a Liberty ship in the foreground. Courtesy of the United States Naval Institute.

The *Eli Whitney*, a Liberty ship. Courtesy of the United States Naval Institute.

information officer for two years aboard the USS *Antietam*, CV-36, and later the *Shangri-la*, CV-37. He is now retired.

I was sailing as junior third mate on the SS *Cardonia* and in March of '42 we made a trip to Puerto Rico, in blackout—no guns, nothing. I guess we had a Very pistol, which was the only gun we had—the captain probably had a gun. A Very gun—that's one you shoot a signal if you're in distress—used to be in the old days. It was like a flare gun. They called it a Very pistol.

So the only armament on the ship was, really, a flare gun for signaling.

Flare gun and the captain's pistol, the sidearm, which nobody ever saw. So we went to Puerto Rico, and when we left Puerto Rico, things were getting rough. German submarines were torpedoing ships in the Caribbean and the Gulf of Mexico, the Windward Passage, all around there. So they built these four rafts on the ship, just for protection. Even though we still didn't have any guns, there were wooden rafts and wooden slides on the side of the ship. When we left Puerto Rico, our cargo was mostly cases of rum and sugar. A lot of American personnel there were shipping their personal effects back to the States because things were getting tough, automobiles, household furniture, all this stuff. So a couple of days later, about four o'clock in the morning, we were off the coast of Haiti, the north coast of Haiti, heading for Guantanamo Bay to load sugar, and a German submarine shot a torpedo at us. We presume it was German, because that's what was going on there.

Did you see the wake of the torpedo?

I didn't. I was asleep. I was sleeping on deck, in fact, under one of the rafts because it was so hot, rolled all my clothes up to keep them from getting damp and my slippers were there. I slept on a cot underneath the raft. It must have been on the four-to-eight watch. The second mate sounded the alarm. He saw the torpedo coming, and he was able to divert the ship and avoid the torpedo. But he rang the alarm and rang the bells, and everybody was excited, running around like chickens with their heads cut off because we didn't know what was going on. All the officers went up to the bridge right away, and the captain immediately decided to head for the shore. We were right off Cape St. Nicholas Mole, about ten miles off, and there was a light flashing every ten seconds or pretty regularly. We headed for that, and then the submarine came around behind and started shelling us. It surfaced, and they were about maybe, oh, about three, four hundred yards behind us and just shelling like mad. Fires were starting in the passageways. We got the hoses out, trying to put the fires out, and that was useless. So finally the captain got everybody up in front of the ship for protection. We were down in the number-two hold or the number-three hold right in front of the housing part. They kept shelling, and they finally damaged the rudder, so that we lost steerage, where we couldn't control the ship.

The captain decided to abandon ship. So he blew one long whistle and six short for abandon-ship signal, and the submarine stopped shelling us at that time. The captain decided to split us up, and the lifeboats were hanging over the side of the ship, as we did in those days. They were ready to go. So he took the port lifeboat with about fifteen of the men, and the rest of us were going to take the lifeboat on the starboard side, but the boats were all full of shell holes from the shrapnel, and we didn't know they were full of kapok. Kapok was like a steel wool that all the water tanks on the sides of the lifeboats were lined with, so that even if they loaded full of water, they wouldn't sink. So they got off in this number-two lifeboat on the port side.

The captain had a dog, a little bulldog, and I took charge of the bulldog, little "D.M." for damn mess. We called him "Dimmie." I had him, and the rest of us were going to try to get off on the other lifeboat. But we first decided a raft would be better, so we decided to let the raft go. I had all my belongings, my money and all my personal belongings in this little zipper bag, and I threw it up onto the raft so I'd have it with me. Of course, I threw it a hundred yards out and never saw it again. We never could get the raft loose. The water swelled the wood. The wooden raft and the wooden slide and the dampness would cause it to just swell like glue. We took a great big crowbar and tried to pry it. We broke the turnbuckle loose and nothing happened. It wouldn't move, couldn't be used.

In about ten minutes, the submarine decided we were all off, and they shot two torpedoes right into the midships of the ship. The ship just hove up, and flames and sparks were coming out of the stack and oil and stuff just all over. Debris was falling. You just panicked. I guess there were about seventeen of us still there. We had a thirty-seven-man crew, and the captain took half. I think fifteen of us were still left, and we panicked. We didn't know what to do. So we ran up to the other lifeboat, and we said, "Well, let's." We tried to let it down with the davits jammed. We couldn't get it down, so we decided to cut the ropes and let it just fall in the roll, which we did. From each end, we cut the ropes and let it fall in the water. We threw a rope ladder over, and then we clambered down and got in the lifeboat. We kind of rode as best you could with a boatful of water: you pushed and you did what you could, and I remember these things. The chief steward started bailing with his cap. He was bailing the water. We convinced him that was useless because it's going to throw up as fast as he did it. So we got about maybe five hundred yards away and rested. We felt we were far enough away to avoid any suction because we knew it was going to sink.

Where the ship would draw down everything near it.

Right. That's what we were afraid of, but we were far enough away then. It was getting daylight. This was about six thirty in the morning by now. It was just getting daylight. The sun was just coming up, and the old ship was just like in the movies. The stern went down, the bow went up, and she just sank under the water. It was quite an experience. We were afraid they might come up and try to machine gun us, because we'd heard some stories of this, and we were very leery. But they didn't. The submarine disappeared, and we never saw it again.

Were there any shoreside aircraft, since you were near the coast, any U.S. aircraft coverage?

Nothing. We knew we had got an SOS out. The radio operator was with the captain near the group. We knew he had sent an SOS out. There was no contact.

After the ship sank, the pressure from the water caused the rafts to pop loose. They finally popped loose, three of them. We didn't see the fourth, but three of them popped loose, so we were able to row over and get them. We tied them one behind the other. There was this lifeboat and these three rafts. We put up the sail, to try to sail, but, of course, with the heavy boat like that you couldn't really sail. We were out there all day, and then the sun came out. I didn't have any shoes, I lost my slippers in all the confusion, and I was barefoot. I had the dog with me. I had my pants, a jacket, and a T-shirt, and we just kind of huddled together.

I claim that the malted milk tablet saved my life because nobody was hungry. We had water, but I liked the malted milk tablets. They were sweet. We also had pemmican. Pemmican: little cans, like little deviled eggs or deviled ham cans of chopped apples, raisins and dates, very rich, to give you nourishment. So we ate some of that and some biscuits, but I thought the malted milk tablets were the best. We could have survived several days. So all day, in the hot sun and, finally, late in the afternoon, the trade winds picked up, and it started getting choppy, and the rafts started bumping against each other. We'd try to fend them off with the boat hooks, and it got worse and worse.

Then the sharks came, and I remember this vividly. I always thought, well, people are just making up stories about sharks, so that's a bunch of bull, but sharks were there. These big sharks were just swimming around, swimming around. We'd try to poke them with a boat hook, and, finally, they went away. They were eight to ten feet long. I mean, big, big, big sharks, longer than a man out there, just swimming around, very agitated. They didn't try to bump the rafts or anything, they were just swimming around. They were there. Finally, they went away, but it got rougher and rougher as the darkness came on.

Just before it got dark, there was a Navy plane that was photograph- ing the coast of Haiti. When they saw us, they came over, and they tried to wave their wings to tell us that they had seen us. They threw a canister over to tell us that help was on the way, which we knew anyway, but we never could get it. It was too far off from where we were. We couldn't row the rafts, so we didn't try to get it, but it was comforting to know that they saw us. They took some photos of us, which I still have, of the life raft, of the lifeboat and the three rafts. I still have that photo, out there, drifting away.

It got a little cold, a little chilly. We were just huddled, and we decided to separate the rafts because they were going to break up if we didn't, which was, in later days now I think back, kind of a mistake. You should always stick together. But at that time, that was the decision we made, so we put about five men on each raft, and we'd let the lifeboat just go adrift. So we split up and just prayed, and that was all we could do. There probably were some oars and boat hooks, but they were square rafts. They were about ten feet long, about eight feet wide. They had seats on them, like U-shaped wooden seats so you could put your feet down on it.

The water was coming up and splashing, and it was pretty harrowing. The next morning, dawn came, and then the sun came out again and it got warm. It got hot, and my feet just got so sunburned because I had no protection for them, but the rest of me was okay. I still had my cap, and I had the dog huddled there with me, all full of oil and grease and dirt, but he was comfortable with me.

Finally, about eleven o'clock in the morning on the second day, we saw smoke on the horizon coming from the west. It was a Navy net tender. They picked up guys on one of the rafts and took them aboard, and then ours was the second. They got to us and took us aboard. As soon as we climbed up the rope ladder, they handed us a big steaming mug of coffee, and that was great to have. Then they let us go down into the washroom to clean up, and, in the meantime, they got the guys off the third raft, so we got everybody.

When I went down to clean up and wash up, I looked in my pocket for a comb for some strange reason. There were my socks [that] I had in my pockets rolled up all the time. I could have had them on my feet to keep them from getting sunburned. In all the excitement, you don't think of things like that. I never once thought of looking for my socks.

They let us go down on the fantail. There was a big, shaded awning, and all of us went back there and laid down and rested. They gave us some food. They were sinking ships right and left that weekend, all over, in the bay, in the Windward Passage, all around there.

U-boats were sinking them.

U-boats, yes. At that time, they took us back to Guantanamo Bay, Cuba, the big U.S. naval base. They had just been building a bunch of new barracks there, and they put us up in those barracks. The doctors kind of checked us over. Nobody was really injured. We accounted for all of our men. As soon as they dumped us off, they refueled and took on some more supplies and went out to get more guys. They were just coming right back and forth. A lot of the tankers were being sunk, and with fires, guys would come in all burned. I remember, some guy brought a cat in. The cat's paws were all burned raw, and we had the dog. The cat and the dog were trying to fight each other, but they couldn't. They couldn't do much.

We had nice accommodations. They had the dormitory rooms and showers and all. We cleaned up, and we were there for about two weeks.

We found out that the captain and his group had actually ridden ashore. When they got near the shore, the natives of Haiti came out in another boat and got them and helped them get in. They were like heroes. They put them up in the best hotel in Port-au-Prince, and they were written up in the paper, about their heroism or whatever. We found out, after we put all the names together, we only lost one man, disappeared, and we never knew what happened to him. Somebody said he got hit by shrapnel, and that he bled some blood. When he got in the water, the sharks ate him. Nobody really knew. The ship was the SS *Cardonia*, a Lykes Brothers old Hog Island–type ship. This was March 7, 1942. And I still have a piece of one of the life rings with the canvas with *Cardonia* stamped on it.

So we got into Guantanamo Bay, and we were there for about two weeks. Then, while we were there, somehow they arranged for a plane to bring the guys from Port-au-Prince, and they stopped off, and they picked up most of our men. The chief mate was a guy named Henry Denker. He was German ancestry, and he was real fearful, for some reason, that the German submarines were going to be after him because he was German. He had only emigrated to the country maybe ten years previously. So he asked me to stay with him on Guantanamo. We couldn't all get on the plane. About five of us had to stay. So I agreed to stay with him, and the rest of them went on to Miami, and they were heroes. They got written up in the paper and all that stuff, and he just stayed back. Finally, they were able to get another Lykes Brothers ship that came into Camaguey, Cuba, to load sugar. They said they could take us back to Galveston, but we had to get there.

We arranged to go. First we got on a train. Then we had to cross a big lake, and then we got on a bus, and we had to drive the main highway from Santiago de Cuba to Havana. We got halfway, somewhere, some little Cuban town, halfway through, and they put us up at a lousy, second-rate hotel. We were all bitching, complaining about that. The next day, they finally got us on this other ship. They took good care of us and gave us rooms and all. We went from there through the other pass on the west end of Cuba and up to Galveston. So we were in the Gulf about two and a half to three days from there to Galveston, and, boy, nobody slept. We would not. We were pacing the deck, watching for submarines all the time; looking out, but we made it back without any problems. So that was a pretty harrowing experience.

The German submarine *U-126* torpedoed and shelled the 390-foot freighter SS *Cardonia* on March 7, 1942, five miles from Haiti. One crew member, a fireman, was killed by shrapnel when the submarine shelled the ship. On March 8, the USS *Mulberry* (AN-27) picked up Douglas Ponischil and his fellow survivors.[2]

James L. Risk, Class of 1942

Hailing from Florida, Jim Risk entered into the Cadet Corps of the U.S. Maritime Commission at the age of twenty. In the course of his wartime experiences, he sailed into almost every theater of military operations. By war's end, he was elevated to shipmaster. He came ashore "for good," as he says, in 1947. During his subsequent career he worked as a district sales manager.

The SS *Delrio* was our ship, and we went down on our "coffee run" to South America. We had no guns. They had managed to get two platforms for the ship, one on the stern and one on the bow, but they were empty! No guns whatsoever. So the captain and crew rigged together a cargo boom and draped it over the stern on the platform in the back, painted it black, and then took some tarpaulin paper and put it over it, to simulate a 4-inch broadside gun, which it was not. And away we went. They had put four .30-caliber machine guns on a platform amidships. We simulated abandon ship, because the captain was real gung-ho on the activities.

He had a ring-tailed monkey that was about 125 pounds, a very vicious beast, as his pet. Nobody could get near that darn monkey except for the captain. He used to take it up in the mornings and chain it to the platform support for this .30-caliber. As a cadet, that was my responsibility, those four guns. Of course, there were no Armed Guards, we just had merchant crew. So I was trying to teach them how to shoot the gun. One morning at General Quarters, we all rushed up to our assigned stations. Some of the crew went to lifeboats. There was this monkey, and he wouldn't let us aboard the gun platforms. Here we were, struggling, trying to get to the guns and couldn't do it.

We continued on this first trip without any guns. We went down to South America and made our trip back, went into Trinidad and refueled, and then on into New Orleans. There we got guns. They brought a 4-inch 50, a 4-inch broadside, on the stern and 3-inch 50 on the bow and replaced the .30-calibers with 20mm guns. At the same time, we were assigned a Navy Armed Guard group. With that, we sailed. We made our coffee run.

Two instances on that particular trip which were interesting: I'm still a cadet. First incident was that we had a merchant seaman who had a very severe case of DTs. The captain had seen fit to lock him up in the lazarette [storeroom] under guard, with chains, to keep him from harming himself or anybody else. Sunday morning came, and the captain decided to go up into Recife, Pernambuco, the northern peninsula of Brazil. That city was a twin city. The other city was native and there was a four-hundred-foot cliff in the lower city down in the bay side, which was German, German Marks [currency] and banks and everything else. German was spoken on the streets.

We pulled in that Sunday morning, and that was the Sunday morning that Brazil decided to declare war on Germany. The captain anchored out, got the Armed Guard commander, and he wanted to form a group to take the kid off the ship, the DT boy, and take him back to the local hospital. Normally that would be the American ambassador's job to do, but the ambassador was very busy with the result of war declared that very morning. So the Armed Guard officer refused to do it. This was not in the Navy regs for having to have any part of a civilian operation, but he did give me his sidearm. He gave me his .45 sidearm, and I, in full uniform, took the kid ashore with handcuffs, and we went into the lower city from the pier. High-quality cigars, which were selling for twenty-five cents apiece, very good, were ankle-deep in the streets. Paperwork out of the banks and the commercial installations of Germany, Marks, were all ankle-deep in the street, and that place was a riot! The natives had come off the cliffs like lemmings, and they would run through the lower city just destroying everything, knocking poles into buildings, tearing everything apart.

I marched this kid through all of this mess down in the lower city, got to the elevators, which was the way you got to the top of the base, and finally got on the elevator, because it was just masses of natives, people all over the place. I got up to the top.

Then I escorted this kid across the town to the so-called hospital on the outskirts of the city. That was a very tough time for me. I did have three cartons of cigarettes with me, to give to the kid when I was going to leave him. I walked into this hospital, and it was not a hospital. It was an insane asylum. The inmates had no clothes on whatsoever, and they were milling around a big yard, a high-fenced yard with armed guards around it. The barrack rooms were just like a jail. There were bars on the room doors and windows. Of course, I'm just a kid, I had my orders, so I left him there. But that was a real tough situation. I knew I brought him some care with my cigarettes, but that's all.

Back to sea we went. The second day out, we're heading toward Trinidad to refuel, which was our standard instructions, and we spotted a lifeboat in the water. It had fifteen English survivors from a tanker that had been sunk over a month before in the South Atlantic. I've thought about that, trying to remember this ship's name and also the captain and the chief engineer and the other people we "fished out." They were in bad shape. They would have been cooked goose because of the hot sun down there. The only thing that saved them was that when the tanker blew up, 40 million gallons or something of fuel oil went up in the air and it all came down.

The chief engineer, I remember particularly, was an older man, and somehow he got to be my responsibility. I had to go over the side and put a breeches buoy on him and gently push him aboard the ship. He was actually stark staring naked. He had been sleeping in his bunk when the thing went up, and nobody had any clothes to speak of. He was coated with oil. That's the only thing that kept them all from getting fried with the hot sun down there, without any protection from that sun whatsoever. They were dehydrated, of course—very, very poor condition. As near as we could figure out, it was twenty-three days that they had been out in the open. We got them cleaned up. None of them died. We got them back to Trinidad, and we turned them over to the English at that point, and away they went.

In Trinidad, we were told to go to New York. This was an interesting little diversion because the ship had been for thirty years going between New Orleans and South America. All of the officers aboard the ship had never been north of the Dry Tortugas in their lives but were long aboard ship. They had no charts. Nobody in Trinidad could give us any charts. But we did have a tide table, and we did have a weather chart, which was eighteen by twenty-six inches, something like that. It had the outlines of the country, prevailing weather, and was brought up to date periodically by radio messages. I was a cadet. I was born and raised in Florida, and I've sailed on sailboats, have worked aboard a full-rigged ship one summer, had worked aboard tankers a couple of summers. All on the east coast, so I did know the east coast and had been up there before. Our instructions were to get into Hatteras at either dawn or sunset. So we went. We elected to go outside of Bermuda and come back into Hatteras in a straight line.

A couple of hundred miles outside of Bermuda one sunset, we saw the outline of this ship on the horizon. We did have the Navy [ship] silhouette books. We looked it up, and it was thought to be a German surface raider. It was not a German surface raider as it turned out; it was a supply ship for German submarines. But there it was. We were on the inboard side, and this ship was on the east side of us, and behind us was this big, very big, storm and rain and very cloudy weather. So our ship was really enveloped in darkness. We could see him, and I don't think they ever really saw us. The captain panicked, and he broke radio silence, which he's not supposed to do, and got hold of the Navy and told them that we had spotted this surface raider, as he was calling it, and we were running west as fast as we could go, 8.5 knots, heading for Hatteras.

The Navy somehow got that all confused, and they thought that the SS *Delrio* had been sunk, and we weren't at all. So we arrived the following morning at Hatteras, at sunrise, as our instructions were, and the Navy didn't believe us. They were convinced that we were sunk, so they felt we were a German ship. They went around us and around us, checking the names. They even went up to the forward part of the ship and checked the Plimsoll marks because the German Plimsoll marks are very definitive, so one of the ways you could tell if it was authentic or not was the Plimsoll marks. They had three DEs [destroyer escorts]. The other thing that was fouling up the Navy was that we were the first merchant ship in thirty-four days to get by Hatteras without being sunk. So it was "panicsville."

We lay overnight, after we convinced them who we were. They still were hesitant about it, but they finally sent an armed troop aboard, and we answered the proper questions about who's in the ball game and convinced them. But the next morning we were supposed to sail under escort, and we went out and a DE right in front of us was destroyed by a German torpedo. So back to Hatteras. We finally got out and back to New York.

For Jim Risk's subsequent trips to North Russia, see chapter 6, "The Murmansk Run."

Robert B. Wells, Class of 1941

Bob Wells was for many years a professor of engineering at Kings Point until his retirement in 1980. His fascination with mechanical devices has never ceased, and he had been seen on numerous occasions commuting to the Academy by motorcycle. He has a chief engineer's license. Cheerful and friendly, he still attends affairs at Kings Point.

In 1941, I was on the MS *America Sun* as third [assistant engineer]. Then war was declared December 7, 1941, and in 1942 the east coast became known as Torpedo Alley. There were U-boats off the coast, but we were very lucky. We never got shot at by a German submarine, but we became, as the Army calls it, targets of friendly fire. We were coming up from Texas in March 1942, loaded one night during a blackout, and a fellow American or an English ship collided with us. They hit us on number-nine tank. The result was the oil from the tank sprayed over the stern end of the ship and into the fire room, and the ship caught fire. Fortunately, we put the fire out, but we had a hole in the ship that ran two-thirds of the way through. The only thing that held the ship together was the keel and one-third or a quarter of the ship on the port side. We then sort of bounced our way up the coast. We managed to limp into port.

Do you think the collision would have occurred if there weren't the blackout conditions that you related?

No, absolutely not, because we'd have lights and so forth. There were blackouts at the time, and it was also foggy, I believe, when they hit us. It was around two in the morning. I was third, so I was off watch and turned in around midnight, twelve thirty or so. Then, when the ship hit us at two in the morning, we thought we were torpedoed. When I got out of my bunk and dashed on deck, I saw the bow of the ship and realized that it wasn't a torpedo. Then I went into the engine room and heard the other ship backing off. Nevertheless, we were still on fire so we had to assemble up the group of engineers, and we proceeded to put the fire out. Fortunately, we got it in time; otherwise, the ship would have gone up.

They sent me home for two weeks to recuperate. I was telling people how I lost a ship with a collision, and nobody would believe me. So I was home for two weeks, and then they called me up and asked me if I'd like to go out to the South Pacific.

To read about Robert Wells's sea experiences on D-Day and in the Pacific, see chapters 8 and 9.

William H. Ford, Class of 1944

William Ford witnessed the loss of two fellow cadet-midshipmen, John P. Lambert and Richard M. Record, who were with him aboard the ship *James Oglethorpe*, for sea training. After World War II, William Ford

went ashore and earned a bachelor's degree in mathematics at New York University. He subsequently worked for the Sperry Gyroscope and Lockheed corporations. Also, he continued graduate education at the Georgia Institute of Technology, where he earned a master of science degree in engineering mechanics. Later, he worked for twelve years for the Federal Aviation Administration designing airport control towers. He has since retired to form his own structural engineering company.

We lost our ship, the *Norlantic*.[3] We were standing off Venezuela, on May 12, 1942. That was quite memorable. I was just an ordinary seaman. It was a small cargo ship, about five thousand tons. We were hit by a torpedo, shelled at first. They wanted to wipe out the radio shack, which they did very well. But in so doing, they killed about half my crew. She was a U-boat. She was on the surface all the time. We saw them with our eyes before sundown. They were taking on after us, and we steamed as fast we could go. We were trying to get into Venezuela.

Most of the shelling and machine gunning took place on the port side of the ship. I was on the starboard side, which was rather sheltered. We lowered away. They came by us when we were on our lifeboat. They wanted to see the captain, but we lied very successfully. We said he was burnt with the ship, but really he was with us. It was dark then.

We stayed in the area until daylight. We didn't know where the other boat was. We saw it in daylight, and we went over to it. Every man in that boat was either dead or wounded, and she was awash. So we took off. We buried the dead and took everyone into our boat. We sailed for four and a half days. We didn't want to go to the Venezuelan coast because at that time it was pretty dangerous. They were all in danger over there, believe it or not. We were picked up by a Dutch sailing vessel and taken into Bonaire, which was under Dutch rule. We were flown back to the United States. That was the first one [ship sinking].

I guess equally memorable was the sinking of the *James Oglethorpe*.[4] I went through the basic school at Pass Christian, Mississippi, and I was a midshipman and cadet then. Four cadets were sent aboard the *James Oglethorpe*, a Liberty ship. It was March 16, 1943, off Iceland. We didn't see the submarine at all. It was a clean torpedo, just one. It was quite dramatic for a short time. I knew she was going to stay afloat for a while, at least for a couple of hours. The impact took place on the starboard side, about number-three hold, in the engine room.

We were in the water first for a few minutes. It was cold. Oh, it was beastly. That was the most horrendous of all. Well, that's what killed everyone. I don't think there was anybody hit with the torpedo. Might have been; I don't know. But we wouldn't have lost all those men had it been in warmer waters. Most of the young men there were inexperienced. We were all in whites. We got on all the warm clothes we could get and put on the rubber suit. This we did, and this is the way we survived. Thirteen survived, out of a crew of seventy-eight.

The engines were out, and the screw was secured and not turning, fortunately. I was one of them by that wheel. We would have been chopped up, I'm sure. The ship was still making way slowly, and she drifted. The ship stayed afloat three or four hours, I expect. But there's no way you can repair a ship that was damaged like that.

Six of us were picked up by a British corvette. I got separated from my brother-in-law to be. He was picked up by a British four-stack destroyer, and we weren't carried to the same place. I was taken into Berwick, Scotland, and he was taken into Londonderry, Ireland. We thought each one was dead.

We came back stateside on the old *Queen Elizabeth*. We stood out across the Atlantic, going about 38 knots. Nobody could keep up with us, even on the surface. As a matter of fact, there's no ship in the world at that time that could pass her. I mean no destroyer, 'cause the seas were too heavy. We had to stay in port for a couple of days to talk to insurance people, the FBI, everyone. They really wanted to be sure the ship went down, I expect. In the meantime, I was taken home by my brother-in-law to be, and I met his sister. It was a year later we got married, because as a midshipman, I couldn't get married. I sat for my license June 1, 1944, and then became a third mate.

William G. Holby, Class of 1944

Proud of his Kings Point education, Bill Holby was for many years an admissions representative for the Academy. After the war, he returned to college and studied music. He achieved a master's degree in organ performance, and he was an organist and choir director for several churches. He retired at age eighty-two.

It was in the fall of '42 that I enlisted in the Merchant Marine Cadet Corps. At that time, you went through a Navy recruiter principally because of a physical exam. Then I was brought out on a bus to Kings Point, and at that time the place was under construction, and there were CCC-type barracks erected on campus. We went to classes, but that lasted only a short while. Around the end of December, I was done with this preliminary training and then was assigned to a Liberty ship, the *Jeremiah Van Rensselaer*, named after a cosigner of the Declaration of Independence. This was a beautiful ship built in Williamston, North Carolina, and I was assigned there as a deck cadet. There was another midshipman, William R. Lindy, on that ship as the engine cadet, and we shared the same room.

The ship had an aborted attempt at getting out of New York. I was assigned to it when it was loading up in Brooklyn and we went out to join our first convoy, but we had a minor collision with a tanker in the Narrows, and that delayed our departure. So we had to wait quite a few days for another convoy.

Our ship then had to go and tie up at a pier on Manhattan, and right across the slip from our pier, was the SS *Dorchester*,[5] a troop ship which was later to gain great notoriety because it was sunk on its way to Greenland. The many soldiers that were lost on this ship was just horrible. And it was on this ship that the famous four chaplains sailed. They were commemorated on a stamp in the 1950s.

At any rate, about the third week of January 1943 we proceeded out on a sixty-two-ship convoy. This was a memorable occasion. We went up north over the Grand Banks, and our position was in the port corner of the convoy. There were ships three deep, and it must have been about thirty ships across the horizon. We couldn't see the other side of the convoy, but we were back in what later got named as "coffin corner" because it was easy picking by the submarines.

And about ten days out, that's what happened. We were about halfway across when our ship was sunk by a German submarine.[6]

Do you recall where the torpedo hit the ship?

Yes! Up on the bow. The first one hit up on the bow, and that didn't sink us so they fired a second one, which did.

And you were in your bunk at the time?

That's right. This was just past midnight. A moonless night. It was like a thunder drum to hear that thing echo through the ship. There was no alarm, and this is the tragic thing. As I look back on that occasion, I remember the crew of that ship. They had qualified people as officers, but there was never an abandon-ship order given, and a lot of the people they had picked up off the street. It was that type of individual that made up most of the crew, because there were no others to do the job (the pressure of the time). People were out to make a fast buck, and they also thought only of number one, and in a way that cost them their lives.

How long did the ship last before it went down?

Probably half an hour. The first one [torpedo], the ship could have survived. But it started a fire. I know that. Well, there were escorts, but I don't know what they were able to do. They stayed with the convoy after that. I really don't know what else might have been done. At that time, you have to think of what's happening and do your best with what you know.

I was one of the very few survivors. It was actually a very disorderly abandon ship. I never heard an order to abandon ship, but we did escape. We got in lifeboats, and I was in one of the last lifeboats to go over the side, and it was only Armed Guard crew. The rest had abandoned the ship on the lee side, the sheltered side. Most of them were lost because they were too hasty in going. They weren't adequately dressed, and this was being in the North Atlantic at that time on the last day of January, a very bad time of the year to be in the water. The temperature was probably in the forties or fifties. The water temperature was cold, but yet we were in the Gulf Stream. We were not in really Arctic water, thank God for that. I was thoroughly soaked myself, and our boat filled with water, pretty well. One very valuable thing I learned from this—and this I attribute to the training at Kings Point—and that was the lifeboat certificate we had to get that qualified you as a lifeboatman. It means you were well versed in the handling of lifeboats. I had, among other duties given to me by the first mate on the ship before we sailed, the job of going around making sure that everything was well lashed in the lifeboats, so I knew where all the things were.

Our ship was sunk just after midnight, while we were in real darkness. The U-boats could see at night; your visual acuity becomes quite sharp for silhouettes, and that's what they did. They spotted our ship, being back in the corner, and they picked us off.

While the night was very dark, you could see the horizon. So as we were floating in our lifeboat, the principal thing was, to me, to do what we could to keep warm, and I got out some blankets. I knew where they were.

Then I saw a small ship on the horizon that I thought could be looking for us. I thought I'd make his job easier, so I found a pistol called a "Very" pistol, which is used to fire a flare. I fired a flare, and the wind being so strong, immediately it went out, and it was swept right into the water, but it stayed lit long enough for them to see where we were. That's how we got rescued.

The swells were tremendous. It was fifty or sixty feet from the crest of one wave to the next, and you'd be in the trough of a wave for a long time and then rise to the crest. But they came over and got us, and they called out over a PA, keep your lapel lights on, those were on the life jackets. So we did, and they were able to spot us and we were rescued in that manner.

What type of ship rescued you?

It was a little steamer, the SS *Accrington* from Scotland. It was a British ship, and its mission was just to do what it was doing, to pick us up. They stayed around until daylight, and they picked up other people on rafts.

The engine cadet was also lost. He dashed out. He was asleep, and I was just sitting in my bunk, reading. He dashed out and probably got on a raft, but he didn't have enough on to keep him from being exposed to that wind. It was the wind that was the chief thing that just takes all the heat out of you. And if you're wet, you don't stand a chance. You can only last a few minutes. So his name is over in the Academy chapel. I've seen his name there, William Lindy. That was certainly a memorable experience. Our rescue ship took us to Glasgow or to Gurick, Scotland, where I stayed until I was sent down to Liverpool and repatriated on a Grace Lines C2 that came back to New York.

So during your sea year [training], you're on the merchant ship, the Liberty ship, and as part of convoy your ship was sunk.

That's right. The next night a tanker was sunk, and we stopped to pick up—well, there were no survivors from that ship. Then I had not been at sea long enough so I was assigned to a troop ship, the *George Washington*,

THE BATTLE OF THE ATLANTIC 71

and that's when we sailed with troops from New York to Casablanca for the North African campaign. We learned on the way across that the German armies, Rommel's troops, surrendered finally in Africa. So from then on, it was a push across the Mediterranean into Italy. We weren't in the Mediterranean. Casablanca is on the west coast of Africa, on the Atlantic, so we didn't go through Gibraltar. We were there several days and then returned to New York. Our ship was then sent down through the Panama Canal to San Francisco, and then we took ten thousand troops to Brisbane, Australia. This was still part of the sea year. By the time I had returned to Long Beach, California, I had been six months at sea, and that was my sea training.

I came back to Kings Point to complete a third mate's license. I enjoyed it very much. I placed second in my class academically and went on active duty in the Navy right away.

See chapter 14, "Navy," for Bill Holby's subsequent career in the Pacific.

Paul L. Milligan Jr., Class of 1944

Holder of a degree in health systems management from Harvard University, Paul Milligan was instrumental in establishing the first health maintenance organization in Pennsylvania. Earlier, after leaving the Navy, he had worked for two telephone systems. He attributes his successful career largely to his Kings Point education.

My training here at the Academy came in 1942. I guess it was about July of '42. I don't have the specific date because all those papers were lost at sea. However, I spent the first six months here at the Academy, scared as heck and raring to go, because I was just a young fella. I was finally assigned for sea duty, the SS *Wade Hampton*, which was sailing from New York. It was a Liberty ship. It was brand-new. We took it on the maiden voyage to shake down and all that sort of thing, and when we finally headed for sea, we were going to Murmansk. I was one of the cadets. There were two of us, a Cadet George Miller and myself. He was the engineering cadet; I was the deck cadet. About four days, maybe six days out of port, we were attacked by submarines, and we were in a very large convoy. We were up in the very cold water. It was February 28 of 1943 off of Greenland. The temperature Fahrenheit at the time was around 28. I remember that. The seas were very rough. The convoy was intact, but fairly well dispersed, and the problem was that we only had two small British corvettes to protect approximately fifty to sixty ships. And they were pretty small.

Did you use a zigzag pattern at all?

Yes, we did. And that was pretty difficult because of the largeness of the convoy. But, up to that point we had no collisions. It was just a cold trip. I was assigned a four-to-eight [watch]. Since being a deck cadet, I was trying to study all the navigation I could possibly get, and that was the time of the navigator watch, four to eight. I had just gone off the bridge and was half-way asleep when I heard this loud thump. The bells went off, and I knew there was some kind of a problem. Mr. Miller, the other cadet, and I were assigned to take care of a lifeboat, to have it lowered in the water and hold it close to the ship until the survivors would come down the ladder into it. There were two torpedoes. As a matter of fact, they were almost midships. The interesting thing about that was that we had in midships mostly general cereal like Post Toasties and Corn Flakes, for Russia. But in the bow, we had a lot of ammunition, and in the stern, the Armed Guards had a lot of ammunition. So the ship did not blow. It just started to sink.

Did the ship become disabled completely?

Yes. As a matter of fact, it blew a pretty large hole in the engine compartment. The fire started on the ship, and the tail section ultimately broke off where the armed guard was. None of them, to my knowledge, were saved. There were not too many saved from the whole disaster. But on top of that, Cadet Miller and I went to our stations, and at that time the lifeboats were lowered by hand on davits, and the seas were very high. It was a storm. They lowered the lifeboats. He was in the bow and I in the stern, and whoever was lowering the lifeboats on the deck let go the stern line so that the bowline held, and the stern line went down and threw us both out into the sea. I don't know whether the lifeboat was ever recovered or not, but Cadet Miller never was found again.

I had a lifejacket on. I didn't have much, because I was in bed. But I did have boots, and they were sucked off, and so I was there with a pair of pants and a sweater and a lifejacket. And it was kind of cold. I had a davit, but the thing went so quickly, that it just let go so quickly. I actually went down under and came back up, and the boots were sucked off. I don't know what transpired for several hours. It may not have been several hours. It seemed like that. I don't know what the length of time was. But I was float-ing around out there, and I was by myself. I couldn't hear anything ex-cept the wind, and a lifeboat bumped me on the shoulder, and guys looked down and said, "Well, here's somebody you know." So they got me into the boat from the *Hampton*. There wasn't anything really around us.

What had actually happened was the *Hampton* wasn't performing up to speed. The convoy, let's just say for example, was going at 10 knots, and we were only making 8. So we kept drifting back and back and back. So we were there practically by ourselves.

I was pulled into the lifeboat. There were several other men, I believe eight all together, including me. Some of them were in bad shape; some of them were not too bad. I had had my chest all caved in, both shoulders broke, and I was pretty cold at the time. We were, ultimately, and I can't tell you the length of time, quite some time, a day at least, picked up by a British corvette. There were only six of us left at that time.

There was another boat, at least one more boat of survivors. So a British corvette picked us up and kept on with us. I can't tell whether it was the same convoy that we finally caught up to, or it was another convoy coming along subsequently, but they took us to Liverpool.

I must say that I really couldn't identify myself. I didn't have anything with me, but they took my word for it, and really treated me like an officer and a gentleman. They put me in a sickbay right away, and they packed me with ice pretty well. At that time, I think that was the treatment for hypo-thermia, to try to bring you down slowly off of it.

I remember a funny incident. First of all, they put me in with the crew, which was fine with me, until dinnertime. So they had me classed a crew-member until dinnertime, and when they served the meal, it was just awful. It was just fat mutton, and nobody seemed to complain. I didn't really ei-ther. But I said, "What are the officers eating?" And they said, "Well, they're eating such and such." I tried to explain to them, well, I'm a cadet, and we were treated like an officer in the United States. I convinced them of that, and they finally changed the chow.

We arrived at Liverpool, England. From there, within twelve hours I was transferred to a train, and they took me to the hospital in Glasgow, where, subsequently, I recovered enough to leave the hospital on crutches and be transferred to the YMCA, sort of a hotel where sailors stayed. I stayed there a fair amount. It was several months until I got passage back to the United States. The shipping company provided me with clothing and some money, because when I came out of the hospital, I had nothing except what they gave me. They gave me a sweater, a pair of shoes, a pair of underwear and a pair of pants. That was enough, and it was wonderful. I couldn't believe how terrific the people there were. They would give you the shirt off their backs, everybody, knowing that you were a survivor on something. They couldn't do enough for you in Scotland.

So, by then I finally got a passage back on a large passenger ship, the *Sterling Castle*, a Castle Line ship. It was an English, very famous ship. I had established my identity then, and I emphasize this, as having been a cadet from the United States merchant marine. So I was immediately, when I was put aboard the ship, put in a room by myself, and ate in the officers' dining room, which was probably, during peacetime, the main dining room. We had great menus, like you have on cruise ships today.

You kind of had a choice, and you could roam the ship at will. I was still recovering from the accident, and I remember one day we were up on deck, not too far from the United States. It was about the second or third day out, and just trying to get a little exercise. We were passing the medicine ball around, and somebody became a little overzealous and passed it to me, and it caved my chest in again. I missed the ball, and so I was almost back to where I was. I was then taken to New York, but there's not much you can do for a sternum and ribs. They just have to kind of heal themselves. I was taken to the hospital, then released, and went on to my home in Pittsburgh, Pennsylvania. That was sort of a kind of an odd, or humorous situation.

I didn't have any uniforms, so they just took me to the large department store in Glasgow and outfitted me. I could have had just about anything I wanted. So I got a suit and all the regular things that a person would buy, and an overcoat. But I also said, while we're here, I would buy a homburg. Nobody wears homburgs anymore, I guess. But I had the homburg and this cane, and I looked like the Lord of Buckingham, or something. When I finally arrived in Pittsburgh, my parents were waiting at the station, and all my dad could do was laugh, and my mother was standing there crying. I had to be about twenty.

On February 28, 1943, the SS *Wade Hampton* was torpedoed by *U-405* after the Liberty ship straggled eight miles behind her convoy, HX-227. She was manned by thirty-seven merchant crew and fourteen Naval Armed Guard. Four crewmen, including Cadet-Midshipman George

C. Miller Jr., and five Navy men were lost, including the Naval Armed Guard commander.[7]

Leslie Churchman, Class of 1944

Born in New Jersey, Leslie Churchman first came to the Academy as a cadet-midshipman in September 1942. Churchman is grateful he survived the war, stating, "I would not have missed it, because the effort was so great that I always think of it that way." After the war, he went into manufacturing within the aircraft industry, utilizing the engineering education he acquired at Kings Point. Later he developed a career in casting engineering and industrial sales.

I left Kings Point for my sea year at the end of February, 1943. I was called into an office at 45 Broadway, with three other fellows. There was a captain there, and he said, "I have two *Luckenbach* ships." The *Andrea*, and another ship I don't recall. He said, "Why don't Churchman and Coonan take the *Andrea*, and Byrd and Miller take the other?" So we did, and we went out to Gravesend Bay in Brooklyn and boarded the ship. We were there for a few days, and then we went up the Cape Cod Canal to Boston.

The *Andrea* was a freighter. It was reported to be the largest freighter under the American flag at that time. It was also reported that it had been built in Japan for the lumber trade on the West Coast, which turns out not to be true. It was built in Quincy, Massachusetts, but it did have a very Japanese silhouette, and they didn't feel they could have it in the Pacific.

From Boston, we joined a convoy that was going to England, although we didn't know it at the time. We were probably ten days out, at the place that they call Torpedo Junction. We had a small aircraft carrier with us. It was one of those Jeep carriers. It left us about three or four in the afternoon, because the seas were so rough that they couldn't launch anything.

We were in the center of a convoy of about ninety ships. It was the largest convoy, I believe, to that date. We were carrying blockbusters. It was all ammunition—five-hundred-pound bombs. I was working the four-to-eight watch, and I had just had dinner. I had just gone back down to the engine room, when we had these two tremendous, earth-shaking hits. It was about six thirty in the evening, and I remember the lights went out, then they came back on. You couldn't see for the dust flying from down through the fiddley.[8] The second engineer said, "Stop the engines!" We had twin screws. We started to crank the engines, the throttles down.

We had been hit with two torpedoes in the stern, and about seventy feet of the stern had been blown right off. So when we tried to crank the engines down, they just kept spinning out of control. There wasn't anything on the end of them. So I said, "Let's get out of here!" and we ran up. I reached in my cabin and grabbed my life jacket. The only thing I had was a short-sleeved dungaree shirt and a pair of khaki pants.

In the afternoon, we had lost two of our starboard lifeboats. During the war, we had to have them out over the side, and they were swept away on the weather side. So the only lifeboats we had were two on the port side. We also had the cargo nets, and I tried to go down one, but my feet kept getting tangled in the webbing. So I made sure there was nothing below me, and I pushed off and fell backwards into the water and then swam to a lifeboat. I got into the lifeboat just in time to see the ship sinking. It took approximately six minutes.

It was a typical picture of a sinking, the bow going up in the air and sliding down into the water. One of the problems was that the blockbusters were floating, and they looked like heads. From the lifeboat, we couldn't tell who was a human being and who was a five-hundred-pound bomb. We thought we had lost twenty-eight people, but I have read since in Captain Moore's book that we lost twenty-two people.[9] They were mostly naval gun crews who were sleeping aft at the time. We were the first of twenty-two ships to be torpedoed that night.

We were in the lifeboats for probably forty-five minutes to an hour. A small British tanker that was supplying the escort vessels stopped for us and took us in. We were very fortunate, because the rule of the convoy was to proceed without stopping and let the escort vessel go back later. They apparently got into quite a bit of trouble the next day for helping us.

We sat through twenty other sinkings that night. They were going up all around us, all through the night. Being on the fuel supply ship, the escort vessels all pulled up alongside the next day to take on fuel. They had prisoners from three submarines that they had sunk, and they felt that they had a possible fourth. Some of the fellows that were on watch on the bridge said they saw this submarine. They actually saw it.

Strangely enough, the next day we heard the German report on the radio. They were very accurate. They knew who we were, and they knew they had sunk the *Andrea Luckenbach*. They were claiming it was the largest freighter under the American flag.

The other two fellows [Cadet-Midshipmen Lee T. Byrd and Francis R. Miller] that were on the other *Luckenbach* ship sailed a week or so later. The ship went down, and all hands were lost. In Captain Moore's book, he reports that there were lifeboats launched, which were seen to be drifting with crewmen in the boats, but they were never found. It had been torpedoed in the same area.[10] It was an area between Iceland and Ireland that the aircraft couldn't cover.

Eventually, we landed in Scotland, and I was in England for three or four weeks. I asked for permission to go see my grandmother in London. I spoke with a woman in Liverpool, and she said, "Your boat sails on Tuesday, so be sure to be back on Monday." So I went. I had never met my other relatives. I went over to Wembley, which is just outside London, and spent the weekend. When I went back to Liverpool, the woman said, "There's been a mistake—there's your ship leaving right now." It was one of the *Queen* ships, possibly the *Queen Mary*. She said not to worry because there was one leaving that afternoon. It was a Mississippi Steamship Company ship that had been in Russia. It had been out of the States for about a year and a half, or more. And it was what we called the Hog Islander, which was a Liberty ship of the First World War. I took it.

Three days out of England, we entered a severe storm, and the quadrant gear on our steering engine broke. Fortunately, on the Hog Islander, the rudder post comes up through the deck, and it has a yoke on it. So we were able to rig the rudder post up to the warping winches on the poop deck, and then steer the vessel from the poop deck. We went into Iceland that way. We were in Iceland for probably six or eight weeks, while the *Vulcan*, the Navy repair ship, repaired our engine.

After graduating from Kings Point with a license of third mate, Leslie Churchman embarked on a voyage to the Mediterranean. See chapter 7.

Francis Bartlett, Class of 1942

Francis Bartlett combined a love of the sea with a life of learning. He joined the U.S. Merchant Marine Cadet Corps in 1941 and faced the U-

boat threat to Atlantic convoys. After World War II, Bartlett entered the world of maritime education at various institutions throughout the world. He received a Fulbright lectureship to teach naval architecture at the University of Alexandria, Egypt, and his last post was also as an instructor in naval architecture at the University of New South Wales in Sydney, Australia. He worked there for three years, until retiring, in order to write, in 1980.

I saw many torpedoed ships. Here is a record from my diary of three days in April 1943 in a North Atlantic convoy:

The battle of the North Atlantic was very much at hand on 16, 17, and 18 of April of 1943, giving me a better understanding of the war at sea in the North Atlantic, a more rugged situation than my former experience in the balmy South Atlantic. The route for this 8-knot convoy that *Atenas* had joined was changed to reduce the distance to England, into warmer weather and hopefully with less submarine action. None of us officers, all under twenty-five, had any knowledge of such matters, all we did was stand our watches to keep the ship in her allotted position behind the one ahead. During the night mid-watch on the sixteenth, the reverberations of exploding depth charges brought everyone not on watch out of a deep sleep, but inspection the following day revealed no serious damage. During my morning watch (eight to twelve) that same day, I was working out a time sight when suddenly off to starboard a corvette let go about eight to ten depth charges and was flying the black pennant of danger and signaled she was using ASDIC [Anti-Submarine Detection Investigation Committee, that is, sonar] equipment to follow a submarine. The convoy steamed along peacefully as though nothing was happening and even after slowing by five revolutions of the propeller, as the corvette followed her path and dropped several more depth charges.

Later during the same watch, the Coast Guard cutter up ahead started belting out depth charges. She must have fired more than a dozen and also had the black pennant flying. She was dead in the water, and the convoy steamed past her, indicating a sub was under us. As the convoy passed, the cutter was soon half a mile astern. Then the other cutter joined her to work as a pair. Suddenly they opened fire at a target off the port side of the convoy. Merchant ships in that region also opened fire. Shortly after, I noticed the small black conning tower of the submarine that possibly was under the convoy. The cutters closed in and captured the sub. They soon passed out of our sight, and later in the afternoon they came back up into position. The score at the time was most certainly one sub captured.

A similar sequence happened just before dark as the cutter went down through the convoy firing more depth charges as the convoy passed, but the score this time was unknown. During the night (eight to twelve) there was no action, but on the twelve-to-four and during the morning there was plenty of it on the port side of the convoy. The score at this time had a corvette damaging a sub, brought him to the surface, then rammed him, and, from what I hear, both must have blown up, which counts for another sub. From then on we had no more trouble. That was a great relief for the naval communicator aboard who was so uneasy about riding that load of bombs through the submarine warfare zone. He refused to sleep in his assigned quarters in the midship house and instead remained in a less than comfortable space on the same deck as the bridge. He should never have had his assignment to the ship, but war being what it is, he had to take his chances with the rest of us. Since we were a faster ship, we and several others left the convoy and proceeded at higher speed than convoy to make a landfall of Northern Ireland. The brilliant green of those Irish hills I shall always remember. We rounded North Ireland and went into Belfast Lough well after dark. At midnight with the change of watch, I was giving the second mate the details of the watch when we suddenly realized that the ship ahead had stopped and we were approaching her too fast. Full astern all engines, and we avoided a collision, but it was still kind of scary.

The orders to go into Belfast were changed, and we turned around to pass through the Irish Sea and go up the Bristol Channel. At this time, several ships in the convoy were flying air defense balloons for protection against dive bombers, but none were present to attack us. The ship had to pass through locks to control water depths at the docks in Newport Harbor due to the thirty-foot tides of the Channel. Once alongside and tied up, the ship was opened up and a load of bombs was slowly and carefully removed.

Richard H. Krause Jr., Class of 1944

Born in Brooklyn, New York, Richard Krause saw service in both World War II and Korea. He received honorable discharges from several

branches of U.S. military service. In 1982, he retired after a thirty-one-year career with Dow Chemical Company.

After graduation, the first ship I sailed on was the *Nashaba*. It was a Lykes Brothers ship I picked up in Boston, and it took us to Halifax. We made up a convoy of about sixty ships. Now, of course, the convoy travels as fast as the slowest ship. We were the slowest ship. It only went about 8 knots. They built it in 1921. I think they only built about three or four of them. We had a lot of medical cargo.

I remember that because we thought the ship was torpedoed. It was February 1945. I found out later that it hit a mine. Well, about two or three ships had already sunk, and I was on the four-to-eight watch. I came up and watched a couple of ships go down. Everyone went down to eat, and I ordered my breakfast, and before it got there, we got hit. The ship vibrated something awful. It sounded like a bunch of broken glass. I remember the chief engineer stood up from the table, and it threw him down in the corner.

The captain gave the order to abandon ship, and we went up to the boats. It hit the number-five hold, and the ship split right before the midship house. I remember seeing about a foot, you know, where it had parted. The gun crew shot in the air. They had their earphones on, and they were bleeding, where they had fallen and hurt themselves. I remember them wading through the water and coming up to the boats. The back end of the ship was already under the water.

About three or four days before that, a pump was blown pretty bad. It was a beam type and condensate pump, and there was a packing gland on it. I put my hand in there to tighten it up, and before I could get my hand out, it smashed my finger up against it. I had it all bandaged, and we put sulphur on it. So, as the boat was sinking, we were cranking out the davits. The third mate, who was in charge of the boat, saw that my hand had opened up and blood was dripping off my thumb. He made me get in the boat, and I remember I wasn't afraid or anything. I got in there, and I saw all these fellows coming through the water. You know, when you are busy, you don't have time to think about it. The rear end of the ship was going down, but the lifeboat was not in the water yet. When it did go down, the forward part of the ship was up in the air. And it was up in the air, the last time I saw it.

When the ship got hit, the pilot was in the first lifeboat with only four other men. He had made a pact with the second mate that one wouldn't leave the ship without the other. The second mate was still on the ship when all four boats were in the water. When he jumped in, he drowned, the water was so cold. I was told that the pilot was lost too. We had pretty heavy seas at this time.

I was in the lifeboat for about two hours before I was picked up by a British corvette. It was difficult to get onto the corvette, because it moved up and down. We had to jump across and it was rough, so I put my oar in the water. We were trying to get away from the boat [*Nashaba*], and I put every ounce of strength I had behind it. We all did, to get away from the sinking ship, and we just couldn't move it. We were concerned about suction from the ship.

We had four boats, and each boat went to a different place. We went to Ostend, Belgium. I was in the British army camp for about ten days. The weather was good, but it's always rough in the North Atlantic and the North Sea in February. When I went up from the engine room at eight o'clock, we would always get the sea temperature. It would be 46 degrees.

We stayed in Ostend, Belgium, and recuperated for a while in the British army camp, until they put us on an LCI and brought us back to London. We stayed on Wimpole Street. I remember that because I walked down to where Elizabeth Barrett Browning lived. At this time there were V1 and V2 bombs dropping all the time over London. They blew up a theater just about two blocks from where we were staying. One time I was in a theater, and I heard the warning. I was going to get up and go to the shelters, but the British just sat there. So I did, too, and watched the movie, and nothing happened. I stayed in London for about ten days.

I came back to the United States on the SS *America*. It was called the *West Point*, and it was run by the Navy at that time. This was a passenger vessel. It was a big one, and fast, and we didn't have a convoy coming back.

Note: While en route from Cardiff to Ghent, Belgium, in Convoy TAM-81, the *Nashaba* struck a mine on February 26, 1945. At 0900, the ship was abandoned as the crew took to the lifeboats. The second mate and the Dutch pilot were killed. Survivors were picked up by a British corvette and a Norwegian vessel.[11]

4

CONVOYS

Convoys provided safety in numbers. Over the course of the war, the Atlantic convoys, in particular, evolved into organized flotillas of supply ships with armed escorts, including aircraft. However, the evolution was agonizingly slow. For the merchant mariner, the early years of the war were perilous in the extreme, and the threat of a U-boat attack was never totally diminished. In addition to enemy submarine patrols, the convoys had to contend with winter storms and the possibility of collisions during conditions of poor visibility. Any ship that lagged behind the convoy was especially at risk. In most instances, standing orders were for military escorts to stay with the main group of ships. German submarine commanders looked for the easy targets presented by an unescorted, lone merchantman.

Kenneth A. DeGhetto, Class of 1943

Entering the Academy at age eighteen, Ken DeGhetto attributes his success later in life to both Kings Point and his wartime service. Indeed, success was his. After the war, he worked for the Foster Wheeler Corporation for over thirty years, filling both engineering and construction assignments. Now retired, he was for several years chairman of the board of Foster Wheeler Corporation. He is an active fund-raiser for alumni projects.

I went to sea. I was at Kings Point just about two months, May, June, and left. In July 1942, I picked the ship up in New York Harbor, and our first trip was to Glasgow, Scotland, with war supplies.

Loaded on deck, I remember, we had jeeps and motor vehicles. In the holds, it was the same. The deck cadet aboard was Woody Schwartz. In port, in Scotland, instead of coming back with an empty ship, we loaded eighty thousand cases of Scotch whiskey. This was in August of 1942. I used to smoke in those days, and for a pack of American cigarettes, the long-shoremen would break open a case, and we'd get a bottle of Scotch. Now, of course, I was only eighteen, and Woody, I guess, would have been nineteen, or twenty. I remember we each got a bottle, and went ashore, and I think they carried us back. To this day I can't drink Scotch. On the way back, we had very rough weather. A couple of the cases must have broken open, and when I pumped the bilges all I could smell was Scotch.

We came back to New York, again loaded up our war supplies, and then went to North Africa about a week after the invasion, and landed in Casablanca. Before leaving New York Harbor, we swung on the hook for a few days, until the whole convoy could be assembled. We had some old destroyer screens, and then we sailed with the convoy. I do remember one night we broke down and we drifted back. Any ship that drifted back was torpedoed. We were very fortunate, though; we weren't down too long and didn't get too far behind. They didn't have enough of a screen to protect the dropouts, you know; they had to stay with the main convoy.

They were, in those days, destroyers, DE class. It might have been even the old four-stacker destroyers that had been converted, and modernized. It could have been even British, for that matter. You know, at night when you went to bed, you always had your life preserver handy. Needless to say, if you needed it at night, it would be hard to find in very rough seas and probably no lights.

The rough seas could be very heavy. These ships from 1915, they used to bounce around. To wash our clothes was another thing. They had in the engine room a big old milk can that farmers used to ship the milk. The wipers hooked up a plunger, tied it to one of the valve arms of the reciprocating engine, and we just put clothes in there. It was like a washing machine.

It was a good experience. I learned a lot about the electrical systems. The refrigeration system would break down all the time; then we would have to get the first or second engineer to repair the system.

After unloading in Glasgow, we came back with eighty thousand cases of Scotch whiskey, reloaded, and started on the North African trip. I saw other ships getting hit in Casablanca. New Year's Eve 1942 to '43 we were in the harbor, and there was a bombing raid by German four-engine bombers, and it was quite exciting. We were all out on deck. Our gun crews, and all the other ships that were there, they were all firing away. The ground crews were shining the spotlights on them so we could clearly see them. I think they were out of range of the 5-inch guns, but they were firing away. Suddenly we started hearing this click, click, click on the deck. What was happening, the shrapnel from the exploding shells was falling back down. We were all out there without helmets or anything on, and fortunately nobody got hit. And we cheered like we were at a football game, or something, to get these bombers.

Captain Douglas F. Ponischil, Class of 1940

Lykes Brothers gave me a job as a second mate on one of the first new Liberty ships built in the Houston Shipbuilding Company, called the SS *Michael J. Stone* [1942]. We took her out on the trials, and, finally, she was ready to go. I remember the things when you take a new ship out. Keys, they had more keys than you could shake a stick at. As second mate, I had the responsibility of getting all the keys in the right places. They had keys for lockers underneath the bunks and for medicine cabinets and this door and that door. Just about everything was regulation.

We had to go to New York, and it was still dangerous. These big Liberty ships were like a big balloon on the water when they were empty. They just floated out there, so we had to follow the Intercoastal Waterway all the way up to New York. We'd go as close as we could to the coast without running aground, and we'd anchor at night and stay in. We went around through Key West, and stayed there. We never had any troubles, but the wind would come up and just blow those things. You had a hard time controlling them.

We finally got to New York, and went to Bush Terminal, which was the big Army base, in Brooklyn. We loaded all kinds of cargo. The North African invasion was coming up, so what we loaded was mostly clothing and things like that for the servicemen over there.

We were, I guess, the first ship to be loaded. After we got finished, they took us out to near the George Washington Bridge in New York, on the Hudson River. We anchored there and stayed for thirty days, waiting for enough ships to form a convoy. So we were able to go ashore every day, and it was wonderful. I loved New York, just got to see a lot of shows and stuff.

Finally, on Friday, November 13, the biggest snowstorm you ever saw in your life came up, and we got orders to sail at night. It was dark, but the submarines were all out there. It was pretty dangerous. We took off and we had a pilot. He took us out through what they call the Verrazano Narrows now, but we just called it "the Narrows" in those days. There wasn't any bridge over there. So we went out to sea, and all these other ships came along. You could hardly see your hand in front of your face. When I think back now, I just wonder how we made it. We were just out there, everybody heading in the same general direction, and we knew the ship next to us had ammunition. How we knew, I don't know, but we knew. The minute it would get close we floated to port, and then we'd see the ship on the port side when we were heading back. For two days it was very harrowing.

Was there any radio contact among the ships?

No radio contact. We had blinkers and semaphore, but you couldn't send any semaphore. You had some blinkers, and you just knew what to do. We heard it was supposed to be six Navy destroyers out there escorting us. Finally, on the third day, it cleared, and the destroyers were hoisting signals: "Form up! Form up!" So we finally formed up. We had five rows of ships, ten ships across. There were fifty-five ships altogether. So I guess the last, sixth row, was just five ships in it.

Then we started zigzagging. We'd go so many knots on a certain course, and then they'd hoist the signal to turn into another course. We got over, across, without any ships lost. We went 10 knots. That was the max we could go. We changed courses, but I don't think we ever changed speed. I just recall the six destroyers out there going ahead of us all the time.

We got over to Gibraltar, and we split into two parts: half the convoy went off to Casablanca, and the group I was in went through the Straits of Gibraltar, and we went to Oran. Where the rest of them went, I don't know. This was all at the beginning of the North African invasion, and there were planes bombing around there at night. There were air raids, and it was pretty scary.

So you actually were in the combat zone shortly after the landings themselves?

In North Africa, right. It was semi-secure, but there were still raids. The German planes and the Italian planes would come over and drop bombs and all. Fortunately, they never hit anything that I could see. We saw aircraft. Yes, they were there. So we weren't there long. We were there maybe a week. We were able to go ashore in Oran, and had some different food. I remember the things that still plague tourists now: the little kids would come up, maybe ten or twelve in a group. They'd kind of surround you and say: "Give me some money! Give me some candy! Some chewing gum!" They'd fool you and take stuff out of your pockets, so you really had to be careful. You had to stay in groups to protect yourselves and fend them off.

Then we went back, and we didn't carry passengers, but there were a couple of Army nurses that had got pregnant. Because we were going back to the States, they arranged to send them back on our ship. So we had these two gals, and we headed for New York.

We were empty. We didn't have any cargo, and we hit one of the worst storms you ever saw in the North Atlantic. That ship was just rocking and rolling, and I had got a hammock somewhere. I was second mate then, and I tied the hammock crossways in my room. Somehow I got it up there, and I was the only one getting any sleep. I had a hotbed: the minute I'd get out these nurses would take it, or somebody else. So the hammock stayed busy the whole time.

It was rough. You thought the ship would just completely capsize from one side to the other. There was a period when it was so rough, we couldn't make any steerage. We just headed into the wind, and kept as much propulsion up as we could. We didn't make any mileage. This went on for about three days. Sitting there, wallowing in the troughs. This was in November or December of 1942. So we finally got back to New York. We made it in safely.

Douglas Ponischil also sailed in the Pacific. See chapter 9.

Perry Jacobs, Class of 1944

Perry Jacobs has had a lifelong interest in the technology of sea and air transportation. Carrying forward his seafaring after the war with the Military Sealift Command, he received his license for chief engineer in 1951, and he participated in several NASA programs, including Gemini, Surveyor, Apollo, and Skylab through the operation and maintenance of range instrumentation ships. In retirement, he was affiliated with a local air and space museum, as well as the Academy's alumni foundation.

I took preliminary training from December through early March of 1943. We had steam engineering and diesel engineering. When we completed our preliminary training, we reported to Paddy Brennan, the district in-

structor in New York. I was in company with a deck cadet. We were assigned to a ship that was under construction at North Carolina Shipbuilding in Wilmington, North Carolina. We went down there by train, checked
into a rooming house, and then reported aboard the ship. The ship had had
her first trials already, but not the sea trials as yet. We just came aboard the
ship, and we were put to work almost immediately in assisting in the final
outfitting of the vessel. I was nineteen years of age. The ship was the SS
William D. Pender, a Liberty ship. I believe construction time for a Liberty
ship in those days was about sixty calendar days to lay the keel, construct
the ship, outfit it, have all the trials, and put the ship to sea.

After we completed our sea trials, we proceeded to Charleston, South
Carolina, where we underwent degaussing checks at a deperming station.
The ships were being built of steel, and, naturally, would be magnetic and
therefore would activate magnetic mines. So they put in a degaussing system, which was a series of electrical cables that would run around the entire deck of a vessel, from stem to stern. It was a continuous circuit, both
sides, port to starboard. In effect, what it did was counteract the magnetic
ability that steel would have. It was a countermeasure in fighting the magnetic mines.

We left the deperming station in Charleston and proceeded down to
Jacksonville, Florida. We went up the St. Johns River, berthed there for
about a week, and loaded general cargo. The only two items I can remember aboard the vessel were paper and tobacco.[1]

We proceeded up the coast to New York to join a convoy. I can remember seeing air patrols, and I don't recall seeing escorts. You have to understand that I was an engine cadet, and I spent most of my time below. I was
on the eight-to-twelve watch. I recall seeing a blimp directly ahead of the
vessels. She was hovering over the water. It was the first time I had known
that they were using blimps on antisubmarine patrols. They had dropped
a smoke bomb, and it just seemed to be sitting there. Whether they were
dropping depth charges or not, I don't know.

Since I was undergoing training, my duties as an engine cadet were
basically anything that I was directed to do. I was under the tutelage of
the first assistant engineer, who had the four-to-eight watch. Ultimately, I
stood watches with each one of the engineers. They rotated my watches so
I would have a full round of experience. I went with the second assistant
who had the twelve-to-four, and the third assistant who had the eight-to-
twelve. I stood a watch of four hours on and eight hours off.

There's one thing I wanted to mention about my recollection of service on a Liberty. The only access you had to the steering engine was on deck, and you had to check the steering engine at least once a watch. If you were in heavy weather, and I can recall some of the waves being thirty-, forty-foot high and the ship in the trough, you knew that those mountainous seas were above you. Of course, the lifelines were strung on deck, and you held on to the lifelines for your dear life, but you had to check the steering gear.

There were two ways of getting to the steering gear. One was across the open deck, or through the shaft alley and up the escape hatch. Because with the ship rolling, it was safer to go across the deck, if you weren't taking seas aboard. In my mind, rather than try and climb a ladder in a pitching and rolling ship (the ladder was at least thirty feet high to go from the shaft alley escape up to the steering engine), it was better to go across the deck. On a calm sea, there was no problem at all. You just walked across the deck. But in heavy weather, when you had to check the steering gear, that was an arduous task.

It was March and fairly cool. There was no mechanical ventilation in the engine room of a Liberty ship. It was all natural ventilation. When we were in the Mediterranean on our second voyage, it was customary to stand under the vent near the throttles and just monitor the other operations of machinery of the engine room on a frequency basis. I would stay on the machinery platform. It was about 90 to 100 degrees on average in the summer in the machinery spaces. If you were near the tops of the boilers, it could exceed 130 degrees Fahrenheit. It was a very hot engine room.

When we arrived in New York, we joined up with Convoy HX-233, which had about fifty to sixty ships. We proceeded to the North Atlantic. We were in the left column, the second ship in line. I don't know if there were destroyers in the escort, but there were four or five DE escort vessels.

Both the deck cadet and I were assigned to the Armed Guard. We had a battle station aboard the vessel. My battle station was a loader in the 20mm magazine aft. We participated with the Armed Guard in various gun drills. As we approached the UK, maybe three or four days out, we had to supplement the lookouts, so I was placed on the bridge. When we were entering Loch Ewe, which was where the convoys arrived, they dispersed all the various vessels to other ports within the UK. I happened to be standing watch on the bridge at that time, which was not normal for the engine cadet, but it was in accordance with my duties as an additional member of the Armed Guard.

We had a "TBS" (talk between ships), where you could communicate between other vessels in the convoy. I heard them all standing around and laughing about something. I inquired what was going on. They said one ship had mentioned to the commodore's ship, "I have only one anchor. What shall I do?" The commodore responded, "Please use only one anchor," which I guess if you're a deck person, was kind of funny, but it didn't strike home with me at all.

I became aware that the Coast Guard cutter *Spencer* had sunk a submarine. I later found out that the submarine was the *U-175*.[2] I know of one ship in my convoy that was torpedoed. About three days out from Loch Ewe, in March of 1943, about five in the morning, we were called to General Quarters. We were going to our boat stations. On the ship directly ahead of us, there had been an explosion. The ship had its masthead red light on, which means, "I'm not under control." It slipped down our column and passed by astern of us. It was a Canadian ship, the SS *Fort Rampart*. It was severely damaged and, as it was carrying lumber as cargo, refused to sink. It was ultimately sunk by one of our escorts, after the German U-boats came back and tried to sink it with more torpedoes. The crew had already abandoned the vessel.

The deck cadet slept in the raw. When we had the General Quarters call, he showed up at his boat station on that cold, bleak, overcast morning completely in the nude. He was carrying his survival suit that we used to roll up and have ready to jump in and put on after you had put on your life jacket. He was ready to abandon ship. I still remember this. It was one of the things that I thought was very funny at a very critical time, and it helped to relieve the tension.

This was my first voyage in the North Atlantic. After leaving Loch Ewe, we went around the north of the UK. We entered the port of Hull, which is on the northeast coast of England, on the Humber River. We were assigned to discharge our cargo. We were going south down the North Sea. Before we had made the turn west into the Humber, a German spotter plane came over. There were only three ships in this convoy. I don't even think we had a DE or a destroyer. I think it was a trawler that was escorting us.

When we were going up the Humber, we passed floating mines. It was lucky we were making the transit in daylight. As we passed, there were two seaman's boots that were inverted and floating in the water. The way they were positioned, I'm sure there was a body underneath. We went into Hull, and I guess there was a severe difference in tide level there. There was an inner harbor. They would open up a gate, and you'd pass into the inner harbor, and close the gate. We were there about a week to ten days. The thing that impressed us upon arrival was the near-complete destruction of the city, which had been attacked by the Luftwaffe.

After our cargo was discharged, we proceeded to a ballast station, and they put stone and rock ballast into the ship. Anyone who's been aboard a Liberty ship can tell you that when you are riding a Liberty ship in ballast, it's one of the worst experiences you can have at sea. The ship was rolling something fierce going back. I believe the ballast was put into number-two hold and number-four hold. There was no ballast in number one, but we had deep tanks in there, which could be ballasted. A deep tank is a tank that is used in a ship within a cargo compartment. They're high. A double bottom is usually about three foot high. A deep tank can be anywhere from ten to twelve feet. In our case, it was used for liquid cargo—fuel oil, water, and that type of thing.

They had used these deep tanks for the carriage of cargo. Unfortunately, when they put the covers down, they didn't bolt them. We were directed to start the ballast pump and pump up the deep tanks in number-one hold. Nobody told the carpenter, who was supposed to take soundings on the vessel. All of a sudden, the ship started going down by the head. They were wondering why they were having so much of a problem steering. They got the carpenter to take his soundings, and they found out that we had pumped seawater up through the covers of the deep tank. We had something like ten to twelve feet of water in the hold. We had to get the water out, so we started up the bilge pump.

We had carried paper in the cargo hold. The battens, which were on clips on the sides of the cargo hold, came loose, and they were floating back and forth. With the ship rolling, all these battens were hitting each other and splintering. They became like wood pulp. We couldn't pump the water out of the hold. When we had taken the water down sufficiently low, the chief engineer, Oscar Peterson, got down and into the bilge wells to clean the strainers. He took his clothes off, jumped in the water, and stayed down there until the strainers were clear and all the water was pumped out. That's when they decided they would bolt the covers back onto the deep tanks. Other than that, our voyage back to New York was without incident.

Captain Arthur E. Erb, Class of 1943

At the outset of his interview, Arthur Erb's friendly nature and kindly disposition gave no indication of the life-threatening challenges that he had faced, both as a cadet-midshipman and as third mate. Coming so close to annihilation undoubtedly seasoned him for life's subsequent challenges. He has been very successful in developing a stevedoring business in Florida. He has served as a past president of the Alumni Foundation.

I completed special training in November 1943, obtained a third mate's license, and immediately shipped out as third mate on a T2 tanker, the *Spottsylvania*. She made four voyages across the Atlantic. We were carrying high-octane gasoline and partially assembled fighter planes on the spar deck. This was strictly cargo from a U.S. port to a port in the UK. We would discharge within twenty-four hours. If we had planes on deck, we'd have to go to another location. Two nights in the UK would mean one night discharging the planes, and then one day discharging aviation gasoline.

By the end of 1943 and the early part of '44, the convoys were better organized. These convoys with the *Spottsylvania* were for the most part 15-knot convoys. They were well escorted, versus the type of convoy that had the *John Witherspoon*, where you allegedly were a 10-knot convoy, but in many instances you were down to 7 knots. These escorts were quite good and very effective. At that point, they were bringing in the new construction destroyer escorts, which were high speed. There were some troop transports amongst those because they were high-speed convoys. The tankers were strictly assigned to carry fuel for shoreside operations. They were not rigged for any at-sea replenishment.

At that time, they had C2s in production, and they were able to maintain the same 15 knots, 14.5 knots, so these were not 100 percent tanker convoys. My recollection is that the tankers were placed all over in the convoy. The convoys were in the neighborhood of between thirty and forty ships, plus the escorts. There were seven to nine columns with four to five vessels per column. In two convoys, we were in a "coffin corner," which was the last two starboard vessels in the outboard column. The significance of the starboard side had to do with the approaches made by the U-boats. They were certainly out there, but we were fortunate on those four transatlantic convoys not to experience any losses.

I was scheduled to get married in June of '44. When we came to New York on this last voyage on the *Spottsylvania*, the skipper called me in. I was third mate. He said, "Erb, you're getting married in June of next year, aren't you?" And I said, "No Sir, next month." He says, "I'm not supposed to tell you, but we're going out to the Persian Gulf for a year to shuttle." Expletive deleted! But he says, "Don't worry about it. I've already called for your replacement, and you can get ashore. You'd better not wait until June. You'd better get married right away." Which we did. I continued to sail until the end of the war.

The average merchant ship crew size was extremely limited and five times smaller, compared to the same size vessel under Navy control. And the merchant marine ships went into the same waters as the combat ships. Going back to July of '42, we went into waters that the Navy kind of pulled away from. We were out in front when the Navy was back in the safe harbor of Seydisfjordur or Hvalfjordhur, Iceland, during that short period.

For Arthur Erb's earlier ordeal as a cadet-midshipman enroute to Russia, see chapter 6, "The Murmansk Run."

Captain Arthur R. Moore, Class of 1944

Seafarer and author, Arthur Moore is the dean of historians of the American merchant marine in World War II. He has remained close to the sea and his home state of Maine. Born on the banks of the Kennebec River, Arthur Moore's affinity for the sea motivated him to pursue a career in shipping until 1986. He became a shipmaster in 1948. His wartime experiences convinced him of the need to tell the story of those unfortunate shipmates who were lost on sunken ships, and he wrote the book *"A Careless Word . . . a Needless Sinking": A History of the Staggering Losses Suffered by the U.S. Merchant Marine, Both in Ship and Personnel during World War II*, which has become the standard reference source on this subject. In 2005, the U.S. Merchant Marine Academy honored Captain Moore with an honorary doctorate.

At the Lykes [Lines] office we were assigned to the Delta Line C-2 freighter SS *Delaires* in October 1942. We were greeted by the marine superintendent, who told us we would be seeing some action on this trip. We boarded at Pier #4 Brooklyn Army Base and reported to the master, Capt. Brote and the chief mate, Henry W. Kinney (later marine superintendent of Delta SS Co.). We all bunked in one room.

After finishing loading a cargo of war materials, we shifted to Gravesend Bay to wait for a convoy. Finally left New York Harbor on November 2 in Convoy UGF-2 (U.S. to Gibraltar fast). I might mention that we also carried 1,500 carrier pigeons in a pen on the flying bridge. The convoy consisted of twenty fast merchant ships including four troop transports plus eleven U.S. Navy escorts including the battleship USS *Arkansas*. The commodore of the convoy was stationed on this ship.

Upon departure I was assigned to the bow with the chief mate, and upon arrival off Ambrose Lightship I saw a sight I will never forget. As far as one could see were running lights of all the ships maneuvering to get into the convoy formation. It was very dark, and the lights had to be on to avoid running into each other. The chief mate remarked there must be some big ships in this convoy because of the distance between the forward and aft masthead lights.

It was about this time I started to get seasick, and I was sick for a week until I got my sea legs, but I never missed a watch. I want to mention here, I was assigned to the third mate's watch (twelve to four). This man detested cadets, and he let me know it. I soon found out that a cadet was the lowest form of animal. During the day watch, I was assigned to the flying bridge with a walkie-talkie in my hand and reported every call to the bridge. At night the third mate made sure I was assigned to the weather side of the bridge out in the open. But I put up with this and said not a word but "Yes, Sir!" I was forewarned to "keep your trap shut and follow orders," which I did. However, I did not learn much about seafaring on this ship. Early in the voyage, I went to see the chief mate and told him I wanted to learn about the shipping business and would appreciate any help he could give me. He said he would try, but he was so busy we didn't have much contact.

The trip to the African coast was very quiet with the exception of depth charges exploding all the time. On the evening of November 17, the commodore on the USS *Arkansas* signaled the *Delaires* via blinking light. There was only one USN signalman aboard, and he was sleeping as he had been up many hours. Capt. [H.C.] Brote asked me if I could read that light signal, and I said I could, so I took the message, which read, "Proceed to Safi Harbor." The captain said I must have been mistaken as there was no such harbor. I asked the *Arkansas* to repeat the message. It came out the same, so the master woke up the Navy signalman, and he got the same message. Well, about this time the master was furious. The Navy man said it might have said "Safe Harbor." At this time I was excused. Anyway, the next morning I awoke, and we were docking in Safi. We docked at the one pier there. It was a dock where they loaded phosphate, discharged all cargo there.

On our eastbound trip over, we had to circle around for five days upon nearing the North African coast as there were no docks available. They were all full with the invasion fleet. We were scheduled to arrive on D-Day plus five. As a result, we were five days late docking. It was fortunate that there were no German subs around because if there were, they would have had a picnic.

We left on November 29 in Convoy GUSF-2 and arrived New York on December 11. I might mention here that we experienced very rough weather. Capt. Brote pleaded with the convoy commodore to slow down as we were without any ballast and were pounding terribly. The commodore would not slow down. Many other masters complained also. The result of this was upon arrival in New York we had to go into dry dock to repair a lot of bottom damage.

Upon signing off, I was allowed three days shore leave. I went home to Maine, and upon my return I received orders from the U.S. Maritime Service to report to the Lykes freighter SS *City of Omaha*, but on January 2, 1943, I was ordered by the U.S. Maritime Commission to leave this ship and join the Liberty ship *William C. C. Clairborne* at Bush Terminal in Brooklyn. I was pleasantly surprised when I found out the master of this ship was Capt. Henry W. Kinney, the former chief mate on the *Delaires*. He told me later I was taken off the *City of Omaha* because she was loading for Murmansk, Russia, and would be over there a long time. The *Omaha* was a member of what is now known as the "forgotten convoy." She was over there for nine months. He also told me that he had asked to have me assigned to his ship.

We departed New York on January 13, 1943, in Convoy USGS-4, composed of forty-nine merchant ships and six USN destroyers as escort. I stood four-to-eight watch with the chief mate. On January 22, the convoy was struck with hurricane-force winds for three days. This caused the convoy to break up, and we found ourselves sailing alone. We continued alone to Casablanca, arriving off that port on January 31, we being the first ship of the convoy to make land. A British destroyer met us and escorted us and another ship to Gibraltar, where we anchored to await convoy to Oran, Algeria. While anchored there, a Royal Navy officer came aboard and left some Limpet mines to be dropped overboard if anyone was seen swimming around the ship. It seems enemy divers were attaching mines to the bottoms of ships while at anchor in Gibraltar. Sailed out of there on February 2 and arrived Oran, where we discharged our deck cargo of four steam locomotives, then proceeded to a port eighteen miles east of Oran named Arzeu. Discharged cargo there and then returned to Oran where we finished discharging. Left Oran in GUS-4 and arrived New York March 12.

I would mention here that when we found ourselves all alone, Capt. Kinney called all hands to number-four hatch, where he addressed us in no uncertain terms. He first told us we were in a precarious position, and then gave us orders in case we had to abandon ship, step by step. Told us he would be in charge and back it up with a .45-caliber pistol. I just stood there with my mouth open fascinated by the whole affair. He also ordered us to carry our life preserver with us at all times and to sleep in them. But, frankly, I never could sleep with one on so I took it off. Nothing bothered me at eighteen years old. Looking back now, I see how foolish I was.

I would mention here that three ships from this convoy were torpedoed and sunk with heavy loss of life. They were the *Julia Ward Howe*, *City of Flint*, and *Charles E. Pinckney*. Also soon after leaving Gibraltar westbound on February 22, a Canadian escort vessel HMCS *Weyburn* struck a mine and sank with loss of life. Also, the Norwegian tanker *Thorsholm* struck a mine and was damaged.

After my arrival in New York on the Claiborne, I was ordered to go back to the Academy for advanced training. While there it seemed somebody fouled up because it was discovered I didn't have enough sea time. So I was assigned to another Liberty, SS *Alfred Moore*. I was sent to Baltimore via train where the master of the ship, Capt. O'Connor, met me in a taxi, took me to Custom House to sign on, and then to the ship. The ship sailed as soon as I got aboard. At 0900 that morning I was on the *Claiborne*; at 2000 that night I was on another ship sailing down the Chesapeake Bay. I remember this being one hectic day. Went into New York to await convoy. Sailed from New York on April 1, in Convoy HX-232 with thirty-nine merchant ships.

On April 12 and 13 during darkness, the convoy was attacked by German subs, sinking three ships and then sinking a straggler (SS *Edward B.*

Dudley) with all hands. There were no survivors. Arrived at Hull, England, April 20 via north of Scotland. Departed Hull April 30 after discharging all cargo there. After clearing north of Scotland, the *Alfred Moore* joined a U.S.-bound convoy, ON-182, with fifty-seven merchant ships and nine Royal Navy escorts. On May 15, we collided with the tanker *Athelduchess* in thick fog. Damage to the *Moore* was a large hole in the port bow. Arrived New York May 23. I left the ship on May 27, and I was given a two-week leave. I returned to Kings Point on June 11 to start advanced training, and graduated on February 18, 1944, with a third mate's unlimited license. I continued in the shipping business until 1986.

Rear Admiral Thomas J. Patterson, USMS, Class of 1944

Enduring the sacrifices of World War II, Patterson served again in Korea, participating in the famous Inchon landing. Later, while serving as director of the west coast reserve fleet, he was responsible for saving the Liberty ship SS *Jeremiah O'Brien*, from going to the breakers, and he served as admiral aboard her for the D-Day celebration of 1994. For several years, he was deputy superintendent at Kings Point. Today, he and his wife still take his sailboat to sea off the California coast.

Well, as most cadets did in those years, you got a Liberty ship, because this was right in the midst of the building program, and they were building two or three a day. This was in July 1943, and we had finished our three months basic training here at the Academy. I had orders to report to the SS *Jim Bridger*. The general agent for the Maritime Commission was James S. Griffith & Son, located in San Francisco. And on the east coast it was handled by a subagent named American President Lines.

She was in Jersey City, and the captain's name was Adolph Zeutsch, an old German skipper, but a very fine experienced skipper. He called the midshipmen "Mister." I was called "Mr. Patterson." I was assigned to the eight-to-twelve watch on the ship, and the chief mate, who had the eight-to-twelve, hadn't been to sea since World War I. He was very honest with me. He said: "My eyes are not good and sometimes my hearing isn't the best. You will be my eyes and ears, and I will tell you what to do. But you have to learn the signal book because we're going to have to be in convoy in daytime and nighttime and you've got to help me with the convoy procedures." I took this very seriously.

The preliminary training at Kings Point stood me in good stead for life-boat drills and for deck seamanship. I was also assigned to work with the bosun. After I'd stood the eight-to-twelve watch in the morning, then I'd be with him in the afternoon. Then I'd get ready for the eight-to-twelve watch at night.

When I went on that Liberty ship, it was the largest thing I'd ever seen in my life. I thought it was really large—442 feet long when you're an eighteen-year-old midshipman, that ship was big. I was really impressed. The first thing I'd noticed, she'd just come in from South America with a load of green coffee beans for the United States. The whole ship smelled like green coffee beans. Forever, when I smell that odor, it always reminds me of my first day going aboard the ship.

We were loading military vehicles, the entire ship. Every type of military vehicle: jeeps, ambulances, staff cars, big, heavy wreckers, DUKWs,[3] every kind I could think of. Not only all the holds, but then up on the main deck. They loaded every square inch, so much that they had to build catwalks from the boat deck forward and from the boat deck aft. We had to get over this cargo to go fore and aft on the ship. You couldn't walk on the main decks.

So then we went over in a convoy. When we sailed from Jersey City and we assembled the convoy out past Ambrose, it was fog. We were sounding our position on the ship's whistle in the convoy. I don't remember our exact position, but we would repeatedly sound the column and the row that we were in. We had, of course, no radar. This ship was fortunate; it did have a gyro-compass. We had a radio direction finder. There were 142 ships. It was a large convoy, and it was composed of a lot of old foreign-flag ships with plumb stems and counter sterns and about 6- or 7-knot speed. So we were going to be in for a long, slow convoy, and we were constantly zigzagging. In fact it took us twenty-one days to go from Jersey City over to Newport, South Wales. We had English corvettes, Canadian corvettes to start out with, and then they left somewhere in the middle of the ocean. Then we were picked up by English escorts, smaller ships. There weren't any U.S. Navy ships that I remember in that convoy's escorts. We did see a couple of B-24s that were coming down from Iceland or Greenland to come out for protection.

The worst thing was that 1943, and all the history books say this, was one of the worst years for weather. The whole entire year, not just the wintertime. I mean this was summer we sailed. We had gales and storms from the time we left the United States until we got over there. It was heavy. I mean we had seas fifty, sixty feet high. Higher than the ship. A lot of times we were rolling with this high deck cargo on. We had a big sail area, and the ship was rolling and pitching. Fortunately, it was well loaded. We had no damage, but bad weather.

The main thing we had for protection against collision was of course standing an alert watch on the ship. All the watches were stood on the flying bridge. That's the only place you can see on a Liberty ship for convoys, up on top. Now you're up in all the weather, above the wheelhouse.

One of my jobs on there was assigned to help the ship's carpenter build what was called an "Alaska house." This was to take the monkey bridge where the helm was and the binnacle and the engine order telegraph and the whistle and the sound-powered telephone and enclose that. It was about twelve feet by twelve feet. We enclosed that with two-by-fours and plywood and actually put in little windows. They brought some wooden sash before we left the United States. The engineers even rigged a radiator up there, which was wonderful because then you could get out of the weather. So that's where we were standing our watches, very alert to ships around us. That was your best protection, always be very alert.

We would use a stadimeter constantly. We knew the height of the mast of the ships around us. So that was one of my jobs as a cadet, to keep particularly away from the ship ahead. We had a special distance to stay within.

Then as soon as it got dusk, we would let out our towing spar, sometimes called a fog buoy, off the fantail of the ship. The main trunk of the towing spar was like a four-by-six or maybe a six-by-eight, and it had a pair of little wings on it that went across like an airplane wing to keep it straight in the water on an angle. Then there was this twelve-foot towing spar. On the back of it, it had a steel scoop, so as it was towed through the water it would scoop the water up and send a little plume. One day I saw the one from the ship next to us by the bridge, and I told the captain, "There's a submarine right off our starboard beam!" He came out and we were looking at this, and then we could see it was a towing spar. But they sent this little plume up like you'd expect from a periscope.

That duty I didn't like. That was really bad. It was so rough that the fantail on this Liberty was going down to the trough of the sea and then the next minute you'd be up maybe sixty or eighty feet above. I was just having problems getting my sea legs. Especially right after that we had to go in and have breakfast. I didn't have much of an appetite. But that was it. Every morning, bring in that spar. Every night, let it out.

On those ships, we had forty men in the merchant crew, and we had those guns manned by the Armed Guard. The merchant crew had to back them up, and we had a lot of drills with the guns. So everybody was very busy, and the midshipmen had to get in there and do the work because the ship needed the work done, like I said, helping to build the Alaska house up there, standing two eight-to-twelve watches, working out on the deck. The weather was so bad we never did any painting, but we always had to be tightening up on all this deck cargo, tightening the turnbuckles up. Things would start to shift and come apart. Because we had some real old guys in the crew, they used the Kings Point midshipmen. If somebody got sick, after you'd made one trip, you could be asked to be third mate, acting.

How long did it finally take to get to the British Isles?

Well, twenty-one days, and I'll never forget that as long as I live. You know, when we grew up, nobody ever went overseas, not in my neighborhood. My dad had come over from Ireland when he was five years old, and he was the only one in our family that had been, of course, and the grandmother. So this was a big adventure, to actually see a foreign country. Big adventure. In wartime, the journey over there, we had many attacks, submarine attacks. We would be up all night. General alarm would go off, you'd go out, escorts dropping depth charges all over the place. These old ships, some of them had foreign skippers, and they wouldn't black out a porthole. Destroyers would come roaring down the rows, you know, "Darken ship or we'll shoot it out!" on the bullhorn. We were happy that we made the trip.

In 1943, that's when they had heavy casualties because of the heavy weather. The submarines and convoys would be scattered all over the ocean. There's no way those escorts could protect all those ships. You were so scattered, and then ships would break down. Fortunately, we had a ship that was built in 1942. We had a good skipper, a good crew, the ship was well loaded, and we didn't get torpedoed. So we were fortunate.

Then we got into England and that, as I said, that was quite a sight! We went into Newport, South Wales. You have to go through locks to get in there. And just after we got through the locks, the first thing I saw was a Liberty ship with the whole bow blown off it, that they had towed in from a previous convoy or whatever. A lot of damaged ships there.

They put us in a berth, and immediately, as soon as we tied up, boy, off came the cargo, these vehicles. They had a big long straight road running out of the dock, and they just parked the vehicles. I can still remember, as far as your eye could see were the vehicles just from our ship. How many vehicles those Liberty ships would hold! It was a graphic illustration to see them parked way out there. So we were in there for about a week. Then we had to wait a couple of days for a convoy to form up to go home. So that was my first experience with blacked-out England.

We returned in convoy. Oh yeah! Boy, that North Atlantic, that was one of Doenitz's' big years. You know, Battle of the Atlantic went from 1940 to 1945. It was six years. And the Allies lost over 2,500 ships and over twenty-three thousand seamen. It was the biggest battle of World War II. So you convoyed both directions.

We didn't have any cargo going back. That was another problem because you still had bad weather, but now you had a ship that wasn't ballasted. We didn't have much ballast. And so the ship rode terribly coming back. You know, Liberties would roll.

We pulled in, back in the same port, Jersey City, and Captain Zeutsch said, "Mr. Patterson, I know you came from Philadelphia." It was late in the afternoon. "Why don't you go home tonight, see your parents, be back tomorrow morning at ten o'clock for the pay-off." I went, "Oh, thank you very much, Captain." So I did that, went home. We were gone ten weeks, nice reunion with my family. Next morning I got down bright and early to Penn Station, Thirtieth Street, Philadelphia, and I got on the train and there was only one seat open, next to a Navy commander. So I sat next to him. I said, "By your leave, sir, may I sit down?" He says, "Sit down." So he says, "What ship are you off of?" And I said, "I'm on a merchant ship." He says, "I know that. Which one?" I didn't know whether I should tell him or not, but he had a commander's uniform on, so I said, "The SS *Jim Bridger*, sir." He says, "Why are you more than twenty-five miles from your ship?" I thought, geez, who is this man? I said, "Well, the captain gave me permission, we just came in from a voyage." He says, "He has no authority to let you go more than twenty-five miles from your ship. It's in the regulations, U.S. Merchant Marine Academy." I said, "May I ask who you are, sir?" And he says, "I'm Commander Patrick Brennan, the district inspector for the United States Merchant Marine Academy." So he said, "I'm going to take you off that ship, and you're going to ship out *today*." So we didn't say another word the rest of the train trip. Very strange silence. As I was getting off the train, he says: "You be over in my office by ten o'clock this morning, at 39 Broadway, with your gear, all your gear. I'm detaching you from that ship."

I got back to the ship as fast as I could, told the captain this horrible story. The captain says, "Well, Mr. Patterson, don't worry. I'll call American President Lines, our agent, and I'm sure they can straighten it out. Because I'd like you to stay on this ship. Do you want to stay on this ship?" I said, "Yes, sir. I like this ship." "Well, I'm sure it'll be straightened out." About a half hour later, the captain called me to his office, and he got in, and he said: "I'm sorry, but it cannot be changed. You have to be detached." And so I said my good-byes.

Now I had to take all my gear, footlocker, uniforms, books, the whole kit and caboodle. It was a very hot day in New York, and I had to get from Jersey City to 39 Broadway. Got there by ten o'clock. Commander Brennan was waiting for me. He says: "Well, you're on time. That's one good thing about you. Now, there's a tanker singling up over in Tottenville, Staten Island, the SS *Seakay*, Keystone Shipping Company. I've called them and they're expecting you. Get your butt over there!"

So now I had to get all the way over to Staten Island with this whole footlocker, seabag full of books and my uniform. I was soaking wet. We wore khakis with a khaki blouse, epaulets, a very hot uniform on a very humid day. Got over there in time, got on the ship, and I wouldn't say they were holding the ship for a deck cadet, but it looked like that to me. As soon as I got aboard, we sailed. That started my career with Keystone Shipping Company, who I sailed with for quite a few years. A most wonderful captain on that ship. So that was my Liberty ship experience until I was later captain of a Liberty ship.

In convoy again, but now, better convoy, 15-knot convoy, fewer ships. I'd say maybe thirty-five, forty ships, all 15 knots, and better escorts—American destroyer escorts. I think our transit time was much less, probably twelve, fourteen days.

Where there any alerts for submarines on the trip?

Yes, yes, there were. Again, a lucky ship, lucky crew. We had no problems. I don't recall whether any of our ships got torpedoed. I know we were constantly having alerts. I mean, we would go to General Quarters, ring the general emergency alarm. The convoy escorts would get a contact. They were constantly dropping depth charges and going through the convoy at top speed. But they kept this convoy tightened up, and being a tanker, we weren't placed next to any troop transports. We were kind of kept isolated in the convoy because we were carrying aviation gas.

Did you have confidence in the escorts during this risky period, and did you believe that they would be able to locate the U-boats?

Yes, I did. I mean, what else can you believe? Again, I was just a young midshipman out there, but I could hear the radio conversation between the commodore and the escort, and between the commodore and our ship. On the tankers, quite frequently we would have a navy radio operator assigned to use the "TBS," talk between ships. Communication was very strictly restricted as I recall, because they did a lot of flag hoist, a lot of sound signals. They didn't want radio communication between the ships because obviously the U-boats could pick all that up too.

Well, I was eight months at sea. We were supposed to do six months. And again, I liked the master of this tanker. It was Captain Alfred K. Jorgensen, and I sailed with him actually from deck cadet up to chief mate—one captain. After I graduated from Kings Point, I went back with the same captain. And the time spent on that ship was really very good for me as a deck cadet, but I should have gone back at six months. But when we pulled into this port, the tanker turned around pretty fast. The Academy training rep didn't come down, and I actually snuck in another trip, which put me two months behind my peer group. I didn't understand "peer group" or that I actually could have graduated two months earlier at that time. I just liked going to sea with this captain and this crew and this great ship.

The *Seakay* was really named for the president, Charles Kurz, his initials. She was a beautiful tanker, built to the company's specification on a basic T-2 design. On that ship the cadet had a wonderful room—big, beautiful bunk. Everything was the best. So anyway, I was going to get another trip in, but the ATR did get me after eight months at sea. "Back to Kings Point! What are you doing?"

When I got off after those eight months, the poor *Seakay* went out, and she was torpedoed and lost, eight days after I got off her, in the western approaches to England. Fortunately, she did not explode. She was loaded with light oil, but the torpedo hit number-one dry-cargo hold and flooded it. The ships went down by the bow and kept going. Everybody got off. One Navy gunner drowned in the lifeboat.

When I came back with Captain Jorgensen in December 1944, after I graduated from Kings Point, they had first assigned us to the *Markay*, and then they assigned Captain Jorgensen and me the SS *Cantigny*, a brand-new ship that was still on the buildingways in Sun Shipyard. We went down. They launched her the next day, and ten days later we sailed for Texas. That's what they would do, "shakedown runs," send a tanker down to Texas to load. You'd clean out the tanks, get all the welding rods out of the bottom of the tanks, get down there and load, get back to New York, get in a convoy.

We weren't escorted down the coast. We had a young lieutenant jg who was in charge of the Armed Guard. He wanted to test-fire the guns. So the captain, finally after two days, said: "All right. Test-fire the guns." He did it at noon mealtime. The 20-millimeters were all fired, the 3-inch was fired forward. The last one to be fired was the 5-inch. Later we found out he had not trained the gun off the quarter, but he had it trained dead astern when he fired this 5-inch. Well, it was a big shock to the ship, and it blew in the wooden hospital door, which is right on the afterdeck. The chief engineer was in taking a little nap after lunch, and it blew the whole false ceiling, which dropped down when this gun went off. The chief came running out, thought we had been torpedoed. The Armed Guard officer was not too popular on the ship. The captain hated to see the ship damaged, brand-new ship. That was our only incident. The ship ran beautifully. We went down, loaded with oil, and back over to South Wales again.

I made ten trips over to England and back. We did go up to Thames Haven up near London, we did go to Liverpool, we went to Glasgow. But a lot of time we were going into Bristol and then down in the Bristol Channel, Swansea, tanker ports along there.

Did you notice any progressive change in coverage or protection during that period?

We had more American DEs. We were building the DEs, and they were more protection. There were more submarines being sunk by depth charges. We were getting into using sonar. They were improving the ASW techniques. The Navy was learning real fast. It was just better controlled. The tides of war had changed from being in the U-boat's favor to the convoy's favor. The convoy is an offensive weapon. It makes the submarines come to these convoys that are well protected with lots of DEs. But the other thing was these merchant ships were well armed by that point. I mean, the guns had been improved on the ships themselves. They started out with machine guns. Then they first put 3-inch guns forward and aft on Liberties, and then they started putting the 5-inch gun on the stern. The U-boats knew that they'd better do all their attacks below the surface, otherwise, Naval Armed Guard crews and those merchant crews were accurate. They were good. They had good armament.

On March 18, 1944, the German submarine *U-311* torpedoed and sank the SS *Seakay* approximately 375 miles west of Ireland.[4]

Eugene Harrower, Class of 1942

I've sailed in many convoys. They generally would have a broad front, and seldom had more than four or five ships in a column, unless the convoy got so big. The idea was that the sides of the convoy would be as narrow as possible, and make less of a target for submarines. In this convoy, we had about nine columns, with maybe four ships in a column. The tankers were in the center column. They were the most vulnerable and most precious ships, because they had to refuel the destroyers that were our escort.

In the fifth convoy [1943], we had about thirteen U.S. Navy escorts that I counted, which was the best I ever saw at any time during the war. The carrier task group near us was one of the U.S. Navy task groups. That would consist of an escort carrier, and probably three or four destroyers. As I recall, when the destroyers required refueling, the tankers would generally fall astern of the convoy and stay as close as they could. They would be clear, in case they had to change course for some reason, but that was about as far away as they would go.

If the convoy came under attack, it would generally stay together. The exception was Convoy PQ-17 on the way to Murmansk. That was a total disaster. But, normally, the convoy would stay together, as best it could at all times, because then they could have protection. In danger, the best we could do was make an emergency turn. On a given signal, you would make a 45-degree turn to port or to starboard, all ships turning together. Then you could make another one. This way, you could actually make a 90-degree turn with all the ships. You kept your same position in regard to the other ships, except you were moving in a different direction. There was a book published by the British and adopted by the Americans that

Liberty Ship John W. Brown *in Convoy*, by Oswald Brett. Courtesy of Oswald Brett and Project Liberty Ship.

contained all the signals that would be utilized and all the maneuvers that you would go through, while in convoy. We called it "Mersigs," which stood for "Merchant Signals."

In 1944, we carried a full load of food items for the use of the British population. This was from New York to Cardiff, Wales. Our next cargo to Port Sunlight, just upriver from Liverpool, was entirely military equipment. The next cargo was unusual, consisting of eight thousand tons of railroad track bound from New York to Cherbourg, France. Also, there were another two thousand tons of vehicles on wheels and in crates. The railroad track could not be discharged at Cherbourg, as the port had not been recovered from the Germans, so the track as well as the vehicles were discharged to barges and landing craft and taken to Omaha beach.

Many times the ships would return to the United States in a ballast condition. This was the case in the five voyages I made from the U.S. to North Africa and Great Britain, as there was little or nothing in those places to be useful in the U.S. But from other parts of the world we loaded cargoes of ore and food items such as coconut oil and copra. Late in the war, we started to bring back damaged military vehicles, and old tires, as well as ammunition containers that could be repaired and reused.

My original plan, prior to 1939, was to go to sea and be a captain in the merchant marine. In 1945, I had achieved that goal at the age of twenty-four. I was a shipmaster.

Eliot H. Lumbard, Class of 1945

We made up in a convoy in the *Thomas H. Barry* that had gotten a little notoriety [1943]. It was Convoy KMF-25A. We had taken trips to Gurock, Scotland. We were held there for a while, didn't know why, and then suddenly ships started appearing in the anchorage in Scotland, and we were told we were going to North Africa, and we loaded troops. There were a lot of foreign troops, American troops, British troops, ANZACS (Australian/New Zealand), and Dutch throughout the convoy. Some Canadians.

The first sign that we were not going back to the States was when a barge showed up and had this huge safe on it. We were told that it contained all the phony scrip money for the American troops in North Africa, and it was very special, and they couldn't use regular money.

So the chief mate decided he would bring it in through the side port of this huge ship, and, to make a short story, he dropped it in the water. One of the most terrifying/hilarious moments in my life was this huge multi-ton thing starting to go and slip out of the ropes. It went plop, and everyone was staring down at the water, and there were millions down there.

But that certainly told us we were leaving. We did make it up in another one of these large troop convoys, and we had, I remember specifically, the *Monterrey* with us, and the *Santa Elena* was just in front of us in line in convoy. It was a big Dutch ship; there were a lot of other big ships.

We left from Gurock with an unusually heavy naval escort; somebody knew something, I didn't know what. We had the impression that we were being tailed, right from the very start, by these long-distance German bombers who would go out and sort of find things and then send the signal back to France. The signals would then be sent out to U-boats.

We were out about two days and a message came, and I'll never forget it. It was from the commodore of the convoy. It was sent by light blinker, which is sort of amazing considering what the nature of the message was. It said: "Secret: Someone is somehow sending the position of the convoy to the Germans every two hours. Please search your ship or try to stop this," and anybody who could, read the thing.

Well, that really terrified me, being at my age and because I couldn't imagine how that could happen. That's a hell of an accomplishment: to know where you are, to have the equipment, to keep it secret, and to do it every two hours. I don't know whether this was to keep us alert or what, but it sure scared the hell out of me. It probably was true, because of what happened later. We went way out into the middle of the ocean and then came straight south, quite deep down, and then turned toward Gibraltar. And it turned out, as I later learned, a lot of the ships were going to fan out to take different kinds of troops and specialists all over the place—North Africa, Malta, Naples, whatever.

I do have this sort of feeling that they took us through at night because they didn't want people on the shore to see what was going through very clearly. I mean, the general lingo was that the Axis had guys on the African side and in Gibraltar who were spies. But we did get through.

We got about just past Oran, and I was on the bridge one night. On that particular ship, one of my duties was to hang around the bridge a lot and be the captain's messenger. That may sound kind of strange, but a troop ship, when it's fully loaded, has so many people on it, and the army would always want to try to get as many of the people up on deck for fresh air and everything, because people were puking down in the hold. It was just incredible. It was pretty hard to run around and to get messengers here and there and so they really needed messengers. There were not many telephones.

I was on the bridge, and as we were going almost dead east, 90 degrees across, I was looking, leaning on the bridge wing and looking astern, at this beautiful sunset. The historical records now say it was just after six o'clock on the night of November 6, 1943. As I was looking exactly at it, a U.S. destroyer suddenly blew up, just exploded in a huge ball of fire, and sank, as far as I could see.

I was in total disbelief, because I was peacefully watching this sunset, and suddenly the thing exploded. This was doubly upsetting because we had been guaranteed heavy fighter escorts from Gibraltar on, and where were all the Navy radars from this heavy escort? We didn't get one single warning. In any event, we were attacked, immediately and very professionally, by the Luftwaffe, with what I've since learned were fifty planes. There were Stuka dive-bombers, but the main effort was with the torpedo bombers. I was told, later, that the new German glider bombs had been dropped on the convoy from very high-altitude planes. They would come in while all the confusion was going on below and drop this newly utilized German bomb, that had quite a lot of notoriety, and guide it from above, keeping the plane's course straight. It was terrifying. It was better for them to do that, while all the confusion was going on and nobody was looking way up high. Everyone was looking at the torpedo planes, so they [the Germans] would have an unobstructed straight run to do this.

Almost immediately, I jumped in the 20mm tub, which was on the bridge wing and which I was assigned to, and started getting the cover off and trying to get into the harness, which I did pretty quick, and got it loaded. There was no else around; it was all so quick. By then, of course, there was the chaotic noise, with the general alarm going off and so forth.

And as I was looking back, here came the German torpedo planes, down between the columns of the ships, and then they would fan out and drop torpedoes at different places. It was magnificently organized. I can't remember seeing a torpedo coming at the *Thomas H. Barry*, but I do remember we took evasive action, and I wasn't paying attention because I was then trying to hit any goddamn plane I could hit.

All these ships came alive, with the 20-millimeters especially, and the planes were flying below the level of the bridges. People were, in their anxiety and nervousness, following the planes down, so we were shooting at the other ships, and that's why they were so clever. I mean, a lot of ships lost their lifeboats, they got just wiped out, and that's what I thought was going to kill me. I really decided that. I mean, the air was filled with guys who were in effect shooting at the other ships, thinking they were tracing along, following these torpedo planes. Some stuff hit the gun tub. The ship got hit a little, my ship. In any event, they would come down, and be gone.

I believe two or three of them were hit. I don't know. I tried to hit them; I don't know if I hit them. Then there were these high-altitude bombers, which were timed very accurately, and right next to us, on the port side, was a very large Dutch ship, which had been traded from Holland before the war with the Dutch East Indies. It had a crew of that nature, Dutch officers and East Indians, whatever, in the crew. She got hit, fair and square, and started to sink. I don't know how many times she got hit, but I saw one that may have been enough.

Also, right dead ahead of us, the *Santa Elena* was hit, a Grace Line ship, and she started to sink slowly, by the stern. It's a very dramatic story, actually. There was incredible chaos. Ships trying to decide whether they would stop to try to pick up survivors, help people, or should they scatter? I don't remember any signals coming from the commodore, perhaps I couldn't have heard them in any event, because there was so much noise, and I was trying to man the gun at that point. I forgot about the captain. He was within arm's length almost; he could have gotten me if he needed me.

But then they were gone. I'd say ten minutes, fifteen minutes this attack lasted. To my recollection, the Germans sank the destroyer and the two transports loaded with troops. There were some real casualties on the Dutch ship. A lot of them went into boats. Our ship picked up a lot of them, the *Monterrey* picked up a lot of them, and there was a lot of really heroic stuff, trying to pick up people as it began to get dark, and then everyone was frightened and chaotic and wondering what the hell's going on. An uppermost thought in everyone's mind, obviously, was, were the submarines coordinated with this? Because, while we were not paying attention to the water, we were all looking up in the sky; it would have been the perfect time for the submarines to attack.

But, as far as I'm aware, they didn't. I'm still mystified. Ultimately, I was told, these German planes had come from the island of Majorca, in Spain, which wasn't supposed to happen under the rules of war at that time, and, was a first-class illustration, if true, of how Franco and the Spanish were helping Hitler. They could never have gotten to us in the way they did unless they had come out of Majorca.

I would like to take this opportunity to praise the seamanship of the American crew of the *Santa Elena*. A tug had been made fast to it, and while it was being towed, a Dutch ship hit the *Santa Elena* during the night, apparently opening up another bunch of seams. They only lost four people. That's a great feat of seamanship, because you have a loaded troop ship with a lot of panicked people. They were mostly Canadians, and there has never been due credit given to the crew of the *Santa Elena.*

The ship that sunk was the sister ship of the *Santa Rosa*. There were four of these great, wonderful Grace Line ships, who used to trade with South America before World War II. One was lost at Casablanca, then the *Santa Elena* sank in front of my eyes, and the other two survived the war.

The effort was made to try to save the *Santa Elena* as she was continuously slowly sinking down by the stern. So they were going to tow her to the first beach-type place that was near Philipville, which is further along the coast. They had to travel at a very slow rate, through the night. And the *Barry*, my ship, stood by. The Grace Line merchant crew stayed on board and tried to see it home all the way. It was just amazing. They tried to save her a number of times during the night, and they didn't leave until she was at an angle of about 45 degrees, and the water had come up almost to the bridge, which takes a lot of guts, too. To my everlasting sadness and to everyone else's, our whole crew was lined on our ship, watching as she sank, two miles off the shore at Philipville. But I would like, somehow or other, to see that the tremendous seamanship that I witnessed of the crew of the *Santa Elena* is recognized.

The *Barry* put into Philipville. There had been admirable conduct among the soldiers on board. When sailing on a troop ship, you were always terrified that if something drastic happens they would panic, and they didn't, and I don't know to this day why. Maybe they sealed the hatches, I don't know. But we discharged, and then we picked up the first really serious American battle casualties, from the North African battle, which included quadriplegics, hoisted in baskets up the side, with a cadre of Army nurses to take care of them. I'll never forget this either. It was one of the most horrifying [sights]. Plus, there were a lot of German prisoners; we took them back, too. We went back to the States after that. I was eighteen years old.

German aircraft torpedoed the Grace Line ship SS *Santa Elena* on November 6, 1943, demolishing the engines and steering gear and flooding her. On November 7, the SS *Manix Van St. Aldegonde* rammed the *Santa Elena* while she was being towed, bringing more seawater into the ship, which eventually sank.[5]

Captain George E. Kraemer, Class of 1944

George Kraemer has always been close to the sea. Growing up on Long Island, New York, Kraemer's family owned a marine engine and boat repair business. He was a natural candidate for Kings Point, and his postwar career also has been in the maritime field. In particular, from 1947 to his retirement in 1986, he had a successful career in managing tugboat and towing operations.

I was transferred to an American Export Lines ship, converted to a troop transport. She was the USAT *Excelsior*, which was Bethlehem Steel–built. She was considered a modified C-2. These ships were built originally in Quincy, Massachusetts, so naturally they called them the "Quincy-class" ships. They were about 475 feet long, also very fast ships. They were 16.5-knot cruising speed. As a matter of fact, they had one of those ships at that time that was called the *Examiner*. She carried 1,200 pounds of steam. Normally they carried, I think it was 450 pounds of steam, but she carried 1,200 pounds. She had a lot of steam pressure. But nevertheless, they converted the *Excelsior* in such a manner that she could carry about 2,500 troops. She had a full-blown hospital aboard. As a matter of fact, the major who was a surgeon and a medical doctor, who was in charge of the medical group aboard the ship, performed a couple of operations: one fellow with appendicitis, and there was another operation performed. They did all sorts of things on the ship.

We were assigned to a high-speed troop convoy (15 knots). There were approximately thirty ships and almost the same number of escort vessels. The escort usually included an escort carrier and a major vessel, such as a battleship or a heavy cruiser, as the escort commander's vessel. We had the battleship *Nevada* in one convoy as the escort commander's vessel. It was on Christmas Eve, 1943. We were returning light from the British Isles, as we took a horrendous beating in the storm. It was a late storm that had come up from the Gulf, I understand, and went across the Atlantic. It was almost like a hurricane when it was up on the coast. But we took a terrible beating. We lost several of our lifeboats. Of course, we had the lifeboats slung over the side. The weather was so bad, we had a tough time getting them in. I think we saved one of the four regular lifeboats. We had two other launches that they had put on the ship when they converted it, and a bunch of rafts slung over the side and hanging in cradles on the rigging. We lost a few of those. The *Nevada* took a hell of a beating. I understand she had one of her turrets damaged, which is quite a thing. I can remember that very, very well. It was a very, very bad night.

In these convoys, we carried troops into the British Isles, and when we got into our destination ports, they would be dispersed into all different areas. I made about four round-trips on that ship, maybe even five. If the ships were small enough, as the *Excelsior* was, we went right up the River Clyde to Glasgow. I saw the place where the *Queens* [*Queen Mary* and *Queen Elizabeth*] were built: I think it was Brown Shipyard. How the hell they ever launched those ships, I don't know, because the river's very narrow. But we would discharge our troops and then go back down. Some of the ships laid out at anchor and discharged into ferries. I made trips into Glasgow and to Belfast and Liverpool.

In one convoy, we had the old four-stack cruisers, *Marblehead* and *Milwaukee*. They were sister vessels. Anybody that knows anything about naval history knows of those ships. They were full-size cruisers. There were several of them in the U.S. Navy. We left those two ships in the British Isles. I later found out—and I saw one of them when I made a trip to Murmansk—she had been turned over to the Russian navy. I forget which one it was, whether it was the *Marblehead* or the *Milwaukee*.[6]

I didn't know at the time, of course, but looking back on it, we were stocking up the British Isles for the Normandy invasion. Also, I understand in retrospect, they were almost like a task force, that particular convoy. Considering there were sixty ships, half of them naval, half of them merchant ships, we could have been diverted at any time to North Africa, or Italy, or anyplace. So I guess according to the way the battle action was going in the various theaters, they would make a determination while these ships were en route.

Captain Lewis J. Heroy, Class of 1944

"LJ," as he is known, still maintains his maritime license as a chief officer. A longtime resident of New Orleans, he served for many years as the Academy shipboard training representative in that busy port. His natural joviality and his keen sense of duty are evident.

Well, after you graduated [1944], the school here turned you loose to give your name to the War Shipping Administration in the area. And you had to register with them, and you were allowed to go home for a couple weeks. I went home to New Orleans. Then, on a T2 tanker, we sailed up the coast to New York and loaded 100-octane gasoline. We waited about three or four days until enough ships were available to form a convoy. We formed what was called a "fast tanker convoy," 16 knots, nothing but tankers, and we had a few troop ships in the convoy also. I went on board as what I thought was third mate, but when I got on there, the captain looked at me and he said, "Son, we're going to make you the second mate instead of the third." I said, "Oh, my gosh!" Here I am, the ink is not even dry on my license, and I'm sailing as second mate.

We got up into New York, and by that time I was a little salt. I had been standing and watching them wait for a couple of weeks. Then we got in the convoy here out of New York, and we had about sixty-five or seventy ships in convoy going over to England.

We formed up past Ambrose, out at sea, and then after you got out there, why you formed up in your columns. I think we were third ship in the column. We had destroyer escorts all along with us out there. I guess the whole width of the convoy was probably ten or twelve miles, and the length of the convoy was probably fifteen, sixteen miles. And there I was. I wasn't even twenty-one years of age yet. It was kind of hairy out there sometimes in the North Atlantic.

Did you communicate strictly with flag, voice, and signal lights?

Flags, that's right, yes, and signal lights. One or two of the people in the Armed Guard crew were proficient in signaling, but it was up to the cadets on the ship at the time and the third mate, who's in charge of the flags on the merchant ship. Of course, he got orders from the captain with the various things that they would be using for this particular convoy. We hoisted first repeat, and this meant something; two or three flag hoists would mean something else to him. We had to check a lot in the book as to what this meant. He had various ships in the convoy that were what they called "light repeaters." At nighttime they would repeat the convoy commander's signals to the rest of the convoy, and in the daytime, of course, you could see them well enough. They had to make the signals so that everybody else in the convoy could see them.

In the column, you had a thousand feet between ships on each side, and you kept station with what we called the "stadimeter" at that time. You knew the height of the mast of the ship, and you knew the depth of the ship, so you took the tip of the mast and put it on the waterline from the stern. You read off this figure, and it told you how many yards you had to the ship in front of you. You either dropped off one revolution to engine room, or you added one revolution to the engine room to keep the speed up a little bit or down a little bit, so you wouldn't want to run up on the guy behind you.

If we got into fog many times in the North Atlantic, which we did a little bit later on in the year, we had to stream a fog buoy up behind us. This thing kicked up about a four-, five-foot spray. Then you got a little bit off-center so that you could see that fog buoy on either your port bow or your starboard bow a little bit instead of dead ahead. And you kept station on that fog buoy. You could see that right off your bow.

You kept a bow lookout then?

Oh, yes, yes. We had a telephone for communication with the bridge. I was still on this tanker, and a big hurricane hit New York sometime in September of '44. This is one that did a lot of damage here at the Academy. We were off the coast, still going over, when the convoy commander told us that this hurricane was coming on. He told us all to disperse on the light signals and on the flag signals, and they gave us the position to rejoin five days later and to continue the voyage. He told us and just turned us all loose, said do your own thing. Everybody had to get the heck out of there and get away from each other. All those ships were carrying 100-octane gasoline; you wouldn't want to hit anything, you know. So it was kind of tough back then, really, in convoy, off the Atlantic in the wintertime or in a hurricane.

Did you see any enemy activity?

No, the only thing we saw was going through the English Channel over to England, why, every so often you'd see one of the buzz bombs, the V1s, come over, which the Germans were pushing at that time. So you knew things were getting kind of tough for them as far as airplanes were concerned, and their only alternative was to put wings on a bomb and the navigation to get it where it was going. We saw those periodically going over day and night, but we never were hit by anything. There wasn't anything to stop us at that time. They were just looking to hit anything. In fact, with the noise on the ship you could still hear those things coming. Somebody said, "Just like a bomb." As long as you could hear it, it wasn't going to hurt you.

We went into London. Right outside of London there was a big oil dock there, a tanker dock, and that's where we discharged our whole cargo of 100-octane gasoline. The T2 tankers were roughly about ten thousand gross tons. She carried a crew of forty-four, forty-five, plus a few of the Armed Guard crew on them. But they did consider them a little bit faster. If you traveled about 16 knots, the U-boat threat was a little bit less than it would have been if it was a Liberty ship.

They had three 20mm guns up on the bridge, spaced about what would normally be number-two, -four, or -five hatch on the Liberty ship. You had a platform there for the 20mm guns. I think 20s were all they had, plus the 3-inch 50 and the 5-inch 38.

We were pretty good coming back, and I think the convoy escorts did a remarkable job in protecting us, really. When they first picked up the sound of a submarine on their sonar, they immediately started running for the position and pretty much kept them under control. I think they did a fantastic job. Those were little things [escorts] out there, and they were not running the same course that you were running. A lot of times you'd run a course and they were rolling out there, 35 and 40 degrees each way. They were small, you know, not very wide either. Those guys really had it tough. I know days on end they wouldn't get a chance to sit down at a table and eat a meal. They were eating standing up.

All of my time during World War II was spent on the Atlantic side. I even made a trip to Russia, not to Murmansk. I went through the Mediterranean, into the Black Sea, and into Odessa, Russia, with a load of raw sugar from Cuba. We were there in February of '45, and the Russians were unloading the ship at the time. It was very cold there, and there was a lot of snow on the ships.

We were just getting ready to be under way. The agent came running down the dock with a message, and this great big arm of flowers, and we said, "Gee, what's this guy doing?" He came on board the ship, and he told the captain that President Roosevelt had died in Macon, Georgia. The captain then told the two deck cadets, another fellow and myself, to take the American flag, go down, take a corner of the saloon, officers' mess, and decorate it with the American flag and have a picture of President Roosevelt down in there. We did that. We draped it with black crepe, and we kept it like that for about maybe four or five days until we got back out to sea, and we took it down. It was a very touching situation at that time. Everybody in the world, I think, was sympathetic to us losing our president at the time.

As the Atlantic war progressed, the hunters became the hunted. The U.S. Navy added aircraft carriers to protect the convoys headed for Europe, and more and more U-boats fell prey to American patrol planes. Germany's "grey wolves" of the deep were pursued relentlessly.

J. Richard Kelahan, Class of 1942

Richard Kelahan's first certificate of service was as a cadet in 1940. In San Francisco, he sat for his license as third assistant engineer. He chose to go into active Navy service. Richard Kelahan was in the right place at the right time to participate in a historic event. He vividly remembers the day his ship helped to capture *U-505* and all her secret codebooks.

There were eight ships, Maritime Commission C-3 hulls that had been requisitioned by the Navy from the Maritime Commission. My duties called for me to be an engineer officer on one of those hulls when it was placed in commission, namely on the USS *Card*, which was known at that time as "AVG-11." The ship was commissioned on November 8, and we moved over to Bremerton for the naval outfitting. Then we proceeded to the east coast, where we reported to the Norfolk Naval Operating Base, which was to be our home port. Portsmouth, Virginia, was to be our home repair yard.

We had been converted to this aircraft carrier, and we proceeded to qualify squadrons, which were to be embarked. Our primary training for the pilots was to see that they could land the planes without pulling the ship apart. Before the aviators, ground crews, or fixed crews took over, one of my first duties as an A Division officer was to repair the arresting gear and the barriers after the planes tore them up. We used two-thousand-pound air-over hydraulics to arrest those planes. That's the equivalent pressure of running torpedoes. There was a C-2 hull that had previously been converted for aircraft service in the Atlantic, primarily for aircraft transport. It also operated out of Norfolk, and was, like ourselves, on a first-time use in support of the invasion of Africa. Our port over there was Casablanca. Our first operation in support was ferrying the Army Air Force and their fighter planes over there. Our second cruise was an operation against submarines, and that's when we embarked aircraft. Torpedo planes were armed with depth charges, and then fighter planes to cover the torpedo planes, when they went in to attack.

The concept at the time, which was developed by the British for escorting convoys, was to use their escorts within the convoy, break convoy, steam out, launch the planes, and then run back to the convoy for protection. When they had to recover their planes, they'd break again, and go out, recover the planes, and get back in the convoy. It was not very effective. Several of the Navy skippers—Arnold J. Isbell, Logan Ramsey, and Dan Gallery, in particular—devised an attack concept of leaving port at least seven days in advance of the convoy and going out and sweeping the convoy route. We were catching subs on the surface, which were forming up in "wolf packs." Then the aircraft from the carrier was able to get sight of the submarines, and the torpedo planes would blast them out of the water under the fighter protection.

I was an ensign, USNR, Merchant Marine Reserve (MMR), on active duty. That MMR designator was on orders all the way until I was detached in 1944.

The *Card* received a Presidential Unit Citation for sinking eight U-boats, and later we were added the Blue Star for an additional three. On one of our assignments, we were holding the *U-505* below the surface,[7] but at the time we didn't know what it was. We knew after having hit that particular wolf pack, that one of these subs was still submerged in the area. Our destroyers and destroyer escorts were keeping pretty good track of her. We would leave our screen of three destroyers aside, and they kept up a patrol. We were watching the sound and the movements of that sub. We knew she couldn't stay under over a certain period of time. We got a number of the other subs in the company with her, but we were running out of fuel and provisions.

We were relieved on station by the USS *Guadalcanal*, under the commander, Dan Gallery, later Admiral Gallery. The *Guadalcanal* was a Kaiser-built escort carrier. It replaced the *Block Island*, which had been sunk. So *Guadalcanal* got the *505*, because they had relieved us on station. We were hardly off-station seventy-two hours and still in the area when they got her. Then the *Guadalcanal* took her in tow. Today you can see that submarine when you visit Chicago. They've got it in the Museum of Science and Industry, and it's the submarine parked right outside, between the museum and the lake.

As mentioned, in our first two operations in the antisub warfare, we had been credited with sinking eight submarines. We had the skipper's hat off of one and prisoners' off the others. We went into Norfolk for our refurbishing and port activities. It seemed like about every seven weeks we'd hit Norfolk for about seven days. We learned that we were to receive the Presidential Unit Citation for our operations. One of the skippers, Logan Ramsey, had been promoted to rear admiral. Our skipper, Arnold J. Isbell, was also relieved and promoted to rear admiral.

When we went to the antisubmarine operations, our designator was changed from AVG-11 to CVE-11, and everybody was curious as to whether they were accepting the *Card* with a C-3 merchant hull. We were lucky when we could make 20.5 knots flank. We accepted that as "a ship of the line," *CV* meant that it was an aircraft carrier, but the *E* puzzled us. The only things we knew at the time with an *E* were some little, smaller destroyer types that were sent to us. Our people in the "black gang" were very agitated about it. A black gang was the Navy's term that applied to us, the engineers, and anybody that worked around machinery. I think it stems from the days when the ships were coal-fired, and the coal dust was all over.

So Admiral Ernest J. King came aboard to present the Presidential Unit

Citation. Throughout the ceremony, he said if we had any questions, we should speak up. As the admiral came down the line to inspect us in the E Division, I asked him what the *E* was for. Now, the admiral was a very tall man, quite a towering individual. He stood there, looked me right in the eye, looked over to the "black gang," and then without batting an eyelid, he said, "Expendable." There was dead silence for a couple of minutes, and then the whole "black gang" broke loose in hilarious laughter. It set the tone for the rest of the day. Everything was relaxed and easy, and everybody had a lot of fun. Speaking of "black gangs," the coal dust got all over like that on the *Mormacrey*. In the lower bottoms, we used to load coal off the Norfolk and Western coaling piers. You could seal the doors on your stateroom, but it still got in there. Your sheets had a black coating on them.

I was on the escorts until September 1944. Then I was detached and sent up to the Merchant Marine Academy, where I thought I was going to have a chance to enhance my knowledge of engineering and be assigned to the Engineering Department. Typical of the Navy, I was assigned to the Department of Naval Science and Tactics. I was training midshipmen in maneuvering and in various naval customs, traditions, usage, and such things as that.

While on antisubmarine duty in the Atlantic, the USS *Block Island* was sunk by *U-549*, which torpedoed the auxiliary aircraft carrier on May 29, 1944. Two American destroyers sank *U-549* during the same encounter.[8]

Captain Lee Roy Murray Jr., Class of 1940

Captain L. R. Murray states, "Altogether I had only two thirty-day periods when I was not assigned to a ship during the nearly four years that we were in World War II." Until retirement, Captain Murray was a ship pilot and a pilotage consultant. He is a member of the Houston Pilots Association.

In 1944, I was sailing as first mate, and I spent nearly the entire year sailing in the large North Atlantic convoys going from New York to England. These convoys, up to one hundred ships, were arranged with twenty ships across in the lead columns and five ships deep. I suppose that the convoys were structured that way to reduce the chances of collision if a ship lost power or got out of position. The convoy would be twelve miles wide. The convoy commodore ship was at the center of the first row and used only visual communications (signal flags) to give course and speed changes, next day's rendezvous coordinates, and other information. Ships on the far corners could not even see the flags on the commodore ship, so repeater ships were spaced throughout the convoy.

Was this at a time before the jeep carriers were escorting the convoys?

I believe that the jeep carriers were in use in 1944, but there were never jeep carriers escorting these convoys that I was in. There were corvettes and destroyers mostly. Air cover gave the best protection to a convoy, and by 1944 the Allies were using land-based planes in the far North Atlantic. There were long-range planes from land bases in North America, Newfoundland, Nova Scotia, Greenland, Iceland, and Great Britain that gave air coverage to the convoys in the far North Atlantic. The weather was usually very bad in the far North Atlantic, and the jeep carriers were not very effective in bad weather. I believe that these new escort carriers were used in the convoys from the east coast of the United States to North Africa and the Mediterranean.

The North Atlantic convoys were run by the British. After all, they had been running convoys since 1939, two years before the U.S. was in the war. The corvettes were Canadian and British. Some of the destroyer escorts may have been American. There were great changes during the nearly four years that we were in the war. It didn't really become a worldwide war until December 7, 1941, when the United States got into the war.

The U.S. Navy had almost no escort vessels at the beginning. The German submarines had a field day the first year and a half that we were in the war. They sunk 592 ships on our coast, in the Caribbean, and the Gulf of Mexico in the first two years that we were in the war. Most of those sunk were American flagships. The Germans lost very few submarines during this time. The first escort vessels that I encountered were 110-foot, wooden-hull submarine chasers. Later there were DEs [destroyer escorts], which had sophisticated sonar and radar.

These surface vessels could make it more difficult for the submarines but could not prevent an attack. The most that they could do was locate the submarine after an attack and drop depth charges in hope of sinking the submarine. The Navy deployed blimps on our Gulf coast and east coast early in the war, and they were some help. However, they were only effective in the daytime and could only operate in good weather.

The answer to the submarine problem in the Battle of the Atlantic came in 1944, when there was land-based air coverage for most of the Atlantic Ocean, and there were escort carriers that went with the convoys or just patrolled the open ocean. The air coverage made it very difficult for the German submarines to operate on the surface in the daytime. In the beginning of the war, German submarine commanders called the Atlantic Ocean a shooting gallery. In the last twelve months of the war in Europe, the German submarines were still able to sink a few ships, but they were being hunted down and nearly eliminated due to the air coverage from land-based planes and also from the escort carriers.

During the nearly four years of the war, I was on three different ships. Altogether I had only two thirty-day periods when I was not assigned to a ship during the nearly four years that we were in World War II.

Peter Van der Linde, Class of 1944

Peter Van der Linde went to sea at an early age. At ages sixteen, seventeen, and nineteen, he spent summer vacations at sea aboard American Export Lines vessels trading to India and the Mediterranean. Later, he became a cadet in the U.S. Maritime Commission's maritime training program. He sailed throughout the war. For many years after the war, he was chairman of the firm Transportation Concepts.

There were arrangements for keeping track of the ships in the convoy and for keeping them in order, so there weren't any collisions at sea. They were very strict, and before each convoy set out, there would be a convoy conference. When I eventually became master, I would go to those conferences.

I remember one time when I was master of an American Export Line ship, the *Exmoor*. We were returning from Rio de Janeiro to Guantanamo, Cuba. At the conference run by the Navy, they said the master of the *Exmoor* would be commodore of the convoy. I said, "I haven't had enough experience." I was only about twenty-five. "I think having a naval man as commodore would be best." They said, "No, you're commodore." So that was it. We had a naval escort of two DEs. They were Brazilian, and, of course, they spoke Portuguese. We signaled them, but mostly they didn't understand what we were saying.

We had quite a few passenger ships in this convoy, and they were to peel off: one at Belem, another one farther up, and so on. I had arranged during the day that when we came off of Belem bound north, we would show a green light through a tube at approximately 2300 that night. That was the signal for two big Brazilian passenger ships to move into Belem and leave the convoy. They signaled back they understood. So it came to 2300, we sent them the signal green light, and nothing happened. They just kept going right along. I couldn't get rid of them, and I had to. So I said to the signal man, can you spell "Vamos!?" He said, "No." So I said, "Spell it any old way," and we sent a blinker with a tube on it, "Vamoose," and boom! Away they went. But it was an interesting voyage because I was responsible for all those people for about two weeks, and I had never expected that.

Charles M. Renick, Class of 1947

For many years, Charles Renick was the director of the Office of External Affairs, which also included alumni affairs and placement. Later, he was a prime mover in establishing the American Merchant Marine Museum at Kings Point, which is dedicated to America's modern merchant marine heritage.

I was assigned to the army transport *Brazil*. The *Brazil* was carrying troops in convoy over to Le Havre, France, and then going across to Southampton, picking up American wounded, and bringing the wounded back to New York.

Approximately how many troops were on the ship?

They ranged from five to eight thousand. So they had a lot of troops on there. I would go down and look at these troops. They were lined up in bunks six or eight high and crammed together. When one got sick, they all got sick because of the closeness. Quite often we were the lead ship because it was one of the larger ships in the convoy, and we often carried the convoy commander. Sometimes they put us in the center of the convoy with the commodore and all the convoy would be around us. I can remember about submarines, as I was worrying about the other ships around us.

It was like being on a busy parkway and having cars speeding sixty or seventy miles an hour on each side of you, and in front of you, and in back of you, and tailgating because one of the things that a convoy had to do was keep very close quarters. You had to be a hundred yards apart and sometimes even closer. If the ship in front of you slowed down suddenly, you could go right into its stern, or if the ship behind you sped up or maneuvered wrong.

You also were zigzagging all the time, and you didn't have a certain zigzag pattern. As the commodore's ship, we had to issue an order, put a flag hoist up, and everybody would turn right twenty degrees, and they would go for five minutes and then turn left ten degrees. There was always some ship in the convoy that didn't get the word. When everyone else was turning right, it was turning left, and that would cause a lot of confusion. So I would lay there worrying about what was happening on these ships on either side of us. One of my jobs on the ship as a cadet in the daytime was to use the stadimeter, which is an instrument that measures the distance, and keep track of the ship in front of us, how many yards they were away from us. At night, they would put up a scoop. They would drag it behind the ship. It would scoop up the water and make a spray of water so you could just see it in front of you because in the blackout, you couldn't see the ship in front of you, particularly if it was a dark night. Yet, you knew it was there. I don't remember the yards now, but it was very close.

You would never, in peacetime, consider ever getting that close to a ship. In peacetime, on ships I sailed on, if we got within a mile of another ship, the captain would want to be notified and be on the bridge. Here you were not miles; you were in yards. These were very large convoys, up to forty to sixty ships. All around the perimeter of the convoy were the naval escort vessels, different types of escort vessels. Occasionally, they would get on something, and they would come rushing up in the middle of the convoy and drop a depth charge or two. The ships never knew exactly what was going on because they weren't privy to that. The cadet on the ship didn't know at all. I was eighteen years of age.

All the ships I sailed on during the war had Armed Guards. But the Armed Guard was just a skeleton force to do the main work on the gun, and to every gun was assigned merchant seamen. They also manned the guns. I mean, the Navy personnel would command the gun and direct it, but the guys who were passing the ammunition and doing the work, turning the cranks, were seamen.

They sent us to a school for training on the 20-millimeters, which was what we used for anti-aircraft warfare on most all the merchant ships during the war. That was really a fun time. They would have a plane drive by pulling a target, and they would be very strict about aiming at the target. One fellow in my section got confused and starting shooting at the plane. Lucky he wasn't a very good shot.

How long did it take for the convoy to cross the Atlantic to Southampton or to Le Havre?

Eight to ten days. After D-Day, we were going into Le Havre. They had already had the docks made, but everything was devastated. The troops were going right from there into combat, and the wounded were coming back. For a young fellow on the ship coming back with the young men with arms missing, blinded, in wheelchairs, it was very, very sad. Very, very disconcerting for a young guy.

For Charles Renick's wartime experiences in the Pacific theater, please see chapter 9.

George F. Koury, Class of 1943

George Koury was a member of one of the first classes of cadets at Kings Point. He was at Kings Point until the early part of January 1942, when he was sent to sea for training. Among the most dangerous positions during World War II were service aboard U.S. merchant ships and duty aboard American submarines; George Koury was involved in both. His perspective was, therefore, quite unique.

As a midshipman in training, George Koury witnessed the use of the zigzag tactic that merchant ships used to avoid enemy submarines. Later, as an officer on the U.S. submarine *Barbero*, he detected a fallacy in the zigzag tactics.

I reported aboard an army transport, the USS *McAndrew*, for training. We went across the North Atlantic, carried marines to Iceland. We replaced the British troops that were there and were air-attacked all the way down past Norway into Scotland. Then we picked up British troops and made a fast run down around the horn, down past Capetown, South Africa, to try to stop Rommel in North Africa. We came up and did a fast transport, fast in those days. We did about 21 knots. I remember we carried sixty-eight passengers, and we were carrying about 3,800 troops, most of the time without an escort. We went by ourselves. Occasionally when we received warning of a submarine, we would zigzag. Otherwise we would run straight through. Of course, my submarine experience indicated that all zigzagging does is slow down the convoy. It was a fallacy. Even the Japanese attacked the convoys. Actually, the only thing that would cause a little problem, if they zigzagged, was what we called a constant helm. The helmsman would try and stay with it, and you wouldn't have set patterns. You would just veer across on a swaying course, and it was relatively difficult to really pin down the angle on the bow in certain target angles.

For Koury's career as a submariner, see chapter 14.

Milton G. Nottingham Jr., Class of 1944

Milton Nottingham says: "There will always be challenges for those who go to sea, for it is a 'risky business.' However war risks impose an even greater danger to those who sail." Nottingham speaks from experience. He describes a near-collision that occurred while sailing close to another ship in convoy. Nottingham served in World War II and in Korea, as port commander for the Port of Pusan. He received numerous commendations for his management of port operations. In recent years, Nottingham has played a leading role in Academy alumni activities.

The *George Washington* was generally assigned to a fast ship convoy and often was the flagship of the convoy, meaning that the convoy commodore was aboard. However, on the voyage I am about to describe in the winter of 1945, the commodore was on another ship. Wartime convoys maintained radio silence in order not to give the enemy their position. Instead, orders were conveyed by the convoy commodore via signal flags in daylight hours and by signal lights in darkness. Each ship was equipped with a light pole on the uppermost deck with red and green lights mounted on the poles in step fashion from one side of the pole to the other. These light poles were called "Christmas trees." Signal lights conveying orders to the convoy originated on the flagship and were repeated by each ship in the convoy. When all ships in the convoy had repeated the light signal, the commodore would order the execution of his order by sounding the whistle on his flagship.

On the night of the incident, I was the quartermaster at the wheel when the commodore signaled for a course change. The Navy signalman on the flying bridge phoned the bridge to report the three-light signal for an emergency turn of 45 degrees. However, the second mate and the two junior third mates did not know if the course change was to right or left and were trying to determine in which direction to turn when the whistle signal to execute was sounded by the flagship. The second officer ordered me to come left 45 degrees, and I started the turn left when the second officer started stuttering, and I realized that while we were turning left, the rest of the convoy was turning right. Without waiting for the order, I started turning the wheel to the right while saying, "Hard right, sir." The second officer said, "That's right, hard right!"

The USAT *George Washington*, loaded with five thousand troops, came within a few yards of colliding with the C-3 freighter ahead of us. Had we struck the other ship at our 18-knot speed, we probably would have sunk that ship and very likely there would have been a substantial loss of life. Had I waited for the second officer to recover his bearings and give the order to turn right, there is no doubt that a collision would have occurred. I am equally certain that had I not had prior experience as a cadet and as an unlicensed deck officer, I would have waited for the mate on watch, in this case the second officer, to give me the order to turn right rather than my anticipating it. Seconds counted!

LIBERTY SHIPS

Liberty ships were the primary vessels that the American merchant marine used in World War II. Called "ugly ducklings" because of their plain utilitarian lines, the Liberties were actually a good example of the principle of form following function. Originally a British design, the U.S. government chose the Liberty ship design for mass production because each ship consisted of prefabricated parts that could be welded together for quick completion and launching. Often ships were completed in forty days. The main objective was to put to sea more ships than the enemy could sink, thus guaranteeing a steady flow of material to the war fronts. The Liberty ship answered that need. Even a single successful trip to its destination justified the Liberty ship's construction.

Over 2,700 Liberty ships were built during the war. Of that number, approximately 200 were lost. Specifications were as follows:

Length overall	*441 ft. 6 in.*
Breadth, extreme	*57 ft.*
Draft	*27 ft. 9¼ in.*
Gross tonnage	*7,191*
Capacity	*562,608 cu. ft.*
Main engine horsepower at 76 rpm	*2,500*
Speed	*11 knots*
Crew size, not including additional	
Navy personnel	*39 to 41 (varied)*
Naval Armed Guard	*12 to 27 (varied)*

The propulsion was by a direct-acting, three-cylinder, triple-expansion steam engine, which drove a four-blade propeller.

Liberty ships were versatile. Basically, they were dry cargo ships that could be adapted for service as tankers, colliers, boxed aircraft transports, army tank transports, hospital ships, troop ships, and animal transports, as well as many other purposes.

Toward the end of the war, newer, faster Victory ships were introduced in growing numbers, but the Liberty ships continued as the mainstay of logistical support. For many Kings Pointers, the Liberty ships were thoroughly appreciated for their ability to deliver cargo and personnel safely under the most trying of conditions.[1]

There are two Liberty ships currently in operation, the John W. Brown *and the* Jeremiah O'Brien. *Both vessels are museum ships and are open to visitors. The* John W. Brown *is located in Baltimore and the* Jeremiah O'Brien *is in San Francisco.*

Liberty ship *Ethan Allen* under construction in 1942. Courtesy of the United States Naval Institute.

SS Jeremiah O'Brien, *Bound for Normandy, From San Francisco—1994,* by Donald W. Patterson. By permission of Donald W. Patterson.

Taylor A. Anderson, Class of 1942

Taylor Anderson served on three Liberty ships during World War II. After the war, Anderson married, and for a brief time he continued to sail on his license. In June 1949, he was hired as a safety engineer. He worked in this field for thirty-one years, eventually becoming a regional engineering manager. Later, he was appointed by the governor of Washington to the State Board of Boiler Rules. In 1981, he started his own firm engaged in marine survey and insurance services. Taylor Anderson has concluded, "It's been a good life!"

I ended up serving on three Liberty ships. The first one was the *Meriwether Lewis*. She was the first keel laid at St. John's yard in Portland, Oregon. They loused it up so badly, we couldn't get it in the water. So they launched the second keel lady, and they called her the *Star of Oregon*. We went in the water behind her as the *Meriwether Lewis*. She was the first keel laid, but the second one in the water.

When we got the vessel in the water and took her to sea, we found a number of serious problems with the construction of the entire vessel, not just the keel. There were many structural problems and slow-downs in the crews that were building those vessels. They probably lacked coordination and proper organization. You had all your components over here, and you had to bring them together in an organized fashion. In the meantime, you had to construct your engines and all your machinery, your piping, and all this sort of thing. Far and away, the leaders were experienced, but the men in the yard, the actual help, were not experienced shipbuilders. So there were lots of things that they finally straightened out.

The second vessel that I took out was built in twenty-three days. She was a far cry from the first one we took out. When we got to sea, we found there was poor welding and a number of things were wrong. Went from Portland to San Francisco, finished loading, and we headed out for New Caledonia. We were out to sea for a week or so, and the weather improved, so the gunnery officer wanted to try this new 5-inch World War I gun. We fired that gun and completely disabled our own ship. The overhead lighting fell off of the gun crews' quarters, the wash basins came off the bulkheads, the toilets snapped off the deck, and we severed the telemotor lines. This was as a result of the vibrations from the gun. The reinforcing wasn't sufficient to properly support the gun. The Navy gun crew was operating the gun. We had no training in armaments at that time.

The third Liberty ship that I sailed on was the *Sam Jackson*, which went up to the Arctic with the Aleutians campaign. Winter trips to the Bering Sea were something else, wild weather, cold even in the engine room. We made trips to Kodiak, Kiska, Attu, Cold Bay, Adak, and other Alaska ports. We were discharging cargo in late December, in Dutch Harbor, and started loading ammunition on the double for the cruiser *St. Paul* in Adak.

We left in a hurry and ran into a severe storm. The light ship rolled and pitched violently. The stowage of the ammunition gave way; the big shells crashing against the engine room forward bulkhead was something of a distraction on Christmas Eve. They sounded more like "Nearer My God to Thee" than "Jingle Bells!" We arrived in Adak, off-loaded the shells, then lay at anchor in the harbor.

We had sudden "williwaws" [violent gusts of wind] and snow squalls all day. While standing on the boat deck under the wing of the bridge with the chief engineer, we watched a heavily loaded lifeboat leave an anchored destroyer escort a short distance away. A sudden squall hit. I watched the small craft pitch in the choppy sea and told the chief, "Two more seas like that and she swamps!" The second sea swamped the boat; the third scattered the men. I called the mate and ran to the crew's mess for volunteers for the lifeboat. I had the motor running before the boat hit the water and had all the men out of the water within thirty minutes. The DE had slipped her anchor and came alongside our boat to pick up their men. The last men we pulled into our boat were so cold, only their eyelids flickered. No casualties!

That night another severe storm hit. We lost our anchor, rammed another vessel, finally sent out of the crowded harbor to ride out the storm. The next day we came back inside the submarine net to pick up our anchor. One Liberty ship had been driven so far up on the beach you could walk out on dry sand and touch the hull. On the inshore side a tug, which had been trying to keep the vessel off the beach, was still moored to the ship. Both vessels were salvaged with the next few extreme high tides. The winter weather in the Aleutians and the Bering Sea is straight out of *Hell*!

On our return to Seattle, we went into the shipyard to clean and paint the ship's bottom and repair damage to the bow. We found the hull had a number of cracks along the deck and side plates due to the extreme cold water and the severe weather. An 18-inch-wide by 1-inch-thick plate of steel was welded along the length of both sides of the hull.

After that, I was second assistant engineer on the *Marshfield Victory*. We sailed to San Francisco, then to Pearl Harbor, and on to the invasion of Guam. On our return to Los Angeles, I was ordered to report aboard the *Sam Jackson*, in San Francisco, without delay!

We went up the river to Benicia, for a full load of bombs, some eight thousand–plus tons of them. This was just after the Port of Chicago Ammunition Depot explosion. We were not allowed to leave the ship while loading, even had an armed Marine stationed in the engine room all the time we were there. Everyone was very nervous and jumpy while loading.

I had no knowledge of the Port of Chicago explosion, having just returned from Hawaii and the invasion of Guam. It had happened just two miles up the river where we were loading; two ships loading ammunition exploded with some three hundred people killed and thousands injured.

We sailed down the river, fully loaded with bombs, and ran aground in San Francisco Bay. We were a little over two days getting the vessel free of the mud. During that time, the pilot, captain, and chief engineer were taken ashore for a U.S. Coast Guard hearing. The rest of the crew was restricted to the ship, while tugs made every effort to free the ship. Everybody in San Francisco knew the vessel was out there and was nervous as hell until we got out of their bay. They didn't want another explosion in San Francisco.

We sailed unescorted to Biak, which is an island just below the Philippines. It was a jumping-off place for the Fifth Bomb Group. They used us as a warehouse. They would off-load the bombs that the group's planes would deliver. Then they would send us around to a bay where we would be far enough away from the base, so that if we got hit, we wouldn't destroy it.

The chief engineer came to my room and said, "I want to borrow your suitcase." I said, "What in heaven's name do you want with a suitcase out here in Biak? Where are you going?" He said, "The captain is sending me ashore under arrest." I was just astounded. I gave him my suitcase. This is the same chief that I had sailed with before on the *Sam Jackson*. We had been together for some time. Sure enough, I walked out on deck, and here is this Marine sergeant taking this man ashore under arrest. Then the first mate came down, knocked on the door, and said, "The captain wants to see you." I went to the bridge, and the captain said, "I understand you have a chief engineer's license." I said, "Yes sir." He said, "You are now the chief engineer of this vessel." That is the way I got promoted.

I brought the ship back. I had one other licensed engineer with me. He had a third assistant's license. We just kind of trained the rest of the crew as we had to, and we kept on. When the bombs were all delivered, we loaded the bomb group, the base group, and all their gear aboard, and we took those people to the Leyte Gulf operation. There were ships scattered around the bay, but the action and such was over by the time we got out there. We brought the Fifth Bomb Group. To help set them up, we made two trips, and it must have taken at least two weeks.

After that was finished, we took the empty vessel to Manila. We were there when the war was over, anchored in the middle of the bay.

The German submarine *U-162* used gunfire and a torpedo to sink the *Star of Oregon* on August 30, 1942. The crew was rescued, but one passenger was lost.[2]

Rear Admiral Thomas J. Patterson, Class of 1944

The fleet of Liberty Ships was built as emergency cargo ships for World War II. To man these ships, we needed thousands of officers for them, and so the U.S. Merchant Marine Academy was formed and being built simultaneously with the Liberty Ships. Admiral McNulty was conceiving the plans for the U.S. Merchant Marine Academy at the same time the British were over here in September of 1940 to see President Roosevelt and Admiral Land to get sixty ships built, which were basically the forerunners of our Liberty Ships. So we shifted from building those English Liberty Ships in Portland, Maine, and in Richmond, California, and started our American Liberty ships.

The *Patrick Henry* was launched September 27, 1941, before Pearl Harbor, which a lot of people don't realize. We had Liberty Ships going before we entered the war. These ships then were coming on the screen in 1942, particularly, and they continued being built all the way through until October 12, 1945. There were 2,751 of these Liberty Ships built. So when the class of 1942 and class of 1943 and class of 1944 were going out to sea as cadet-midshipmen for their shipboard training, in the war areas, your chances of getting assigned to a Liberty Ship were excellent. That's what most of us received.

Then, after you got your license, your chances of going on a Liberty Ship as a licensed officer, again, were excellent, and we found that Kings Pointers fleeted right up; we had young masters and chief engineers—twenty-two, twenty-three years old. So you went on with a third mate's license, and immediately were sailing second mate. You'd get your second mate's license, and you'd be sailing as a chief mate. During the voyage, older masters would get ill, maybe masters from World War I on these Liberties, and Kings Pointers were fleeting up to masters and chief engineers. Cadets were sailing as acting third mates and third assistant engineers. So they [Liberty ships] were part of the roots of Kings Point. O'Hara Hall at Kings Point is named after Cadet Edwin O'Hara, sinking the German raider *Stier* from the stern of the *Stephen Hopkins*. A Liberty ship proved that these were offensive ships: these weren't defensive ships. So that's why I say that the history of Kings Point and the history of Liberty ships are one. They were inseparable.

Well, they started out with light armament. The ship I went on had the regular Liberty ship armament of eight 20mm guns and a 3-inch gun on the bow and a 5-inch gun on the stern. The early ones had less than that, two 3-inches, for example, or, even before that, machine guns. I know the ships in the very early part of the war had .30-caliber machine guns. They didn't have armaments. Then it just evolved as the weapons became available. But the average Liberty ship, then, as the war progressed had these eight 20-millimeters: two forward and two aft, four on top of the superstructure midships and a 3-inch 51 forward and either a 5-inch 38 aft. Usually the Navy Armed Guards operated them with mariners as loaders. We had twenty-eight, which was about an average number in the U.S. Naval Armed Guard. Usually a lieutenant (jg) for the gunnery officer.

Unfortunately over two hundred cadet-midshipmen and Kings Point alumni could not be interviewed because they died in World War II. The story of Cadet-Midshipman Edwin O'Hara illustrates the sacrifices Kings Pointers had made. As noted earlier, the Kings Point training program required all cadet-midshipmen to undergo training at sea. As with Edwin O'Hara, these undergraduates frequently went into harm's way, as did most of the graduates. A fellow Kings Pointer and World War II veteran, Rear Admiral Patterson comments on O'Hara's final hour aboard the Liberty Ship *Stephen Hopkins*.[3]

Cadet-Midshipman Edwin O'Hara was down in the engine room, and *Stier*, the German raider, was firing its 6-inch shells and going right down the stack of the *Stephen Hopkins*, and so the engine room was abandoned. There was nothing but steam down there. O'Hara went back through the shaft alley and up through the escape trunk up by the 5-inch gun, and he discovered that everybody in the gun tub was killed. There was live ammunition up there, so he started to load the gun and fire it himself—five shells that hit the waterline of the *Stier*. Much to the German captain's horror, his ship sank from under him. The German ship *Tannenfels* picked up the *Stier*'s survivors. That was a sister ship that was with the *Stier*. They did not attack the lifeboats filled with the [Liberty ship's] survivors. There were fifteen left from the *Stephen Hopkins*. You know, he [O'Hara] sank

Cadet-Midshipman Edwin J. O'Hara, who perished while defending his Liberty ship, the *Stephen Hopkins*, September 27, 1942. By permission of United States Merchant Marine Academy.

that German raider. I mean, this is why I say, these [Liberty] ships were offensive ships. They were well armed.

Edwin O'Hara died at the gun station as the wrecked *Stephen Hopkins* slid to its watery grave, September 27, 1942.

Robert Glenn Smith, Class of 1944

Robert Glenn Smith drew the illustrations included in this book while on location for sea training as a cadet-midshipman in World War II. Bob's affinity for artistic creation continued after the war in a very successful career. Smith states, "On returning to the States in spring 1947, prospects for a career in the Maritime Service were bleak." He finished his education at Pratt Institute in Industrial Design, and he has held several positions in product design and development. He was also president and chairman of the Industrial Design Society of America.

Arriving on the overnight train from New York to Wilmington, South Carolina, Cadet-Midshipman John Maloney and I entered the bustling shipyard ready for sea duty aboard our assigned vessel, the SS *Roger Moore*. It was an awe-inspiring sight to approach seven shipbuilding ways, six with a Liberty ship in measured states of construction, and a seventh conspicuously vacant. That was to be our ship, which would sail north in about two weeks to be loaded with war materials.

On December 7, 1941, I was studying design at Pratt Institute in Brooklyn. Within a few weeks, the art of camouflage had been added to our studies, a specialty where most of my classmates would soon enlist. I had just learned about Kings Point through a relative who lived on Long Island. During my teens, I had read much about the sea including Conrad's adventures sailing the globe. Add to this, years of being fascinated by the views of the world described by the monthly National Geographic Society magazine, I eagerly sent for my application in the spring of 1942. To my chagrin, there was a long waiting list, and it wasn't until that December that I was signed into the Naval Reserve and shortly thereafter received my orders to report to the Academy.

The three-month basic training gave us enough discipline, enthusiasm, and a working knowledge of navigation, cargo handling, seamanship, and gunnery, etc. to be useful before being assigned to sea duty and the rigors of war.

Seven days after we arrived, the ship was launched, and in another week she had been completed, ready for our crew to take it out for a one-day sea trial. Experiencing the unprecedented speed of building these ships firsthand was an inspiration, and opened my eyes wide to what was meant by American ingenuity and its application to efficiency, capability, and determination. In about three weeks since we had arrived at the shipyard without even a keel laid, we had threaded our way past the masts and funnels of sunken ships on the Cape Hatteras shoals, and were entering Norfolk to be loaded with mustard gas and sundry other war materials. By this time, I believe the U-boats could no longer come alongside to determine whether it was worth their limited arsenal to sink the ship, so we proceeded to New York without escort to be assembled in convoy.

After three days of waiting for a convoy to be assembled and my waiting with a sharp abdominal pain, the captain finally sent me ashore to see a doctor. Unfortunately the launch went to Coney Island, not Staten Island. I arrived at the Marine Hospital four hours later with a ruptured appendix, and the convoy sailed the next morning with one less deck cadet. A month later I was fully repaired and assigned to another ship.

See chapter 7, "The Mediterranean," for Robert Glenn Smith's subsequent wartime experiences.

George H. Bark, Class of 1944

In his early youth, George Bark set his course on a seafaring career. While still in high school, Mr. Bark says he "pestered a friend of mine to get me a job with the Standard Fruit and Steamship Company, for at least a trip or so. . . . I wound up on a banana ship . . . for a two-week cruise to Jamaica and Honduras and back to New York." He sailed throughout the war. After war's end, he continued to sail for almost eight years, or, as he states, "I stayed long enough to get my master's license." He was twenty-four years of age (1949). In his later career, he was the principal marine surveyor for Hull and Cargo Surveyors, Inc., in Florida, until his retirement in 1986. He says, "Throughout the years, I continued my strong interest in ships and the sea."

I guess it would have been '42. It was called the CT *Jaffray*. She was an old vessel from the Great Lakes, and she was operated by the Army Transport Service at that time. But this was in the Gulf, out of New Orleans. They put her to work. She was laid up, and they brought her down the Mississippi River, and she resembled something like the C4s that were later developed by the Maritime Commission that had the engine aft and so on.

It was on that ship that we had a close call when we rounded the eastern tip of Cuba, which was known as Coffin Corner. As soon as we came around the tip at a location that is only about thirty miles from Guantanamo Naval Base—that's how audacious the subs were—they attacked, and the ship next to us got it, and she was an ammunition ship. She was the Liberty Ship *James Sprunt*, but there was nothing left of it, and the impact of it was so severe that it tore apart our blackout ports and the doors. The concussion was felt throughout the whole ship.

I had just done my watch at four in the morning, and I had been drawing coffee from the urn, and I just sat down, and the heavy blackout screen went flying across and smashed the coffee urn, missing my head by a few inches. That was close as I came to being killed. It would have been very embarrassing getting killed by a coffeepot!

After that we had no more problems, and we had a very unusual trip going up from Panama to Alaska, bringing coffee from all the coastal ports of Central America. We were in convoy only in the Gulf. Then we got to Panama. We were on our own. We loaded coffee. There was already a coffee shortage in the States. And then we came with a full load of coffee into San Francisco, and you've never seen such a parade of officials and semi-officials coming aboard with some kind of little bags, and so on, to get a little bit of the coffee.

Phillip M. Torf, Class of 1944

Phil Torf has always been close to his family. After the war he continued at sea and achieved a chief engineer's license. However, in 1948 he joined his father in business as a manufacturer's representative. In 1991, he inherited his uncle's business supplying props and objects of art for the motion picture and television industries and is still very active. He's also active in Academy affairs on the west coast. He's married and is very proud of his family.

I think the Liberty ship was probably the most serviceable ship possible that could have been built at that time: the technology, and the ability to go fast. There was very little complication in terms of the engine and the engine room. They seemed to withstand the seas very well. They were good ships. In fact, most all of the ships that were built, even the T2s, held up very nicely. The Victory was a step up from the Liberty ship, because it had steam turbines, so it traveled faster, and was a little more deluxe, but they were all good ships. Those ships were even serviceable after the war and were sold to foreign governments.

John J. Burke, Class of 1945

John J. Burke states proudly, "I am enjoying all of my eight grandchildren and getting old." He was a cadet-midshipman during the war and graduated in 1945. Contending with the postwar recession, Burke managed to sail on his license from 1945 to 1947. He served in an active unit in the Navy Reserve until 1953 and subsequently worked for several tire companies until his retirement in 1989.

What was your feeling about the construction and the seaworthiness of the Liberty ship?

Great. You can see how many of those ships came back to the boneyards that had gone on so long. One ship in particular was the *Jeremiah O'Brien*. I was on her in a typhoon off Okinawa, with Captain Jahns. When the trip finished, we found footprints on the walls of the galleys of the cargoes, where she had taken such a list that the crew had put their feet on the wall. We split up on the side gunnel,[4] which was normal for a Liberty, but she rode on. She could take anything. She was an old ship. I think she was built about 1943 or 1942. And she was a good ship. She could do a job without spending the time in port, and she could hold an excellent load.

Did you see any advantages to having steam as a major driving mechanism in the ship, especially during wartime?

I don't know about that. We did have a machine shop aboard, and we could make parts for the engine. We broke down one time, in fact. I was going to be married, and I had to wire my wife to cancel it for a week, because we were broken down. But we fixed it ourselves. The ships with turbine engines couldn't do that. They would have to come in for repair.

The only one thing against the Liberty ship was she didn't have speed. We were in trouble if we got into submarine attack. I was in a convoy one time when we were going to Tarawa and they had a sub alert. The escort boats went after the sub, but we just turned and scrambled. Our skipper steered her 180 degrees and headed right back. That's all we could do; we were too slow.

6

THE MURMANSK RUN

Several Kings Pointers stated that the Murmansk run posed the greatest challenge to survival. Treacherous seas, foul weather, the Luftwaffe, German surface raiders, and waiting U-boats conspired to make the runs of supplies to the North Russian ports of Murmansk and Archangel a hellish ordeal. Distances were formidable. Ships sailing out of New York Port had to carry cargoes a distance of 3,948 miles to Murmansk and 4,320 miles to Archangel. Convoys forming up in the British Isles for the final leg of the trip to Murmansk still faced voyages of approximately 1,700 miles past German-occupied Norway. When reaching their Russian destinations, merchant mariners were greeted with suspicion that bordered, at times, on hostility. Kings Pointers made the best of their circumstances and delivered trucks, locomotives, and other materials that enabled Stalin to maintain the Eastern Front.[1]

Captain Arthur E. Erb, Class of 1943

I was a twenty-year-old deck cadet on the *John Witherspoon*, one of the earliest Liberties delivered. Witherspoon was a signer of the Declaration of Independence from the state of New Jersey. The engine cadet and I reported to the ship at nighttime out in Baltimore. It was all new to us. However, in the next few days before we sailed, we were able to get acquainted with the vessel and certainly with the three mates on board. The skipper was somewhat removed from involvement with the cadets. On board ship you were supposed to learn the trade six hours and study for two hours. However, the master didn't believe in that type of regulation. He said: "The day is twenty-four hours long. Anything less than that would be slacking on your part." So I didn't have these six hours of work and two hours of study. The skipper seemed to think that I was learning by doing.

We sailed out of Baltimore and worked up the coast, anchoring at night in the various ports. We just hopscotched up to Halifax, where we were anchored for several days. At that time, they took the merchant crew ashore and put us through "gunnery school" training. They gave us a stripped 303 Lewis machine gun that we held at the hip. We were supposed to fire away at an aircraft sleeve target. The training was minimal, to say the least. We had a very small Navy Armed Guard aboard, but you were expected, as a cadet or a seaman on the crew list, to serve in the gun tubs. Unfortunately, our armament consisted of two .30-caliber machine guns, two .50-caliber machine guns, and a World War I 5-inch deck gun. We thought that was rather inadequate, but later on we found out we were probably one of the best-armed ships in the convoy.

From Halifax, we sailed in a small convoy to Hvalfjordhur, Iceland, in June of 1942. We laid anchor there for approximately thirty days. No shore leave granted. The occasional service boat would come along shoreside with Royal Navy people, who would predict our grim future as part of a Russian-bound convoy. At that time, the ports of entry for the lend-lease cargoes were both Murmansk and Archangel. I found out later that the Port of Murmansk was abandoned as a port of entry for the simple reason that the Germans were about eighteen miles away, and they deemed it inadvisable to bring any future cargo vessels there.

The convoy was made up in Hvalfjordhur. There were some vessels in anchorage there from thirty days prior to our arrival. Our convoy was named "PQ-17" and had several books written about it, one being entitled *The Destruction of Convoy PQ.17.*[2] To my knowledge, PQ-17 was the worst convoy disaster of World War II.

On sailing from Iceland, we all had felt pretty comfortable because visible on the horizon and close in was a sizable escort of Navy ships, including the U.S. cruisers *Tuscaloosa* and *Wichita*, two U.S. destroyers, two Royal Navy cruisers, corvettes, and trawlers. So we thought that we were going to be well protected, and upon sailing from Hvalfjordhur, we *were* well protected. Unfortunately, on the Fourth of July, the escort's commander was given a direction from the British Admiralty to scatter the convoy and for the escorts to withdraw to Iceland. Needless to say, the Navy people were shocked at these orders, and, naturally, those of us on the merchant vessels were in total dismay that we were then to scatter and proceed independently as best we could to Archangel.

The U.S. Navy escort vessels were under British Admiralty, which gave the orders. There have been investigations as to the "why's" and "where-fore's" of the escort command to scatter the convoy and withdraw all the escorts from them.

Of course, the masters of the vessels were instructed not to group up. Each had to proceed on an independent course, which we did for another two days. There were thirty-eight ships total, which scattered, including three rescue vessels. We were under radio silence, but our radio operator was receiving messages from various vessels that were being attacked by submarines or land-based planes.

Prior to scattering on July 4, we were hit by a heavy force of aerial tor-pedo bombers. The *Witherspoon* did not withstand any damage the first time. But two days after scattering, on July 6, at about two in the afternoon, I was standing on the bridge with the second mate. I asked him if he really did see a periscope on his earlier watch, and he said, "Absolutely, that was a periscope." And with that, there was a "Bang!" and we were torpedoed. The torpedo blew up the two lifeboats on the starboard side. She started to sink, and the order was given to abandon the ship, which we did. We lost one man right away. Just as we cleared the stern of the *Witherspoon* in the lifeboats, the submarine put another torpedo in the opposite side. This Lib-erty ship folded in half like a piece of cardboard.[3] The submarine surfaced after the *Witherspoon* went down. We were in the lifeboat. There were no other ships in the area, and the sub questioned us. They knew the name of the ship, where we came from, and what cargoes we had. The cargoes were plainly marked at the time of loading at the port of origin, as going to Technoprom, USSR. There was only one way of getting it there, and that was through the two northern ports. But he questioned us and, naturally, told us the obvious: to head south for landfall.

What he didn't tell us was that two hours away was the pack ice. The other lifeboat had a small motor and went on its way. We were slower be-cause we just had oars, so the two boats separated. We ended up in the ice fields, where we were for about fifty hours. It was almost solid ice. It was pan ice at the time, so the water temperatures had to be fairly close to the freezing mark. Although, bear in mind, this was in the summertime, and we had twenty-four hours of daylight.

From there on, somebody upstairs was looking out for us. We were in absolutely thick fog, and we had set the leg-o-mutton sail. There was some discouragement among the crew, after spending two days plus jammed together in the lifeboat. Just at that time, another freighter from the convoy ran into some heavy ice and stopped her engines in that particular piece of the ocean, outside the entrance to the White Sea. We took turns sounding the whistle. We had it fixed to our life jackets. This other cargo vessel heard us, and the mate on watch was able to spot us. There was very little visibility, but we were not more than fifty yards away from the vessel at the time. So she maneuvered to alongside us, and we were hauled up out of the lifeboat. One British book described this rescue as "hauling up these half-frozen logs." This is one of those half-frozen logs that survived.

The ship was called the *El Capitan*. She was a Panamanian flag vessel, which was under management of a U.S. steamship company. But because of circumstances at the time, the crew was from almost every seafaring nation. The skipper, as I remember, was a Scandinavian. They had all sorts of nationalities on board.

We were aboard her less than a day when the bombers came out and started attacking us. It appeared that the Luftwaffe was using us as a training target. They were at us for eight hours, before they finally dropped the stick just outside the engine room and opened up the seams of the ship.[4] The *El Capitan* started going down.[5] So, once again, the nineteen of us from the *Witherspoon* took to the lifeboats with fifty-odd people from the *El Capitan*.

We were picked up shortly by a small converted fishing trawler entitled the HMT *Lord Austin*, which had sighted the sinking of the *El Capitan*. These trawlers were used for escort duty, and they carried depth charges. The *Lord Austin* had a regular speed of 9.5 knots, and when they dropped the depth charges, she did 10.5 knots. We were rather crowded on board, and we remained on board the *Lord Austin* for two more days. They were out of food, and the only thing we had was the lifeboat rations from the *El Capitan*.

At that point, the reports indicated that most of the ships were sunk.[6] We were heading independently into the port of Archangel. On landing there, I was taken to a Russian hospital for two weeks, suffering from exposure and immersion, and dehydration. The Russians did everything they could, gave us everything they had, but really, they didn't have an awful lot. So, for the two weeks in the hospital and a subsequent five weeks plus, we were not eating in proper fashion, unless you want to refer to the cabbage soup, yak meat, and black bread. And oh, yes, they did give us a ration of vodka on a daily basis. When I joined the ship I was a pretty skinny young fellow, but I lost probably twenty pounds through this little experience.

I actually got no credit for this sea time. According to my continuous discharge book, I signed foreign articles on April 29, 1942, and I was discharged on July 6, 1942, the day the ship [*Witherspoon*] sunk. But I have some more comments to make about what I thought should have been credited sea time.

Before getting evacuated from northern Russia, there was no U.S. military presence in Archangel. The engine cadet and I were wandering around town one day, and we bumped into a British army sergeant. We were telling him about our concern that our families didn't know we were OK. He suggested we send a commercial cable, which we did. I wrote: "Safe and well. Please reply c/o Intourist Hotel, Archangel, Russia," and addressed it to my father. Now, this is an indication of the confidence that a young cadet from the Merchant Marine Cadet Corps had. Strange as it may seem, seven days later, I got a reply from my father. It said: "Anxious for details. Please write home." Well, there was no way of doing that, but at least I knew he was advised that I was still alive. Now, my father knew the ship that I was on. One day, he was listening to a German newscast that mentioned the names of the ships that were sunk in the latest Allied convoy, one of them being the *John Witherspoon*. He didn't dare tell my mother, but he agonized over this until he got that cable, and I would say my father aged more with worries than I did with the experience.

During a total of seven weeks that we were there in Russia, there were fourteen American crews "on the beach," survivors. A decision was made that they had space to take care of five American crews, plus all the hospital cases, i.e., the amputees, frostbite. We didn't know why the Brits weren't brought out, but they weren't. As it turns out, the *John Witherspoon*'s crew was number five, so they boarded us on a British destroyer, the HMS *Blankney*. She had just been on the Malta run, which was another disastrous run for some smaller convoys in the Mediterranean. The *Blankney* took us down to Kola Inlet, where we went aboard the USS *Tuscaloosa*, one of the escorting cruisers that abandoned the convoy on July 4. Needless to say, the Navy personnel on board were terribly embarrassed at having to abandon the merchant ships at the time.

Soon the *Tuscaloosa* sailed. The situation was bad. She was employed to run aerial torpedoes to the Russians because it was hopeless to try to load cargo on conventional cargo vessels, and there was a need for aerial torpedoes up in the Archangel area for the Russian air force. There was a small British air force detachment up there as well.

So we sailed out of Kola Inlet, which is on the approach to Murmansk. Then we went back to Seydisfjordur on the northeast coast of Iceland for fuel. From there we proceeded to Glasgow, where we debarked for two weeks, awaiting repatriation. Finally, the order came, and we were put aboard the *Queen Mary*, which at that time had not been fitted for troops. She was still, for the most part, rigged as a passenger vessel. So I had the luxury of living in one of the staterooms, although they had built upper bunks over regular berths on board. But the lounges were all intact. Strange thing about it, part of the *Queen Mary* gun crew was United States Coast Artillery personnel, in conjunction with the Royal Navy gun crew. So we had a desperate situation, as far as providing people to operate within the convoy structure. The *Queen Mary*, incidentally, did not sail in convoy. She sailed completely independent because of her speed. She could outrun any of the submarines on the surface and was therefore considered safe to operate independently.

We arrived in New York Harbor on September 19. Three weeks later, I was assigned to a new C-2 freighter that was scheduled to sail in the second convoy to Casablanca in October of 1942.

I had to make other short trips to complete the official credited time because all of that time that I was a "tourist" in North Russia was not considered as credited sea time.

See the chapter 4, "Convoys," for Arthur Erb's subsequent service.

James L. Risk, Class of 1942

I got my third mate's license in December [1942] and was assigned to the SS *City of Omaha*, operated by the Lykes Line. The thing that she had, which most ships do not have, was double 'tween-decks.

But anyhow, World War II came along, and the *City of Omaha* had been pressed into service. We put guns on her; we had a 3-inch 50 on the bow together with a couple of 20-millimeters. Amidships we had two tubs of 20-millimeters on each wing of the bridge. Off on the boat deck and then in the stern, we had two more 20mm tubs plus a 4-inch 50. When I boarded the ship in New York Harbor as third mate, I should have been a little bit more observant because the bow of the ship had been heavily reinforced with extra plates welded in place. She was not a welded ship as the Liberty ships were later on. She was all riveted—World War I. But these heavy big plates at the bow should have given me an inkling of what was in store for me. She was about 12,200 deadweight tons. She was a bigger ship than the Liberties, a beautiful ship.

We sailed on January 19, in convoy, for Scotland. The ship had P-51 aircraft, fighter planes, on deck loaded as whole planes ready to fly, and we had parts of P-51s in the double 'tween decks. It was ideal for that. And in the lower hold we had guns, ammunition, wartime supplies, food, and clothes.

And where were you going?

Secret. Nobody knew. We couldn't find out. I went to the convoy meeting with the captain, and we still couldn't find out where we were going. Our instructions were to follow the convoy to Lochbuie, Scotland. We should have known.

We had fifty-six ships in the convoy. This is January [1943]. We proceeded in the wintertime, and, sure enough, we ran into the typical North Atlantic hurricane. The convoy was dispersed in blizzard conditions. Everybody got all screwed up. The English, by the way, ran the convoys in the North Atlantic. The Americans had responsibility for convoys in the South Atlantic. In the extreme weather conditions that existed, about three-quarters of the way across, the rudder on the SS *City of Omaha* broke. So we took some hatch covers and lashed them together, and we rigged them up on two lines, cargo wire runners, over the stern of the ship to the steam winch on the port side and the steam winch on the starboard side. Then we could drag that back and forth and get some semblance of steering to the ship. We were also dead in the water for a day and a half, and we blew some tubes. It was a thirty-year-old ship.

I've got to say right here, the engine crew that kept that old ship going for nine and a half months was remarkable because we blew tubes practically every day. Later on, during the summer, we broke the ship down and broke the engine room down and replaced tubes, which was unheard of in this particular part of the world.

We eventually dragged ourselves independently into Belfast, Ireland. From there, they sent over some British navy tugs and towed us across the Clyde up to Glasgow, where the ship was put in dry dock, and the rudder was installed and repaired, and away we went.

We lost our convoy, of course, way back. We headed north by ourselves to Lochbuie, and just as we got up there, the convoy was forming outside of Lochbuie and heading out. So we were told to take position, and off we went.

In identifying ourselves and getting into convoy position, we asked where we were going. They said, 'We cannot tell you; it's secret, but wear your 'long handles.'" Again, I should have gotten off the ship.

We proceeded north, and a day later we ran into a wolf pack. They started sinking some ships, and we scattered. The convoy broke up, and we all headed for Reykjavik, Iceland. We got into Reykjavik, and we laid there for a day and a half while we regrouped and got some stuff going. We had only eight American ships. All the rest were Allied, English, and all the rest of the Allies. We reformed, and as we were going out of Reykjavik Harbor, there was an English frigate escort ship. With the weather conditions, snow and so forth, it was misidentified by somebody, and all of a sudden somebody started opening fire, and all of the convoy ships started shooting at once. They actually destroyed that little English frigate. The Armed Guard commander on the SS *City of Omaha* was a very intelligent officer, nice guy, and none of our guns fired. I never knew what happened to the survivors; they were gone. Two minutes later, after we were out heading north, we knew that our destination was going to be Murmansk.

This was convoy JW-53. We later became known as the "Forgotten Convoy of North Russia." To jump ahead, we got back to the United States in December of 1943. We were gone for nine months, and that's the reason we were called the "Forgotten Convoy."

Two days after leaving Reykjavik, we got picked up again by a German spotter, Luftwaffe. From then on, in between the snowstorms and the blizzard conditions, we had twenty-four hours of bombing. Between the submarines and the high-flying bombers, when we got to Murmansk, out of fifty-six ships that we sailed with, we had only twenty-four left. All eight American ships got through. We had damage. Talk about lifeboats—our lifeboats were actually riddled with incendiaries. That was an unusual weapon. We had no experience, no idea what would happen, but they would come over with these big, big baskets of little incendiary bombs, magnesium. They'd drop them, and as soon as they'd hit, they would fire. They'd burn right through the deck of the ship or anywhere else. We had an awful lot of reconstruction work on our lifeboats because of that condition when we got to Russia.

When did the submarines attack, at dusk or at daylight?

Twenty-four hours a day—it didn't matter. It didn't matter a bit. Wolf packs are a unique group. Just sort of an aside, many years later I sold my house in Riverside, Connecticut, to a doctor that was on the wolf pack on that particular patrol at that particular time. So we compared notes. To them, he told me, it made no difference. They'd attack anytime, especially up there, because the weather was so bad. They had complete freedom. The sonar detection equipment in 1943 had not been developed to the state where it was sophisticated later on. At first, we had no defenses against underwater craft.

How successful was it to position lookouts on board vessels? Was that how sightings were made, or was it after an explosion?

After an explosion had occurred. So very quickly. We had a tanker, presumably an English tanker, right in front of us. He got a direct hit from one of the big bombs, one of the high-flying bombers, and in thirty seconds there was nothing there. We went right over where he had been, and in thirty seconds there was not a thing. Nothing visible.

Attached to the convoy we also had three seagoing tugs or trawlers, English, and they tailed along behind. When sinkings went down, they'd head over and try and pick up survivors. In that water, you had forty-five seconds life expectancy, the water was so cold. Forty-five seconds wasn't accurate because we've had people in the water for five minutes and got pulled out and survived, but pretty close. You didn't last long. Off of that one particular tanker, according to a crew member of the ship, only five people were pulled out of the water. The rest of the thirty-two personnel were gone.

We proceeded north. We had no gyros in those days, just old magnetic compasses, and a blizzard going on. All of a sudden the second mate called all his hands to the bridge one night, and we went rushing out. The magnetic compass was turning around, spinning in circles. That's all we had, of course, blizzard conditions, ships on all sides, and everything else. "Panicsville." The whole convoy was the same way.

There's an island up in the middle of the Bering Sea called Bear Island; it's on the charts. It's an iron mountain, solid iron. And its proximity to the magnetic compass caused it to misbehave, resulting in "panicsville" in the convoy because now we had nothing to steer by, nothing whatsoever. So we told the helmsman to put the wheel amidships, and stay. Don't budge it and hope. I was out in the starboard wing; another officer was in the port wing. We looked over, and there was a ship right alongside of us, within twenty feet, it looked like, or ten feet. Those things are so heavy, if you just touched them, you'd destroy it. So hard aport and ten degrees port emergency turn. Over we went, and then all of a sudden you thought that there was a ship over there too. Fifteen degrees back, and man, we finally got through!

Everybody complained. We were in close formation. There were several different degrees of keeping convoy formation, particularly on the Russian trip. Later on, down in the Mediterranean and some of the South Atlantic convoys I was on, there was much more space. On the Russian trip, the ship separation was about three hundred yards, in other words, about the size of a football field. Down in the Mediterranean when we went through the Straits of Gibraltar, the separation was close too. Out in the open ocean we were several miles apart, still within visual distance but not that close at all.

We finally got to Murmansk. Murmansk is way up the river. The area had been practically destroyed. The docks were blown up time and time again. A ship would be tied up at the docks, the Germans would come over and sink it, and there'd be another ship right over the top of it. That river was the deepest water I've ever seen in my life. We had an awful difficulty in anchoring because of the depth of water. It was a hard bottom, and there was no real traction. At anchor, all the ships would drift back and forth in the river.

At the same time, the Germans were occupying Finland. The Messerschmitts would bounce over the mountains and down the river and the harbor of Murmansk so quick that nobody could defend against them. They would sink ships right and left. This was all part of the loss of our convoy. On the *Omaha*, we discharged the P-51's deckload, and then we moved around to the White Sea to a harbor called Molotov. It was a city that had been built in the White Sea by the Russians to handle the Allied cargo that was coming in.

This was a February-March time frame, 1943, and the White Sea was frozen over four to six feet thick with ice. That's what those reinforced bows were all about. We were escorted through the White Sea by two big Russian icebreakers. Russian icebreakers have spoon bows. They ride up on top of the ice and crush it, versus American icebreakers, which are cutters.

They cut through the ice. American icebreakers never could have handled the White Sea in the wintertime.

As we were going through, it was the birth time of the seals. In daylight you could just see twenty-five miles across the sea in the glare of white-blue ice, and all the seals were giving birth. The red afterbirth and everything else was quite a sight. Did you know that baby seals cry just like a human baby? It's true. Believe me. We were stuck in the ice with these thousands and thousands of crying babies around us. It was quite an eerie situation.

The second day, we were constantly attacked by Stukas. We were stuck firmly in the ice and over comes a Stuka bomber and says, "Ah, a sitting duck!" So he peels off and comes down for his dive, and, of course, they're noted for their sound when they dive. It scared the living devil out of everybody. Just as he peeled, we hit him with a 3-inch 50 and blew him apart. He cascaded down in a fiery tumble down on the ice. Of course, being stuck in the ice, outside we went. We hustled over, but nothing. We couldn't find him; the plane was completely destroyed.

Eventually, five days later, we got to this town of Molotov. Molotov was a hand-built wooden city. The streets were wood, the docks were wood, the apartment houses that they had thrown up were all wood, and it was a unique experience. We had a little Intourist [facility] there where we were to go for recreation. They had an old wind-up Victrola with some American records on it, and it was staffed by young ladies from the University of Moscow. They just pushed us and pushed us and pushed us to speak English, to practice their English. I remember dancing cheek-to-cheek with a lovely young thing from the University of Moscow, and she was spouting Leninism and partyism the whole time. Three officers formed a group ourselves—we were quite selective—called the "Bewildered Order of Baffled Britches Busters of North Russia." Our favorite expression, which got to us, was a Russian expression which very loosely translated means "You sleep ship."

We were there in Molotov from early March of 1943 to November of 1943. We learned what to do. We went up to Archangel, which was eighteen miles away, and went to the opera, ballet, lived at the Intourist up there and back on the ships. They had American ships there. We organized baseball teams. They didn't know the game at all, and they used to come in droves and watch us play. And everybody said, "Where in the heck did you get baseballs up in Russia?" Well, we took hot shellman's mitts and made fielders' gloves and catchers' mitts. We took dunnage and some Russian lumber that we got hold of and took them down to the engine room, turned them out on lathes and made baseball bats. The balls were a challenge. We had a very talented engineer on the SS *City of Omaha*. We cut off the tops of Navy-issue sea boots, and we had little rubber balls in the engine room to stuff in the tubes so they could operate the steam turbines and stop up the tubes that were split. We took those little rubber balls and strung them round and round and then took the tops of these sea boots and cut them down and sewed them into baseballs. Good! Better than some I've seen stateside. We had five tournaments. I must admit that the Armed Guard was very spirited to our emergency. We passed time. We had put on plays with seamen dressed up in all kinds of costumes we made ourselves and so forth and so on. We went up to Archangel and went to the civic activities that they had in the city. We got to know quite a few people. Quite a bunch of nice people.

One little incident: I was walking by myself in the outskirts of Archangel. Archangel's a big city. A very attractive, American-looking young lady appeared, and I followed her a little way, and finally she got me off behind some bushes, and we started talking. She was an American. Russia had a program in the 1930s to attract the best way they could a lot of intellectuals from America, to come over and experience life as a communist. We all knew that there was a whole mess of communist people in the United States at that time. Her family was one of them. Her father was a professor at the local university. We had to be very careful because she indicated to me that if she was ever caught talking to me that she would be sent off to Siberia. An awful lot of the young ladies that we did have contact with in that convoy, and with the other convoys, were sent off to Siberia to the labor camps, and some of the men too. In any event, I learned an awful lot about that particular side of Americanism and communism.

The last three months up there, we had almost run out of food aboard ship. The Russians had none to give us, and we had also run out of barter material for their black market. The Russians themselves, of course, lived and worked by government chit. You worked, and you got a chit. That chit was good for clothing, food, and housing. If you didn't work, you didn't get chits. If you didn't get chits, you didn't exist. We saw corpses on the street every day as we went around our duties. Of course, in the summertime they grew vegetables, fertilized by human materials, and there was a big flourishing black market. So we did do a lot of black marketing. A friend of mine formed a "potato company," and he would barter, get potatoes, and bring them back aboard the ships. For the last three months that we were there, we had Spam, dehydrated carrots, dehydrated potatoes, and water. That was all except for what we could scrounge. Our health deteriorated rather dramatically by the time we sailed. But we finally did sail.

Just before sailing, we had been issued a little Russian passport. The name "Risk" in Russian on the passport was spelled "Peru," which is unpronounceable. But I had this little Russian passport, and I decided that as I was going home, I'd just report this as being lost and I'd keep it and take it home with me as a souvenir. The day of sailing, early in the morning, I had to go next door. We were forming a group called the "Forgotten Convoy of North Russia." We needed to do some final work on it, and I was going from my ship to the ship behind me to a friend with some last documents to put together for this society that we formed. As I wended down the gangway, I flashed my Russian passport to the Russian guard at the bottom, which of course I had to do, and I took off down the dock. I was immediately apprehended and taken up to the local NKVD office and interrogated for over two and a half hours. Very strong interrogation. They didn't touch me, but it was mental beating. They would not accept the term "souvenir" in their language. They just couldn't get that at all. So, needless to say, I did not get my Russian passport as a souvenir.

People would always ask, "Why was the convoy kept there [in Russia] nine months?" As I said earlier, the North Atlantic was operated by the English. They had their capital ships, the *Hood*, and their supporting forces up in the north Atlantic. They kept the *Prinz Eugen* and the *Scharnhorst* and the other big boys holed up in the Norwegian fjords. So, as long as that was under control, the convoys could at least get by without danger. Churchill decided when we were first in Russia that the North African campaign was to begin. He drew out of the North Atlantic all of the defenses that they had, all the capital ships, and put them down in the Mediterranean. So that left the big boys of Germany in the Norwegian harbors free to do as they wanted to. So they had to cancel all convoy activity in North Russia for that period in Europe. We just happened to be at the other end. We finally sailed back to the United States in good shape after visiting in England. We survived.

Almost a year later, I made a second trip up to Murmansk. This time I had eighty-ton locomotives on deck. We went right into Murmansk. The equipment that they had couldn't handle these narrow gauge eighty-ton locomotives, so they moved us around to the White Sea, then up the northern Dvina River, past Archangel on the river, where they had heavy equipment. Again wintertime, again icebreakers, and all the rest of it. We had had one heck of a North Atlantic winter crossing again. I was chief mate. I had nursed these eighty-ton locomotives. By putting extra eye bolts on the deck, welding them in place, chains, and all kinds of things, the crew and I had lived with those locomotives because the ship was rolling. This was a Liberty ship, the SS *Cardinal Gibbons*. Twenty-five, thirty degrees and eighty tons were moving around. We got there without any structural damage. We had a split between the number-three hatch and number-four hatch, with a split across the deck, but it was not in critical condition. Anyhow, we got there and got into port, and I wasn't about to let the Russians handle my eighty-ton locomotives. They were mine at this point! They weren't anybody else's. I rigged up double jumbo booms and with fifty-ton jumbos we got those locomotives off the deck and down on the dock. I had been living with those things for all of these weeks. I had not shaved, and I had no officers' insignia, no designation of rank or anything else.

Word came out to us that my ship crew and I should come in to pass immigration. We had American passports, of course, also. So we came in, and my crew, in heavy woolen winter gear, and I put our American passports down in front of the NKVD officer. He took one look at mine, and he leaned back, and he looked up at me, and he said: "Mr. Risk, welcome back to North Russia. We hope that this time our laws and your inclinations will not conflict and that you and Russia will have a better, happy understanding."

They assigned interpreters to all the ships. We had two interpreters. One was assigned to me, and one was assigned to the ship. Mine was an attractive young female, and she later admitted that her sole job was to get the secrets of the United States from me, as if I had any. As acting chief mate aboard that ship, what secrets did I have? None.

Anyhow, I had an incident coming up the White Sea on the SS *Cardinal Gibbons*. The Navy had warned us before we left the United States that the Russians were in a position of piloting up in the river and deliberately putting Allied ships on the sandbars. Of course, the Allies had no salvage equipment or anything else there, so after a time the ships would be abandoned and miraculously the Russians would produce some big seagoing tugs and pull the ships off the sandbar and acquire a ship. The pilot that was assigned to us going up the river—I didn't like him, number one (taking him aboard the ship), and number two, he was not following the speed, course, or the direction or anything else. So I threw him off the ship, literally. I threw him over the side, and they had a boat there to pick him up. He wasn't lost, but, nevertheless, over the side he went. When the news of the incident with the pilot got up the river to port, the girl interpreter was replaced by an armed Navy officer. I deliberately didn't go ashore on the second trip at all because anybody I'd have talked to or contacted would have been under suspicion. This was March of '44, and we came back in September of '44.

In 1992, the Russian government honored Jim Risk with a commemorative medal for his wartime voyages on the Murmansk run.

Henry H. Evans, Class of 1944

Henry Evans began his maritime training at the Florida Maritime School in St. Petersburg, Florida. He studied basic seamanship and sailed on the sailing ship *Joseph Conrad*, which is now at Mystic Seaport. He later went to the training center at Pass Christian, Mississippi, and eventually to Kings Point. Mr. Evans is currently president of his own business, Evans Fleet Services.

We had twenty-nine escorts in total. We had locomotives on deck. At one point, the locomotives shifted, due to rough seas, and the deck crew had to get out and reanchor it. All our cargo was to help the Russians come in from the backside of the German line.

We went by Murmansk and went on across the Arctic, over into the White Sea to Archangel with this load. We broke ice through the White Sea. It was about four feet thick. We would break it, and it rolled over, and then it would be eight foot thick. Then we'd break it again, and then it bowled over and got to be twelve foot thick. Three layers about twelve feet. We couldn't move any further, and so we had to sit in the bay about a mile from the dock until the ice started rolling over. The icebreaker was behind us. It was Russian, naturally. They didn't get in front of us. (*Laughter*)

Richard M. Larrabee, Class of 1944

One of the first students to arrive at Kings Point in 1942, Richard Larrabee sailed throughout the war and witnessed the D-Day operation of 1944. After the war, he established his own business.

The first ship I was on was a Liberty. This was 1944 now. We were in Murmansk Harbor alongside the dock with two ships at the dock on Easter Sunday, and the Germans bombed the daylights out of us in the harbor. The Germans had quick access by air from Finland. The water temperature was around 36 to 38 degrees. There were probably no survivors. For escorts we had British destroyers. That convoy, I was told, was supposed to draw out the German battleship *Scharnhorst* from the yards, but that never occurred. We had a pretty heavy escort. They [the Germans] were looking for tonnage, and we just happened to be there. I don't think they really were too concerned very much about five thousand tons of chrome ore, which we discharged in Portland, Maine.

For Richard Larrabee's participation in the D-Day landing, see chapter 8.

Captain George E. Kraemer, Class of 1944

I was assigned to the *Joshua Thomas*, which was a Liberty ship. We shipped out of New York and made the trip across the North Atlantic to the British Isles. We went into the Firth of Clyde, and we anchored. We laid there for quite a while, a couple of weeks. Meantime, we were waiting for some other ships that were due in to form up the northern convoy. Cargo was all loaded here in the United States. It was a full wartime cargo.

The merchant marine, in their supplying Russia with wartime material, also rebuilt the Russian rail system. They had lost so much of their track, so much of their equipment, that they had nothing, literally nothing, to transport their war supplies by rail. So every American Liberty ship and every American freighter that went into those convoys had some rail equipment aboard. We had several locomotives and tenders, and we had two big diesel-powered cars. They were rail cars that were diesel engine operating generators, and they could light up a good-sized city with one of those cars.

The rail cars were on deck. I think we had some railroad ties, and we had some railroad track. Of course the European gauge is different than the American gauge on rail equipment, but that wouldn't affect that because they were broken down into small segments. But we also carried much wartime equipment—arms, munitions; all those ships were all topped off with some kind of munitions.

We proceeded north. That was late winter 1944, early spring of 1945. Weather conditions were quite favorable for the first few days of the voyage. Then it got a little bit tough; it blew a little bit. As a matter of fact, when we got into heavy weather, we had taken over a number of these small patrol vessels on deck on some of the ships. They put them in the water in Scotland, got them running, and they put Russian crews aboard them. They were going to the Russian navy. Those Russian patrol boats used to come alongside and lay in the lee of the Liberty ships in heavy weather. We used to throw fruit and candy bars, and see if we could get them on deck for them.

We had a few real bad days of weather but nothing really tough. It was favorable weather for the submarines, but fortunately they didn't get at us. The sea temperature was probably in the forties, maybe the low forties. And the farther north we got, I think it dropped even below that. The air temperature ranged from, probably the low point would have been 20 degrees and the high point probably in the forties or fifties, after we left Scotland. Of course you were still in the influence of the Gulf Stream up in that area. That sweeps in as far as the coast of Norway.

I can remember one particular thing. We were under submarine alert. The black sock on the escorts was flying continuously. It's a black pennant that they ran up. In this case, we had some British frigates. Let me just tell you that the escort was excellent. The British by this time had had tremendous experience in escorting vessels up around that area. We had a CVE [escort carrier] with us, and they used to fly off morning and evening patrols. They had some Wildcats aboard, and they had these old Swordfish. They were biplanes that they used for torpedo bombers. As a matter of fact, I think one of those was instrumental in slowing down the *Bismarck*. They hit her with a torpedo and knocked her steering out of commission.

Anyway, they would fly these patrols off. But in between, the Germans would send out Focke-Wulf Couriers. They were long range. They weren't too fast, but they were very, very good. They had long sky-keeping capabilities. They could fly for long periods of time. They would send them out to observe the convoy. They would be spotted on the horizon, and they would shoot off a group of planes from the escort carrier. As soon as they'd shoot off those planes, the Germans would disappear. So I think that had a lot to do with the fact that the submarines didn't really catch up with us en masse. The escorts were dropping depth charges especially for the last two days out. For smoke screens, they would run up ahead of the convoy and drop "smoke pots" all along the outside edge of the convoy.

We had about sixty ships in the convoy and maybe a dozen escort vessels. As a matter of fact, it split. Some of the ships went into Archangel in the White Sea, and some of them went into Murmansk.

There were some things I can remember very distinctly. As we approached the coastline, I remember noticing hundreds of dead fish (victims of depth charging) floating dead or stunned on the surface. In entering Kola Inlet, which is the entrance to the river that takes you up to Murmansk, we would have to "single down." Of course, that's a very critical situation because if there were any submarines in the area, they could get very close to you. The convoy might have been eight columns wide. When we got into that area, they would split down into two columns. And two columns would proceed ahead, then the next two columns would drop in behind them, and then the next two columns would drop in behind. Then when you got very close to the inlet, you would single down into one column and make a run for the inlet. That's how they would break it down into a single file going into the river.

When we were in the process of doing that, I think we were in double file; we weren't getting the response from the engine room that we wanted for whatever reason. We kept ringing down for more revolutions, more revolutions, and they wouldn't give it to us. And the escorts came over and called on the loud-hailer, "Ship number so-and-so, speed up, speed up. You're causing stragglers." They were getting a little indignant about this. All of a sudden, one escort vessel came right across the stern of the ship, and he dropped a depth charge close to our stern. And boy, I'll tell you, that shook everybody up! So then we sped up. I never found out what was the reason for the delay in getting extra revolutions.

I can remember sleeping with my clothes on, continuously, day after day. I forget how long it took us to get up there, probably four or five days. We all had a "scram bag" packed. It's a small handbag with extra equipment in it. On our life jackets, we had a knife, a whistle, and a safety light that was battery operated. We also had overboard suits, survival suits. In those days, you had to have your life jacket on under the suit. If you didn't, you'd sink like a stone. But you try to get into one of those, and you might have a problem. So we all had a bag packed with extra gear in it, foul-weather gear, extra clothing, gloves maybe, or a scarf or a woolen cap, whatever. Just in case you lost any of your gear, you would have something to hold on to. We had some candy bars, and if you smoked you'd have cigarettes and matches—just extra stuff that you might not have available in the lifeboat.

We were in Murmansk for a couple of weeks. It was not a very, very fast operation, and Murmansk was a very, very strange place. There wasn't much you could do; there wasn't anything available to you really. The foreign seamen were only allowed in certain places. There was an international hotel, as they called it, which wasn't much. And there was another place like a seaman's club. They were about the only two places you were allowed in with any degree of freedom. Of course, it was under very high security.

They had Romanian prisoners of war working the ships as longshoremen. They were all under strict military discipline. The Russians controlled the Romanian officers and noncoms. They had a sergeant that was in charge of each hatch gang, and then I guess it went up the ranks: a lieutenant in charge of maybe four or five gangs. But I remember they had a problem with pilferage. We had Pet Milk, canned evaporated milk, and they were stealing it. They blew the whistle, and all these Romanians came out of the hatches, were marched out on the dock, lined up in military order with a sergeant and a corporal in front of each platoon. A Russian officer came down the dock with two armed guards and with a can of Pet Milk in his hand. He went over to one sergeant and was berating him and calling some soldier out of the ranks. The sergeant was giving the Russian officer an argument for some reason, and the Russian officer hit this fellow right full in the face with the can of milk. Then they marched the two of them [the sergeant and soldier] off. That was the last we ever saw of them. They put somebody in charge of that gang and sent them back on the ship. But it was a very rugged thing to see. You knew you were involved in a very, very tough situation.

Karl J. Aarseth, Class of 1943

I went back [to sea] in February [1945] on a ship called the *William Tyler Page*. I must have made about three trips to Russia in it. I remember she was loaded up different than any other ship I'd ever seen. Boy, they had everything on there. We carried at least ten locomotives, and they would separate the boilers and the chassis and the tenders. She had the two seventy-five-ton units of a railroad train. When you put the six or seven of them together, I think it would generate electricity for a bombed-out city of two hundred thousand population.

Then off we went. We sailed north and anchored in Loch Long, Scotland. The convoy left once a month. We went ashore occasionally. So deep was the loch, we lost an anchor. One must anchor very close to shore. Finally we got together in the shape of a convoy of about fourteen ships. We must have had twenty escort vessels, including an anti-aircraft cruiser, with all the guns pointed up to the clouds.

Things were rather quiet. We ran into snow. They must have had fifty of these Russian torpedo boats around. They were throwing over grenades twenty-four hours a day. Finally we got around the North Cape. Half the convoy went to Murmansk. We proceeded further east into the White Sea. Now there were two ports in the White Sea. One was Archangel in the Dvina River. Strange enough, my father was there in 1917 with the Norwegian merchant marine.

When we got there, we couldn't proceed because of sixteen feet of white, hard ice. It was springtime, and the noise was like thunder. Finally, all seven of our ships were stranded there in the ice. So what did you do? You waited there until the freshwater in the river breaks it up. In a couple of days, the river broke, and in no time at all, the river was clear, and we got up to the dock.

When we finally got alongside the shore with our floating train, we were two miles from the city. They didn't have a road in the permafrost, but they did put railroads down. They put two pieces of lumber together with wires. It was like a roller coaster.

In April, we went up to the Intourist hotel. They had a little party for us where everybody was served drinks and listened to speeches by the commissar with toasts for everybody. So we had a good meal. The Russian people treated us well. Sometimes you would get a lift and ride in a jeep. They never drove the way we did. They had one speed, and they kept stepping on and off the clutch.

One time I saw a group of people walking. Their heads were bent down, and their hands were behind their backs. I saw a little kid who could hardly keep a submachine gun out of the snow and some wretched woman in rags wearing burlap bags for shoes who begged for cigarettes every morning. Perfectly at ease, the commissar said, "They're orphans of people who were killed in the war." I'd been in my first gulag, and I didn't know it. We had aboard a Greek who could speak some Russian. He said they came from a place called Bessarabia. It was a pitiful sight. They were longshoremen and wood choppers.

I remember the music. I think it was the only cheerful note I had in Russia. We had a half-baked orchestra. There was a guy who was a fiddler. Another put a broom handle on a gallon oil can with a string and could get music from it. We had a young guy who was a single parent. His wife divorced him, and he was trying to do his thing. He used to work in a carnival. He could play the fiddle upside down. To Russians, of course, this is wonderful entertainment.

One day, a Marine, sort of an attaché, came down with the Moscow newspapers, and we found out the war was over. I saved that paper. We sailed for home. We came back to Scotland for bunker [fuel]. No more convoys.

THE MEDITERRANEAN

The Allied invasions of North Africa drew heavily upon the ships and men of the American merchant marine. The campaign started out as a way to open a war front in the West, until a major cross-channel invasion of France was attempted. The Mediterranean theater acquired a life of its own as American and British forces defeated General Erwin Rommel in North Africa and then fought their way up the Italian peninsula. Allocations of men and material for the Mediterranean area of operations were limited, and those Kings Pointers who delivered troops and supplies often found themselves in the thick of the conflict as the Luftwaffe sought to demolish their cargo-laden ships.[1]

Perry Jacobs, Class of 1944

We went into Sullivan Shipyard in the Red Hook section of Brooklyn and stayed there about three days. The holds were used for military cargo on this voyage. Of course, we didn't know that we were headed for the invasion of Sicily. This was May of 1943. We were loaded with engineer torpedoes, and we had gasoline in drums on the deck. We had all types of ammunition, all the articles of war. We had mustard gas in number-four hold. The galley range on a Liberty was coal-burning. They took sacks of coal and placed them over number-four hatch, after it had been secured. That was our protection against aircraft bombs.

We went in convoy through the Straits of Gibraltar to Algiers, which was an assembling point for convoy. While we were waiting in Algiers to proceed onto Malta, our next stop, we put the lifeboat in the water and took a tour around the harbor. One ship we visited was the SS *Gulf Prince*, which was a tanker that had been hit by a torpedo. The hole in the side of the vessel was literally the size of a room. It was hard for me to imagine that a ship could be punctured with that large a hole and yet stay afloat. She was just sitting there. When the torpedo hit, there was a gun tub directly above. I understood that the gunners that were in the tub were killed.

The Royal Navy had a group sent on board. They installed a barrage balloon that we towed from the mizzenmast of the Liberty ship. When we were proceeding to Malta, I was on watch down below when I heard the guns firing. We had eight 20mm Oerlikons on board. We had a 3-inch 50 forward and a 5-inch 38 aft. A wiper was coming down below. I said, "Are we being attacked?" He said, "No, we're not being attacked." I said, "How do you know?" He said, "Well, they haven't given that guy a chance to jump that's up in the balloon." So you have an idea of the mentality of some of the crewmembers. He was convinced that there was a man in that balloon. It was strictly a barrage balloon. It was flying when you were in a hazardous area.

We proceeded to Malta and anchored in Valletta Harbor. The ships didn't stay in port at night because Valletta had air raids literally every night. At night we went out, cruised around, then came back into port and anchored in the morning. They were afraid that the ships would be attacked if we stayed in port. There was one daylight raid. It was a Sunderland flying boat [British patrol aircraft]. The plane was circling around, and there were some splashes near it. We didn't hear a group of aircraft, only one or two. It must have been a single-plane attack. They did sound General Quarters,[2] but the gun crew took no action at all. After we were relieved from General Quarters, we just went back to normal routine.

I recall the captain wanted to test the efficiency and utility of the survival suits. He asked the deck cadet if he would put on his life preserver and suit. Smitty got up on the side. He stood up on the bulwark and jumped in.[3] When he came up, everybody applauded. He said, "I guess those things work." Apparently, you had to be very careful to hold the life preserver down. Otherwise, it would come up and hit you in the chin. He demonstrated it two or three times.

We proceeded out. At that time, we heard we were going to the invasion of Sicily. We proceeded to the port of Palermo. The city of Palermo must have just been captured. They were still sweeping for mines when we entered the harbor. We docked at the breakwater, and you could see that there had been some enemy action there because the breakwater was littered with rifles and hand grenades and other items of war. Some of the crew got down on the breakwater. They brought the rifles back, the radio operator being one of them. In testing one of the rifles, he put a slug through the slop chest, almost into the captain's quarters. The captain decided to confiscate all of the weapons at that point. Unfortunately, I had an Italian carbine with a folding bayonet that got swept up. I'd planned to take it home as a souvenir. When we got back to the States, we weren't allowed to keep any of these weapons. They were turned in to Customs. They said we would get them after the war, but that, of course, never happened.

Apparently, they were "softening up" the port. Some ships were sunk alongside the piers, which negated the use of the piers for discharging cargo. I have to give these people a heck of a lot of credit. The Army engineers came in, and they built piers over the sunken ships. They were arranged so that there were five skidways or piers. When a Liberty ship came alongside, each roadway (basically that's what they were) would fall in line with the hatch of a ship. We came in and moored alongside this sunken vessel. The ship's cargo gear was used by the Army port battalion stevedores to load the truck. They would fill up the trucks with these engineer torpedoes, mustard gas, and the gasoline in drums and so forth, and they would take off. That's how they discharged the vessel.

I recall one air raid while we were there. I was ashore at the time. We had heard the ships firing. There was still fighting along the coast. The U.S. Seventh Army, led by Patton, was landing behind the German lines as they were going up toward Messina, which hadn't been taken yet. That action was about ten days or so that we were in port.

I had wanted to go up to the front. I talked to the drivers of the trucks that were bringing the munitions and the gas, "Redball Express," I think they called them. I asked them if I could take the trip up to the front, and they invited me to go along with them. We went along the road of the north coast of Sicily, going up toward Messina, where they were still fighting. Patton's army was coming up, and General Montgomery had the Eastern Shore. It never dawned on me—here I was entering into an actual area of combat. They were still fighting. They were landing GIs behind the German lines every night. We could see these MTBs [motor torpedo boats] that were taking the GIs aboard. You could hear the firing. We were getting close. The driver turned off and steered his truck so that it was facing the road. He went in reverse at about forty miles an hour, slammed on the brakes, and the drums of gas rolled into the forest. Then he said, "Now let's get the hell out of here." We took off down the road again, and we went back to Palermo.

It was a crazy idea that I had had, wanting to get up to a combat area. I didn't realize that he was going that close. But I guess he was as scared as I was. It was a really bumpy, shaky ride going back. He was very careful going, but he was in a hurry to get back!

When we left Palermo, we thought we were going home. They had only stored the ship for sixty days. We were running out of food. We were eating Army rations, five-in-one and K rations, until they could get us replenishment. We loaded equipment for the Eighth Army, which had come across from El Alamein. They were still going into Sicily. Their lorries were put below in the hold. We loaded troops with all their equipment. When I saw their lorries, it was hard to believe that equipment that looked so unreliable and obsolete could have made it across the desert. But there they were with these British Eighth Army soldiers. They came aboard, and they were put into some of the troop areas that we had. We went back to Palermo, and they replenished the ship with provisions for the trip back to the U.S. I enjoyed the five-in-one and the K rations. To me they were very good, and I couldn't understand why the GIs were complaining about the food. I guess when you're eating the same rations day in, day out, you have a cause for complaint.

We went to Newport News [Virginia] and signed off the vessel. I didn't get my war souvenirs back.

Richard H. Krause Jr., Class of 1944

I worked in the shipyard for about two years, and I met some cadets there. That was the first time that I ever heard of Kings Point. I became interested and applied. I had a congressional appointment and came to Kings Point on December 4, 1942. I stayed in the CCC barracks and took engineering courses. I was assigned to the *Edmond B. Alexander* in February 1943 as part of the Army Transport Service. It was the second-largest reciprocating engine job in the world, and it was a German ship. I believe it was built before 1914, and it had a steel alloy hull about an inch thick, and it had two quadruple-expansion twin steam engines and twin screws.

We were headed toward North Africa in convoy with troops for the North African campaign. We had about ten destroyers, and I remember the battleship *Texas* was in the convoy. Going over there, I had been reading the Bible, really for the first time. As I was reading, I heard this noise in the engine room, "Bang-Bang!" The cylinder head on one of the pistons blew off. We worked about two days straight and bypassed the engine of that cylinder. With the other engine, we were cut down to about seven-eighths [speed]. We left the convoy with a destroyer, because we had six thousand troops on board.

We landed near Mers-el-Kebir, not far off from Oran. We were supposed to be in the invasion of Sicily, in the seventh wave. But they took us out of there, and we went back to the States. The troops debarked in Oran, and we brought back some German prisoners from the Afrika Korps. There were no incidents with those prisoners. In fact, they were well educated. They spoke English real good with an English accent, you know. They had been told that New York had been bombed, and they were surprised when they could see the buildings and everything.

I stayed on the *Edmond B. Alexander*, and on the second trip, we made it over to Liverpool, England. Then we came back to the States and made another trip to Oran. We were a troop carrier, and we always had an escort. Sometimes the troops would come up on the deck. They took turns, eating and sleeping. I remember one time in Africa, one of the deck hands killed somebody over there. They had a trial for him and hung him before daylight. I mean, it was that quick.

After about seven months at sea, I returned to Kings Point. I was twenty years old. I graduated on July 21, 1944.

Robert Glenn Smith, Class of 1944

I joined my new ship, the SS *Cape Cod*, in Manhattan [1942]. She was being loaded with war material bound for Russia. Word had passed back to the Academy of the havoc and heroism to be faced on that passage. It wasn't a happy thought, but at least winter was over. We tried on our rubber survival suits and readied for the journey as the convoy finished assembling. About fifty ships set out, and my luck held. Halfway across the Atlantic, our orders were changed. The Suez Canal had just been cleared, and we were to bring our cargo around to Iran, where the Russians would be ready to bring it overland to their homeland.

When we entered the Mediterranean, our ship was selected to be commodore. We led the pack, and the sixth night, past Sicily, there was a great blast astern, and a Liberty ship had been torpedoed. It was the SS *John Bell*,

Above: From SS Cape Cod—
*Commodore Ship, Submarine
Attack off Sicily on Convoy
Diverted from Murmansk,
September 1943*, by Robert
Glenn Smith. By permission
of Robert Glenn Smith.

*Left: USMM Cadet-
Midshipman 1943*, by Robert
Glenn Smith. By permission
of Robert Glenn Smith.

Dog House—Quarters for Supercargo, by Robert Glenn Smith.
By permission of Robert Glenn Smith.

loaded with drums of gasoline. I learned later, from the cadet-midshipman on the *John Bell*, Larry Passell, that all but one man, who was trapped in the engine room, were rescued. Fortunately, if there were other torpedoes, they had gone astray.

The convoy broke up in the western end of the Mediterranean, with many of us proceeding through the canal, missing by inches the remains of torn hulls, smokestacks, and masts that had been recently cleared from the main channel. Just before leaving the canal, our drinking water began to have a very bad taste. As we approached Aden, it had become so bad we couldn't drink it, even as coffee so strong you could cut it. Upon pumping the tank at Aden, our inspection revealed a complete change of dirty clothing, from socks to sweatshirt, quietly riding at the bottom.

Above: Khorramshahr, Iran—Market Place '43, by Robert Glenn Smith. By permission of Robert Glenn Smith.

Left: Army Supercargo, by Robert Glenn Smith. By permission of Robert Glenn Smith.

Several days later we arrived at our destination, Khorramshahr, Iran. The two engine cadets joined us in hitching rides with the Russians to Basra and one of our Army bases on our free hours. Two weeks later, we departed on a very watchful but uneventful return to the States.

The experience at sea and the Academy changed my course in life from being like a ship without a rudder, to one of self confidence and an attitude of "can do," whatever the task, location, or opportunity.

Leslie Churchman, Class of 1944

I took my license exam immediately after my training. It was a third assistant engineer license. I never sailed as a third. I happened to get on a vessel that picked up a second engineer as we were leaving. He was a diesel engineer, and he didn't know a thing about steam. So I sailed as second, and he sailed as third, which was very agreeable to him, because he was a little bit "lost." And that worked out fine. I went to North Africa, to Casablanca, Oran, Algiers, and Marseilles in southern France. We were helping supply the war effort.

I was also in the invasion of Sicily. I remember the British warships, the *Rodney*, and the *King George V*, shooting over the top of us. Later, we came to find out that the Germans had been shooting at us, and we didn't even know it. Then I made a couple of trips to supply the troops in Sicily. The troops were just getting off the beaches as we came in.

We made a trip up to Palermo after our troops had taken it. We were taking supplies. We were involved in a very, very heavy German aircraft raid there in Palermo. I remember them hitting a freight car, a train that was carrying ammunition, and just watching the explosion, car by car—just like dominoes falling.

Karl J. Aarseth, Class of 1943

I got a job on another ship called the *James Lykes*. She was loading ammo in New York, and we ended up in Philadelphia in Hog Island. The number-one hold was sheathed lumber and copper nails. When they came to load the ammunition, the longshoreman didn't smoke. They could only smoke at the end of the dock. We loaded 1,500 tons of smokeless powder in Philly.

Later we shaped up a big convoy of over one hundred ships in Hampton Roads.

When we entered the Mediterranean, we had to come down to about four columns. We knew the Spaniards were a neutral country. They had two volunteer divisions fighting on the Russian Front called the Blue Division. I'm sure that that night the Germans knew everything about us, but nothing happened. I remember we had barrage balloons put aboard all the ships on 150 feet of wire to keep off Stukas, and we had to drop them at Port Said. They would send this thing up about 5:00 p.m. An airplane couldn't come through, or it would tear the wing off. It worked well. We stayed close to the coast, and we were never attacked. The British had protection at that time. They had the RAF in Malta.

We captured fields in North Africa and Bone, so the Germans sort of transferred operations from Africa to Russia. While we were going down the Suez Canal, I found out that at one time, the Germans had used what they call teller mines, which they dropped from airplanes. The first bomb had to be crossed ten times, the second nine times, right on down the list. Then, when the first mine was detonated, nine others would go off at once. This would bring down every ship that followed. The canal company had large steel workboats. For some reason, they sent the workboat out early in the morning to check the canal. The workboat blew up on the tenth mine. But at least they found out that the canal had been mined. They soon cleared the other nine mines and saved the day.

Then I got my second voyage. I joined a ship called the *James Turner*. She was a Liberty ship that carried troops. We went to Newport News and loaded her full of military supplies for Naples. When I looked down on the dock, I saw all these Japanese American troops. There was half a combat team there and half on the other ship. That way, if anything happened to us, half the combat team would be saved. Then about three or four hundred of the Japanese Americans came on the ship. It took us twenty-five days to get to Naples. It was strange on board.

In Naples, the Germans sunk the ships right alongside the pier. The Army engineers cut the mast down and built a dock right into the ship, so it didn't take too long to discharge. That night, air raids went off as the Germans were coming over. The radio was on. You could listen to this Berlin woman from Livorno. She was saying: "Welcome to the four hundred and forty-second combat team. Enjoy your stay in Italy. You look rather heavy in that old British ship that's loaded with scotch whiskey. But you're not going to get any. That's going up to the officers' club." This was the way she talked. Then they played the best American music, and you couldn't help listening to it.

They [American forces] just invaded Anzio beachhead, and they captured a lot of prisoners. They first landed in May, but they [Axis forces] gave up quickly. In Monte Casino, it was defended by Hermann Goering's First Parachute Regiment.[4] These poor Japanese Americans, Nisei,[5] attacked, and the Germans killed most of them and drove them down the mountain. They stayed there two months. Churchill said they were going to invade the soft underbelly of Europe. He said the Germans were second-rate troops on rest and cure from fighting on the Russian Front. And you find out it was not so easy. It was terrible.

When we left there, we had three hundred German prisoners of war and thirty Italians. Two guys from the Hermann Goering parachute regiment went around and told the Wehrmacht POWs: "There's too many of you here. Why did you give up so easily?" They said, "We were wounded and left for dead." They [parachute regiment] had guys every morning to clean their boots, and they would march about the deck. The other POWs stayed away from them, but they seemed to be reasonable enough. Then I found out that they were up on deck reading the signals. That's why the commodore had said, "Whatever you do, don't keep anybody on deck."

We came back to Newport News, where we put them all ashore.

George H. Bark, Class of 1944

We were going to Naples [1944]. This was during the Italian campaign. But the Germans were already pretty well defeated, and they were now just sending observation planes over the harbor. The place was full of sunken ships all over the place, including an old German troop ship, a famous passenger liner, the *Resolute*. It had been converted to a hospital ship, and yet it had been bombed. You could still see the red cross showing on her. She was lying on her side there in the port. Even the hospital ship had been bombed by the German aircraft. Hardly anybody was safe at that time, I guess.

Eliot H. Lumbard, Class of 1945

The *David G. Farragut*, which was a Liberty ship, made only a trip or two before I got on it. And we carried ammunition. I think we left the New York area. In any event, we carried ammunition first to Sicily, in convoy. We went to anchor at Syracuse, on the east coast of Sicily. It was a big bay where they sort of regrouped the ships that arrived with different cargoes and going different directions. It was a staging area.

We were sent up the east coast of Italy, around the heel, to Brindisi, and discharged there. That was an amazing experience for me, in all kinds of ways. The port was guarded by British Gurkhas, and to this day I admire them and I fear them and I don't understand them, the way they would let you in or out or not from the port area. It was just a mystery to me.

It was very dangerous. They were quick on the trigger. The port of Brindisi, like all of the east coast, had been taken over by Montgomery's forces. The British went up the east side of Italy, and the Americans went up the west side, basically.

There were lots of experiences there. I got to meet some guys from the nearby American airbase, at Lecce, or some such. This was before Foggia was developed as a big airbase further north. Anyway, they said, "Come on out." I went out, and the next thing I knew, they were sort of saying they just wanted to check some stuff on a B-24. They took me on a mission. They thought this was funny as hell. I wound up going over, straight across the Adriatic, together with some other planes, over Yugoslavia. To this day, I don't know what the hell happened. I was so stunned. At first, I couldn't believe anyone would do that to me, and they were all hilariously rolling along. They've got this kid, sailor, sitting there.

I got back all right. They told me, later, that was a mission that would count. You had to have twenty-five. It was an official deal. There was no manifest. I could have vanished. Our cargo was essentially five-hundred-pound bombs, and they were actually headed to the Lecce airbase.

There was an unpleasant thing that occurred while we were there. The British were upset about the Americans generally, about Patton and the incidents that occurred in Sicily, or the rich Americans who had this or that, and we [the British] didn't have anything. There was hostility. I never did understand. I don't really know the whole story, but I do know that the British army visited our ship just before we were going to sail and requisitioned most of our food; they just took it. Certainly, we didn't give it to them, that's clear. And we sailed from Brindisi back to Syracuse with practically no food. When we got to Syracuse, they sort of said we should never have sailed. We went to Syracuse, and all we got were cauliflower and oranges. We came back eating endless amounts of oranges until your mouth was sore, and throwing them in the ocean when you're finished.

But it was just among the "wacky" things in the war, things like that. *Mr. Roberts* was actually true. People think it's a joke, but most of what's in there is true.

8

D-DAY

*D-Day looms large in the history of World War II because it
marked the beginning of the end of Hitler's domination of Europe.
Participating in the Normandy operation were all manner of supply ships, including ones with Kings Pointers aboard. Stationed off
the French beaches, Liberty ships helped guarantee that the door
created by the first Allied assaults was kept open. After the con-
solidation of the beachhead, merchant ships brought the troops
and supplies that had been collected in Britain for several months
before the decisive day.*

Robert B. Wells, Class of 1941

I signed on a big tanker. The company operating this ship, the MS *Sabine
Sun*, was the War Emergency Tankers Corporation, which was a merging
of various oil company ships. Then I sailed on convoys to, I guess you'd call,
the United Kingdom today. We went to England, Scotland, Wales, Iceland,
and so forth with aviation gas, fuel for ships. We also had a deck cargo of
fighter planes on these tankers. They made a regular rig for them, and we
carried maybe a dozen. They were single pilot fighter planes, I believe P-40
aircraft.

**Was there any discussion as to the ultimate purpose of all the supplies?
Was it known or surmised or thought that there would be an invasion
of Europe?**

Yes, it was pretty obvious. When we went into various ports in England,
Scotland, and Wales, American troops were all over the place. There was
a big build-up there. In fact, I was there when they had the invasion of Eu-

rope, the Normandy invasion, June 1944. I was in Bristol, England. It was very hush-hush. I remember, I was a first assistant engineer at the time, and we were just one ship of many hundreds. When we came into Bristol, we came ashore and usually the place was crawling with sailors and soldiers. However, when we came ashore in June 1944, there was nobody. We were the only Americans in Bristol. We went into a pub and started chatting, and we were looking around, and there's not a soldier in sight. Nobody, no ships in the harbor except a few merchant ships. While we're sitting there chatting, we saw some Englishmen coming in and sitting around and listening. So we assumed they were some sort of English Secret Service. Whatever they were, they wanted to know who the devil we were. Some of the officers were in uniform, but most of the crew were in civilian clothes. But I think it was pretty obvious as soon as we opened our mouths, we were Americans. So that was the beginning of the invasion at that time. I didn't know where our troops were. I was in Bristol, which is on the west coast of England. I believe our ships went around the south coast and were on the east coast ready to go to Europe. In fact, they were going when we were there—all convoys. And the aircraft that we carried were taken off the ship, were serviced, and away they went.

When did you first hear of the invasion of Normandy?

When we got back to the States. We suspected it, but nothing was said. Everything was very hush-hush. But when you see thousands of troops there on the trip before, and then suddenly there isn't a soldier in sight, there's something up. We didn't hear about it due to the news blackout coming back, and the radio operator didn't tell us anything. So I guess the skipper figured it out. Well, anyway, we found out when we got back to New York.

Captain Walter J. Botto, Class of 1944

Displaying a youthful zest for life, Walter Botto declares, "Nearly 98 percent of everything I've ever wanted to accomplish in life has been done." His maritime career after the war included creative design projects for cargo handling, especially in the area around the Port of Cleveland, Ohio. He has been an enthusiastic participant in alumni affairs.

I graduated on February 18, 1944. Then I sat for license exams, USNR commissioning, etc. I managed to earn twenty-five more mast demerits just a day before check out! My fiancée, Judith Rebello, and I were married March 4, right after graduation and working off the demerits! Then I signed on with the War Shipping Administration to ship out.

My first vessel was the Liberty ship SS *Benjamin Hawkins.* As a newlywed, lacking a decent honeymoon, I requested a short UK run, so I could get home in six weeks. I got home about six months later.

We were sent to the UK. We went to Liverpool in convoy, discharged our cargo, and then we were sent up the Irish Sea to Oban on the Firth of Lorne in Scotland, to join a fleet of Liberties already there. They put us at anchor, in quarantine. Unknown to us, they were getting us ready for the D-Day invasion of Normandy.

We just "rode the hook" for three or four weeks, awaiting orders. We were incommunicado: we could get mail, but couldn't send mail out. Then we were ordered to Cardiff, Wales, to be fitted out for carrying troops and their assigned equipment in the holds and on deck, as well as two Piper Cub surveillance/reconnaissance aircraft and their pilots. When on watch, the crew let some of them use our rooms for comfort, trying to help make it as comfortable as we could for the fellows that we were getting to know. When ashore, those two pilots took off, and the "feedback" was they didn't get up in the air for long when they were shot down. But I don't know. I can't confirm that. We laid over for two days in Cardiff, until the weather proved conducive to crossing the English Channel. Eventually, we were sent to Omaha Beach for D-Day. We crossed as an armada of vessels and planes overhead.

At Normandy, the troops were having a very difficult time landing on shore due to enemy action. To make it easier for the unloading of the troops and their equipment on the landing barges, we had to come in very close. When the tide went out, our ship sat high and dry. And at night we were all getting attacked. As third mate, my assignment was to be on deck for possible fire damage control. In Wales, they had put two portable gas engine commercial water pumps on board. The idea was you hung a hose over the side to pump seawater to fight the fire. Well, we were so high above the water, the pumps couldn't lift seawater, so they were ineffective. Also, anchored to our decks by fine aircraft wires, we had two barrage balloons floating aloft for aircraft protection from enemy strafing.

How long did you stay off the Normandy coast before you got under way for your next assignment?

We were there for a couple of days. The problem was getting the equipment ashore. The enemy action was so severe, and with the inclement weather they were having, they were really fighting both the enemy and nature.

But the hard part was the high casualty toll of our troops in making the landing, we were told. There was one story that there were some persons (best left unidentified) spotting for the Germans from one of the church towers, by helping direct their artillery fire. To what extent that was valid, I didn't know, but that was the report from the landing craft crews taking our discharged cargo and troops over the side.

Once our troops got their foothold on the beach, it became somewhat easier. But the first wave on June 6–8 was very rough for those in the landing. There was nothing we could do because we could only unload with the ship's cargo booms as equipment came up, onto the "Rhino" barges, as they arrived alongside around the clock.

Did you subsequently come back to Normandy again?

Yes. We were in a repeat shuttle service. Northbound, we loaded German prisoners of war on board, because we had troop accommodations. Then we sailed back to Plymouth, England. We unloaded the POWs, reloaded with fresh troops, and brought them southbound to either Utah or Omaha beachheads, all aboard the *Benjamin Hawkins* and other merchant vessels assigned for same duty.

We were escorted by four vessels, U.S. destroyer escorts (DEs) and Canadian corvettes. D-Day, however, consisted of a "sea of ships" armada and a sky blanketed with planes—as far as one could see!

How many months did this shuttle service run?

We were in service until the weeks of early August. We made three or four shuttles, then we were suddenly released and sent home to New York in midsummer.

Richard M. Larrabee, Class of 1944

In late May, we went immediately to England. We discharged and reloaded material for the Normandy landing. We made Omaha Beach. The ship was the *Edmund Fanning*, a Liberty ship. We were at Omaha Beach about six hours after the initial landing on June 6, 1944. There was just a beehive of activity. We were carrying tanks, ammunition predominately, and food (C rations), that type of thing. It was just a melee of activity. As soon as you got in, you had an assignment. You had landing craft and were off-loading as soon as you could. We did not have much time at that point to do much observation. We had an Army captain on the ship who was in charge of that equipment, mainly the tanks. He had said to me: "If you get back here, look me up. I will probably still be here for a month or two, on the beach." We went back, reloaded fast, came back again, and did go ashore, had the opportunity to walk around the beach area and see what the [German] bunkers looked like. We were more concerned really with what the job was at hand. We knew it was bad. A lot of bad weather. But we were also very busy at the time. We had one more trip to Omaha Beach after the landings, so we had a total of two trips. Then we went back to England and back to the States.

Captain Richard A. Cahill, Class of 1943

A respected shipmaster for many years, Captain Richard Cahill decided to draw upon his seafaring experiences in order to help his fellow ships officers avoid common hazards of the sea. He penned three books widely used as reference works throughout the maritime industry and as textbooks in maritime academies and classrooms. He was the Academy's first visiting professor. He has lived both in England and the United States.

I went down to New Orleans, and I got a job with the U.S. Army Transportation Service as chief mate on a little Army tanker. We went from New Orleans to Charleston, where we joined a convoy, went to northern England, and then I was appointed master. We ran around the Bristol Channel for several months, waiting for the invasion of France, and then we participated in the landings at Omaha Beach. It was an interesting experience. We refueled landing craft, PT boats; and then, about two weeks after the invasion, we went into a little French fishing village, Port en Bessin, and they set up a submerged pipeline there. We were the first ones to off-load gasoline for the troops in Normandy. We sailed from Swansea, and we didn't arrive off the beachhead until the morning of the eighth. The weather was cold, typical June weather in the English Channel.

Was there still some fighting in the area near Omaha?

Yes, there was. We didn't witness any fighting, directly. You could see the planes attacking, and there were a couple of minor air attacks during that time. But the beachhead was secured by the time we arrived. My ship was called the *Y-23*.

I'd say about early September, we were assigned to a British minesweeping force to refuel minesweepers that were going down to clear Brest harbor, which had just fallen. We spent about two weeks around there, acting as sort of an oiler for the minesweepers, this British minesweeping force and also American minesweepers attached to it, but it was under the command of the Royal Navy, a commander.

When they broke out of the Normandy beachhead, they bypassed several of the Channel ports. Then, as they began to surrender, they sent this minesweeping force down to clear the harbor so that it could be used. Brest, I don't think, became a significant port during that time. It was pretty badly damaged. There was still some resistance when we arrived, but that ceased a day or so after we anchored. We got ashore in Normandy and in Brest. We established contact with this local resistance commander and traded him some gasoline for fresh vegetables, which didn't turn out too well: we all ended up with dysentery.

Captain Edwin C. Kaminski, Class of 1940

I had my master's license. I was assigned to a Liberty ship called the *George Dewey*. We made our first trip from New York to Liverpool by way of Londonderry. After that we were fitted out for troop carriage from England to Normandy beaches, such as Le Havre. The *George Dewey* was assigned as a commodore ship to about twenty-five or thirty ships from Glasgow to Southampton to join the main invasion force. I felt very good about that convoy because we had cruisers and battleships and all kinds of escorts that we never had with any other convoy. I didn't realize it at the time, but they were not our escorts. They were just going over with us for the D-Day invasion of the Normandy beaches. It was just a coincidence.

After I got to Southampton, we were under the control of the British Sea Transport Service, which is part of the Ministry of War Transport.

Routinely the ship and I were assigned as commodore. I was assigned as commodore for over fifty-five convoys going across the Channel and back to the beaches of England. Only one convoy lost a ship where I was acting as commodore. That was the last convoy that I was supposed to be commodore of. I was delayed by weather in Le Havre, but I had managed to relay the information that I could catch up with the convoy and assume my position as convoy commodore. In the meantime, the vice commodore took over the job as commodore. As we got near the southern tip of England, we were attacked by submarines, and the vice commodore was torpedoed and sunk. I was two ships away from the position at the time; otherwise I would have been torpedoed. So you see, I had a very lucky career in World War II.

As noted by Captain Kaminski's entries in the Bridge Log of the *George Dewey*, on several occasions during this period the Royal Navy sent aloft barrage balloons to deter enemy aircraft attacks. On June 8 and 11, 1944, and on other dates, Kaminski noted in the log book that air raid alert signals had been sounded.[1]

9

THE VAST PACIFIC

While convoys were used in the Atlantic Ocean, the expanse of the Pacific Ocean allowed American ships to get "lost" in the vast stretch of blue between the west coast of the United States and the Pacific areas of military operations. Although Japanese submarines were a threat to merchant shipping, the Japanese naval command preferred attacks on U.S. Navy ships. In fact, while German naval strategists in the Atlantic sought to break the logistical supply line of American merchant ships, Japanese strategists never fully recognized the vulnerability of the long supply lines that American military operations in the Pacific required. Nevertheless, the Japanese submarine threat was present, and U.S. merchant ships plied routes well to the south on their way to the war front. Because American merchantmen often entered into combat areas hot on the heels of the American task forces, the most prevalent danger came from Japanese aircraft, which strafed and bombed many ships in port while discharging their cargoes. Later in the war, Japanese kamikaze planes posed an even more nerve-racking challenge. Another element of contention was the weather. Storms in the Pacific could reach major proportions, a perilous circumstance for overladen, lone merchant ships. As the Pacific war was brought ever closer to the Japanese home islands, Kings Pointers and their fellow mariners plodded over much of the 63,855,000 square miles of the Pacific, delivering their essential materials.

Taylor A. Anderson, Class of 1942

I made my first trip to Japan in 1940, the year I started as a cadet. The Japanese people were very friendly. We were warmly welcomed. By our last trip into Yokohama, I can remember the customs officials being quite nasty. As I recall, I took a package of cigarettes out and laid it out on the counter for them to stamp it. This fellow had a heavy stamp. When he got through, I didn't have anything left but shreds of tobacco. This was totally foreign. They were itching for a problem. The air was just tense. It was very, very difficult for me to understand.

We were in Manila for about ten days around Thanksgiving of 1941. They were drilling troops. In Manila, there were wooden guns. When we went to Cebu, we were blacked out every night. The entire port was blacked out. The feeling there was that the war was imminent at any time.

Then we sailed down to Torres Strait and came out behind the Hawaiian Islands. We stopped in Honolulu because we were running out of chow to eat. I got home to Seattle on December 6. The following morning, the Japanese bombed Pearl Harbor and Manila, hit the whole works. I remember I was absolutely astounded that they came in there and took them so completely unaware.

Robert B. Wells, Class of 1941

I signed onto another ship with Sun Oil Company, the MS *Pacific Sun*. The tanker that I was on joined other ships anchored at Virginia Beach. There was a bunch of us there sitting around waiting for escorts and the Navy had very few ships available. When they found out that we were going to the South Pacific, they said they'd give us two escorts, destroyers, to go as far as the Gulf of Mexico, and then you're on your own. So they took our ships as far as the beginning of the Gulf of Mexico, and then they turned around and went back. We went through the Gulf of Mexico, continued through the Panama Canal, and then on to Hawaii. After staying in Honolulu for a couple of days, we proceeded to New Zealand. This was in the early summer of 1942.

During the spring, well, early summer of 1942, when we came back from New Zealand, we came back to San Pedro, California. We then made three more trips to South Pacific alone. We went to New Hebrides, New Caledonia, the Fijis, and so forth. We carried fuel oil for the warships. We also had drums of aviation gasoline lashed to the deck for air bombers at the various island airports. It was around the time of Guadalcanal. It's in that era, summer of '42. Actually we were there over a year, but back and forth. We made five trips. We'd get rid of our cargo wherever we were, New Zealand,

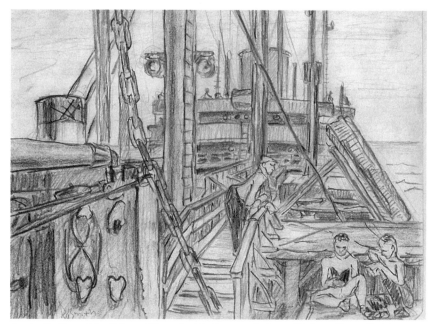

Australia Bound, by Robert Glenn Smith. By permission of Robert Glenn Smith.

Australia Bound—Passing Time—Spring 1945, by Robert Glenn Smith. By permission of Robert Glenn Smith.

Aussies Lounging in Crew Mess—Spring 1945, by Robert Glenn Smith. By permission of Robert Glenn Smith.

New Hebrides, and so forth. We'd come back to San Pedro, and we'd load up again with fuel for the ships and aviation gas for the airplanes. Then we'd head out alone again. The Navy would say, "Get lost for three or four weeks." And of course we'd zigzag and so forth, and then we'd arrive three or four weeks later to where we were going. We'd unload our cargo and then head back to California again. It was a real fast ship, 10 knots, which is actually quite slow.

I don't think they had any ships to convoy us. In other words, practically everything was on the east coast. We still had submarine problems off the east coast. On the west coast, basically, we were in danger when we were in the South Pacific, in other words, below the equator when we were off the coast of New Zealand, Australia, or the islands, New Guinea, New Hebrides, etc. I guess they felt the Pacific Ocean was big enough to "get lost," which we did.

See chapters 3 and 8 for more of Robert Wells's sea experiences.

Phillip M. Torf, Class of 1944

In April 1943, my first ship as a cadet-midshipman engineer was the Liberty ship *John H. Couch*. It was a new ship. We made a shakedown cruise to Hawaii and came back. Most of the cargo was essential cargo. It would have been supplies—munitions, foodstuffs, kind of a mixed cargo. We made a second trip to Samoa, and we had a Marine unit on Samoa at the time, and came back to the States.

Then, on the third trip, we lost our third engineer; he had to leave the ship. He had some illness I can't recall, and I was very fortunate. The chief engineer had a lot of trust in me, and made me acting third engineer. I was kind of really a greenhorn, but I sailed as third engineer on that ship, although I was still a cadet-midshipman. And it was very interesting. We didn't know really where we were going to wind up, but we went on our third trip to New Caledonia. We had some small repairs done there, and at that time we did not travel in convoy. From there we went up to the Solomons, and at that time we were carrying all fuel cargo: diesel, aviation gasoline, and bunker fuel. We carried it in barrels.

When we got to Guadalcanal late at night, and we were offshore, and broke sea watches, because we were going to start discharging cargo. In fact, we started immediately, and in those days they had Seabees, which are the Navy Construction Battalion, who came out to the ship on cargo lighters to discharge the ship,[1] and they started probably shortly after we arrived.

I don't know what time I turned into my bunk, but it was around two in the morning that there was this tremendous explosion. I just grabbed the first thing. I slept in my undershorts, and I grabbed my sneakers, and just ran up to my gun station. They did sound General Quarters; in fact, the alarm stuck; it kept ringing and ringing and ringing. I got to my gun station. I was first loader on a 3-inch gun, which is in the after part of the ship, and I said, "Let's shoot the gun." The answer was, "Well, what are we going to shoot at?" I said: "I don't know. Let's shoot something." I wanted to shoot a gun at least at something during the war. Well, the next thing I knew the abandon ship was sounded, and the whole forward part of the ship was on fire. I don't think we got any boats off, so most of us just slipped over the side. I think it was October 11, 1943. It was not a submarine; it was an airplane. As a matter of fact, he came over and sank two ships. He just dropped two torpedoes and sank two ships, one not far from us. Japanese aircraft.

Was there any anti-aircraft protection?

At that time, I didn't see any shots fired in retaliation, so I doubt very much. I think it was kind of a surprise thing. The Japanese were on islands really close by, and they used to come over and harass shipping and whatever in the American controlled areas, and it was continuous. I mean, every night while I was on Guadalcanal this plane used to come over, and we used to give it the nickname of the "Washing Machine Charlie," and he'd drop a few bombs around. We had our places where we were supposed to go for bomb shelters, and most of the time it was mud, because it rained almost every day, and so we were slipping and sliding in the mud, and looking for our bomb shelters. It was kind of interesting, but it was exciting to me. I mean, I was a young man. I was twenty years old. We were in Guadalcanal for about a month, as survivors, so we had no actual duties. Unfortunately, my sea project, which was mandatory during your time at sea, was lost, and all the books were lost, so I had no way of studying.

Guadalcanal was pretty secure. I think there was some fighting on the furthest part of the island, but nothing of a major threat to us. In fact, they had moved up the line. I think the next island that they were fighting on was called Bougainville. We were there for about a month, and really just reading, and kind of acting like a bunch of beach bums. We were given a SeaBee issue, and they treated us very nicely. As a cadet-midshipman, I had an officer's privileges, which is they gave me a couple of beers, which I traded. I brought home a Japanese rifle.

In any event, a T2 tanker came into port, and they took back all of our ship's survivors, and I became very friendly with the engineer cadet on the ship. There were some losses. In fact, we had a funeral there; nobody that I knew close to me. Before the attack, I think the total amount was probably around fifty merchant seamen, and around twenty or so Armed Guard gun crew. We came directly back to San Pedro, California, because they had already discharged, so they were going back to reload.

Most of the time, ships traveling by themselves would do what they called a zigzag route. There was no effort to take any particular lanes to avoid submarines or whatever, but I would imagine we came back pretty direct, but zigzagging all the way. A T2 tanker empty would do around 14 knots.

I remember coming home in exactly the same clothes that I had brought back from Guadalcanal and nothing else. I probably came into San Mateo [California] with those clothes, because they gave us a new issue of uniforms at San Mateo. Then, we were given examinations, the deck cadet and myself from that ship. We were given examinations to cover our sea project that should have been completed at about that date, and I came through fine. The deck cadet was washed out, and he was immediately placed in the Navy, as a seaman. We were in the Naval Reserves. He was a midshipman in the Naval Reserves, but since he didn't complete the course, he came in as an enlisted man.

I sat for my license September 1944. I went to sea continuously through 1944, 1945, to the conclusion of the war, and then I served in the merchant marine through 1946 and 1947.

On October 11, 1943, at 0150 local time, a Japanese airplane torpedoed Weyerhauser Company's *John H. Couch* and sank her while she was discharging her cargo off Koli Point, Guadalcanal. Her five thousand tons of cargo consisted of highly flammable materials, including grease, kerosene, motor gasoline, diesel oil, vehicles, and pilings loaded on deck. Her crew was composed of forty-one merchant mariners and twenty-five Naval Armed Guard. In addition, there were one hundred members of the Naval Construction Battalion on board handling the cargo. Four crewmen were injured while fighting the fire.[2]

John J. Burke, Class of 1945

I first came on board at Coyote Point, San Mateo, California, in August of 1943. I did the basic training there, and then was sent to do my sea duty out of Richmond on a Liberty ship, the *Mary Bickerdyke*. She was brand-new. It was her first voyage, and we took her straight into the battle of Tarawa in the Gilbert Islands. We were loaded entirely with pontoons. We were absolutely unsinkable. When we got down there, there was too much activity on the island, so we laid offshore. Then they finally brought us into the lagoon.

There was still fighting on the island, and on November 20 [1943], they invaded. We arrived on the 23rd, in convoy, but we had to lay off the beach for quite a while. There were air raids—it seemed like every hour we were under attack. Fortunately, we never got touched. The Navy LST[3] next to us, which we were loading and unloading onto, got sunk. As a young nineteen-year-old, it kind of scared me. I was a little nervous at the time, when I got ashore and saw the island was leveled—nothing left.

One of the fellows had a couple of rabbits aboard the ship, which we left with the chaplain on Tarawa. I was often questioned whether anything became of them, whether we'd have a population, but I never checked it.

My second voyage as a cadet (we had to serve six months or better) was on the *Matsonia*, which was a troop transport at that time on the Matson Line. We just ferried troops to Honolulu, to the camp where they learned to fight in the jungle, and then we took the seasoned troops to Langamack Bay, New Guinea. We could hear the fighting. We weren't that close, but we could hear it, so we were anxious to unload and get out of there. Then we went on to Australia to pick up the wounded and bring them home to San Francisco.

Captain Douglas F. Ponischil, Class of 1940

I sat for my chief mate's license. They had a big Coast Guard office in Galveston. Then I went on up to Wilmington, California, where there was a shipyard. They were building C1s there; so I got on board a C1 light, one of the first new C1-type ships. I made one trip on that. We went to Honolulu and to Pearl Harbor. Pearl Harbor was still in a state of devastation from all the bombing, but they were cleaning it up. You could see all those battle-ships that were there, the *Arizona*, of course, was there. We were able to dock and unload our cargo.

We just went to Pearl Harbor and went back on the *Jean Lykes*, and then I transferred to another C1 called the SS *Cape San Martin*. There were four ships, all C1s. We got attached to the Fifth Amphibious Force. They kind of leased us from the Maritime Commission, so we were really under Navy control. We loaded the stuff, like heavy earthmoving equipment. The first trip was mostly these steel grates that they used for airfields on the coral. We invaded, took over the Gilbert Islands, Makin and Tarawa. About four days after the islands were secured, the merchant ships, these four ships would go in. We went in to Makin Atoll with this cargo. On our ship, we had these mats. That's all we had: all these heavy steel mats, like criss-cross, like gratings. They would lay them down on the coral to support the planes. This was for the airfields. We weren't supposed to go ashore, but I went ashore. I managed to get ashore in a boat, and ran out and I got a few Japanese souvenirs. Saw some dead Japanese lying there and flies around them, and it was pretty harrowing, but that's war. After we unloaded, we went back to Pearl Harbor and then back to the States again.

When you were in the Gilberts, in this area, was your ship armed?

At that time, yes. We had a 5-inch gun on the stern and a 3-inch on the bow, and we had four 40mm stations. We had a naval gun crew—Naval Armed Guard, they called it.

Did you have any training in that?

Yes, I did. I was still second mate, even though I had a chief mate's license then. I had these strings of 40mm shells, and I had the starboard 40mm gun on the starboard bridge. The starboard side of the bridge was my station.

So if there was combat, you would have been expected to operate that.

Oh, yes. Yes. And I have to confess how frightening it was. While we were there, there were a couple of air attacks from Japanese planes, and, you know, just panic. I can vividly remember standing underneath the port side of the bridge. There was like a passageway, and it was like protection. I would just stand there, just shaking, not knowing if we were going to be bombed or whatever. I had these 40mm shells, and I had to run up there when they needed them. But the air raid passed, and we got by. We weren't hit or anything.

The rest of the war in the Pacific, the same ship, after the Gilbert Islands invasion, we went to the Marshall Island, Kwajalein, and then we went up to a wonderful place called Espiritu Santo in the New Hebrides Islands. This was a big base that they had built, a huge refueling base, and there were ships all over the place. Had a big bay, this was in preparation for going to Guadalcanal.

First we were in the main channel, and then, since we weren't ready to go up to Guadalcanal, we went back to this bay on the other side with about ten other ships and just anchored there for about thirty days until it was our turn to go up to Guadalcanal. They'd only take two ships at a time up to Guadal, to unload, because they were still fighting vividly up there. We had a complete disassembled hospital on board. That was our cargo, which they needed desperately. There was a little Navy patrol boat that went out ahead of us. Espiritu Santo was such a wonderful place. This was '43 and '44; all this happened now, all these invasions.

Espiritu Santo was like a rear bay, like a reserve base where you could have fun. Like they had an officers' club, and you could go up and get martinis. We'd go up and drink, and they had candy and beer and things that you just couldn't get anywhere else. As merchant ships, we weren't really entitled to it, but because we were part of the Fifth Amphibious, I swung some things, and we were able to get some beer on our ship, and, boy, everybody was just happy, thought it was a great thing.

After we went up there and back to Pearl again, and back to the States, and then we made another trip to Saipan. That was a rough one. We went all around the coast, and we were anchored off Saipan for, oh, it must have been a couple of weeks. That was terrible. We lost a lot of Marines there. It was just tough going, and the bombardment was just going on night and day. The big Navy ships were out there. The battleships all went boom! boom! boom! boom! Just constantly. We were right there, I guess half a mile off. We had to unload into barges because there weren't any docks or anything, while the shelling and the shooting and the fighting was going on. We'd get reports that the marines were being set back, and they weren't making any progress. Then they got some more troops in, and they finally overcame and got the island.

When we left, we took a lot of Marine troops, not casualties but Marine troops that were just worn out, took them back to another base, some other base that was further west than Espiritu Santo. It was like a big naval base. We took them back there. Most of these Marines were officers, so they were entitled to a fifth of booze every week. It built up while they were gone, and when they got back, they all had lockers full of Scotch and good booze and all. Oh, we had the wildest party you ever saw. I was a good friend because I had let some of them sleep in my room or on the couch, and get where they had good food. So I was a big friend, and grapefruit juice was all they had to mix with it, so you had whatever you had and grapefruit juice. We got stinko. That was one of the worst drunks that I've ever been on. I actually went back to the ship, and I was throwing my cap up in the air and the heck with it. We made it back, and we took off.

The last invasion I was in was in Palau Island. That was north of the Philippines. We went there and unloaded. Then we had to tow a ship, an LST, and another smaller naval ship back to Pearl Harbor. Without any cargo we were empty then, and, fortunately, the weather was good. We didn't have any trouble, but the submarines were still out there. You wonder how you did all these things, but we towed them all the way back to Pearl Harbor. Then we had some liberty.

The terror of fire at sea has bedeviled seafarers since humans put to sea. Except via lifeboats and rafts, escape from fire aboard ship was well-nigh impossible, and the swiftness of a fire in a cargo-laden merchant ship was devastating. The flammable liquids and stores provided ready tinder for a conflagration. In World War II, the possibility of fire aboard a merchant ship was magnified with the explosive nature of war materials carried in holds and on deck, such as ammunition and aviation fuel. The frequent practice of overloading the ships increased the possibility of a swift end if fire erupted.[4] Douglas Ponischil relates an incendiary incident.

The port captain who took a liking to me said: "I know the port captain at Weyerhaeuser Steamship Company in New York, and they're looking for some skippers. I'm pretty sure, if you go up there, I think you can get a job." Weyerhaeuser, the big lumber company, was acting as agent for a lot of ships in the war. So I went up: "Yes, we need a skipper right away. We've got a ship in Norfolk, the *George L. Baker* needs a skipper." They put me on a train and got to Norfolk. Here was this little twenty-four-year-old kid walking onto the ship with the suitcase, everybody looking down: "Who's this?" So I took over and had a chief engineer who was an old-timer. He must have been about sixty-seven, and I'm sure he wondered, too. I did it, took over and made it. I befriended him and asked his advice, and took it, and we became really good friends. He respected that, even though I was young, I would do the right thing.

We loaded at the naval base in Norfolk; they loaded, and I knew it was wrong, but, anyway, the Navy was in control. We couldn't say anything about what they were loading and how they were doing it. They loaded these bales and bundles of underwear and clothing for the Army and servicemen, and then they put some dunnage down, which were pieces of wood to tighten it up. Then they loaded five-gallon cans of cooking oil on top of that, and then other stuff. So we took off and went through the Panama Canal, and I was real proud being the captain at that age. I was one of the youngest captains that had commanded a ship in those days, at twenty-four; and real proud, taking it through the Panama Canal.

Then halfway across the Pacific to Pearl Harbor, the ship caught on fire. The number-four hold caught on fire. Spontaneous combustion from the oil that always leaks off these cans and dripped down. Somehow it got onto the clothing and started the fire. Well, this was a Liberty Ship, and they did have a CO_2 system. We engaged the CO_2 system, which didn't do much good, because the cargo was so tightly packed. We put hoses down the ventilators to try to put some water down in there, in the forward hold. We couldn't open the hatch because we knew it would just blow up if we did that, and you could see the side of the ship on the starboard side, a big bulge that just got red from the heat of the fire and just bulged out, and then actually expanded the bulge like a boil or a blister. Then the water from the ocean would hit it, and it would steam and sizzle.

We were kind of panicky. We were still under radio silence in those days because the war was still on, so we broke radio silence to let them know in Pearl Harbor that we were on fire and all. They very curtly said, "Keep proceeding to Pearl Harbor and let us know if it gets worse." That was about it. So we kept going. About two days later we made it, and it was still contained or controlled, but it was there.

They met us with some big fireboats, and they took us to a dock way inside Pearl Harbor. I think it's something like way on the west side of Pearl Harbor, where there wasn't any other traffic. It was tied up to a remote dock, and it took them about two days to get down to the cargo where the fire was and to actually put it out. So that caused us to be there and have to get repairs. We were there for about a month.

Douglas Ponischil's odyssey continued. See chapter 15, "End of the War."

Rear Admiral Thomas A. King, Class of 1942

Within days of obtaining my second mate's license, I was on my way across the country, by rail, to an assignment, in my new licensed capacity on US Lines SS *Cape May*, a General Agency, C1 ship just completing construction in Consolidated Steel's yard in Wilmington, California. I made two voyages to Australia, New Guinea, New Caledonia, New Hebrides, and the Solomon Islands. We steamed independently with the exception of a run into Guadalcanal during which we had the convoy commander on board. We carried combat troops while we were a cargo ship. We carried combat engineers. When we went to Guadalcanal, I remember we had P-38s stacked on deck nose down, and when we were off Guadalcanal, the airstrip was in sight. We could see P-38s taking off from the airstrip at the same time we were discharging new P-38s to be taken ashore there. An air raid while anchored off the beach at Guadalcanal and a later reported submarine sighting, from which we ran while firing away with our 5-inch stern gun, was the totality of our exposure to enemy action. Upon completion of the second voyage, I took my chief mate's exam and passed as 1943 concluded.

With my new license, in January 1944 I reported as chief officer on board the US Lines, General Agency, C1 design, MV *American Packer*, as she lay at her berth in San Francisco. I made three trans-Pacific and one coastwise voyage on that ship. For me, those voyages provided both valuable experience and the time in-grade required for my final license exam. The *American Packer*, carrying military cargoes, voyaged to the Marshall and Gilbert Islands with stops in the Hawaiian Islands. We also served as an ammunition ship, replenishing the Pacific battleship fleet in the New Hebrides and carried wartime cargo to Australia and New Zealand. Returning to San Francisco, with one year as chief officer, I was ordered to New York, where I successfully took my final license exam as master; then came a too brief vacation time.

Early in 1944, I was assigned as master of US Lines MV *Snug Hitch*, under General Agency assignment. The ship was completing construction in San Pedro, California. It wasn't until several years later that I fully appreciated how rapidly I had moved through the ranks from cadet to shipmaster. I was, of course, aware that the six months between grades up to chief mate and then one full year to eligibility for the master's exam was not the norm, but was due to the war and a massive shipbuilding program. I certainly did not then think in terms of having secured my master's license in about the same period of time that I had originally expected would be required for completing the four-year course and obtaining a third mate's license. I do recall, however, feeling the weight of the world on my shoulders when the pilot, who had taken the *Snug Hitch* from the loading dock to the open sea, was safely away, and it was then my responsibility to give my first helm and engine orders as the master of an armed merchant ship, sailing independently and bound for contested waters.

The *Snug Hitch*, down to her marks with a wartime cargo ranging from weapons and ammunition to military vehicles and PX supplies,[5] was under sealed orders with the first checkpoint being Diamond Head in the Hawaiian Islands. Passing that landmark without incident or changed orders, we proceeded west, crossing the International Date Line, to the Palau chain of islands. There we entered an atoll, anchored, and awaited further orders. When those orders came, we were directed to join other ships and proceed in convoy to Manila in the Philippines. Ours was to be the second merchant convoy into Manila Bay following our invasion. Enemy resistance was still being encountered there within portions of the old walled city.

Proceeding, as a multicolumned convoy, we sailed through the Surigao Straits, and then the convoy headed north toward Luzon and Manila. We passed many islands, during the hours of darkness, hoping that the escort and commodore were navigating with greater confidence then we felt. There were, of course, no navigational lights and at night, lacking radar, with no moonlight and many islands, it was difficult to be certain of your ship's exact position amongst reefs, rocks, and islands. Some comfort was derived from knowing that our ship was not leading or in an outside column. Hopefully any error in navigation would affect others first. At one juncture, on a very dark night, a large number of scattered, low-powered lights came on; native fishing canoes out of self-survival instincts were attempting to let us know that they were there. The convoy did not, and undoubtedly could not, deviate from its restricted course. Within minutes we had steamed through them, having seen some of the canoes, with their feeble lights, pass down between the columns of the convoy. We consoled ourselves that we had not struck one of them and wondered, but never found out, whether the lead ships had been less fortunate.

The convoy arrived off Corregidor, broke formation, and steamed into Manila Bay in a single line of ships. We took our assigned anchorages amidst multiple sunken wrecks of ships. We were soon informed that shore-going should be limited to absolute necessity as fighting was still going on. When our time came, we shifted to a dock and discharged our stateside cargo.

We then entered the service for which the *Snug Hitch* was ideally suited. For the last six months of World War II, we shuttled from Manila to the military units engaged in taking back the outlying islands from the enemy. Unescorted, the *Snug Hitch* made most, if not all, of the major and many of the lesser islands in the Philippine chain. On one trip, however, we carried cargo for discharge in Hollandia and Oro Bay in New Guinea.

In August of 1945, the ship was sent to the northern coast of the largest of the Philippine Islands, Mindanao. There we discharged our cargo at a temporary pontoon dock and then became a prison ship loading almost one thousand enemy POWs to be taken north to a prisoner of war camp at Tacloban in the Leyte Gulf. We were in the process, virtually in the process, of loading eight hundred Japanese prisoners, which we took down in the hold, and we had probably a thirty-six-hour run up to Leyte, something on that order, when the word came. The radio operator gave me a message. It was the conclusion of the war, but to be alert, not to let your guard down, almost precautionary advice, and I think it was rather dramatic. I think we celebrated; we blew the whistle, we did things of that sort, that we could do. I'm sure the Japanese who were marching down this long pontoon dock couldn't quite figure out what it was that was taking place at that stage. We proceeded north to Tacloban and discharged our POW cargo.

Edward Lewis Scott Jr., Class of 1945

While at the Academy, Ed Scott was editor of *Polaris*, the student magazine. After receiving his license, Scott sailed for American President Lines. Years later, he started his own import-export business. He holds a master's degree from the University of California.

I took my basic training at San Mateo in California, and then went to sea from there. In San Mateo, we had basic training courses in seamanship. I was a deck cadet, so I had a big course in navigation and piloting, and then just basic courses to prepare you for your year at sea. I was there three months. Then I was assigned to the SS *Pendleton*, a tanker.

We went to Aruba to pick up 6 million gallons of high-octane gasoline. Then we shuttled gasoline for the aircraft carriers. We went to ports on the West Coast, to Honolulu, and then they sent us south of the Palmyra Islands, to take us over to the South Pacific. We had off-loaded most of the gasoline in the Solomon Islands.

We were going through the Great Barrier Reef into Brisbane, when we struck what at the time they thought was an uncharted rock, but turned out to be a reef. It put a gash in the ship 181 feet long. So that ended that ship's life right there. We didn't quite sink in the harbor, but we got close to it.

It was a mistake on the part of the chief mate. He forgot to calculate the distance. When we hit the reef, I immediately went topside, took some bearings on some lights, and put the bearings on the chart on my own. I discovered we were not at the position that we said we were at the time.

So I was involved in the Coast Guard hearing, because of the fact that they had erased the bearings. They said it was an uncharted reef in the Great Barrier Reef, and it was going to be a considerable expense. This was 1944, and I was twenty-one at the time.

After the Coast Guard hearing, I was sent down to Sydney. They had a holding station there for a bunch of us that were coming back to the Academy. We came back as passengers on a Liberty ship there, directly into San Francisco.

After about a year at sea, I came back to Kings Point in September of 1944.

James W. Gann, Class of 1944

Starting with preliminary training at San Mateo, California, Jim Gann graduated from Kings Point in 1944 and sailed on his license until 1947. He worked for Waterman Steamship Company and Moore McCormack Lines as chief mate.

I originally went through the cadet program at San Mateo. Training was very complete, but hurried because of the situation. I took general courses in seamanship, navigation, Rules of the Road, and so forth. I was there in May of '43, and then to boot camp for two or three months and then spent about seven months at sea in the Pacific on a troop ship.

I was on a C2 ship, converted to an XPA. It was a merchant ship with landing barges. We were outfitted while I was aboard ship for the campaign to Tarawa. We had our own landing ships, troops, and crew to discharge and handle the boats. We were backups. We were at the island about D plus three or four, and people went ashore at that time. We shuttled people and mainly equipment back and forth between some of those islands for a few months, before I came back to San Francisco. I was twenty-one years old.

We zigzagged whether we were in convoy or not, but we didn't really get into convoys until we were way out in the war zone, during the last part of that voyage. Our escort vessels were destroyers, DEs, and sub chasers.

One time, after the Tarawa invasion, we came up to Roi Island in the Marshalls, which had been taken by Marines. We were in there something like D plus 4 or 5 and discharged our troops. The first night we were in there, why, "Washing Machine Charlie" came over and dropped a string of bombs on the beachhead. I'm talking about this little putt-putt type of thing. It sounded like a washing machine when it flew over at low elevation. Well, there was a huge explosion with high casualties. As the original casualties were already moved out, they made us the hospital evacuation ship. We only had two doctors aboard, so they brought on more. We brought back over two hundred casualties to Pearl Harbor.

I returned to San Francisco, changed ships, and got on the SS *Eagle Wing*. Originally, when I signed Articles, the ship was at Alameda with floating general cargo. After about two days, they closed down the operation and transferred us to Port Chicago, which was a Navy ammo depot about thirty-five miles from San Francisco Bay. There, we were loaded with cargo that wasn't marked as to what it was. Basically, they had a number of tongue-in-groove boxes, completely encased, and all painted an olive green type of a thing. They had specific orders on them, like, "mail" or "deliver to John Jones," and gave an address somewhere.

We left Port Chicago. Near San Francisco, they had trouble with some type of a fan in the engine room, and so they wanted to stop and repair it. Well, they wouldn't even let us into San Francisco Bay. The pilot had orders that they had to drop anchor, and so we did, up in San Pablo Bay. On the Fourth of July [1945] we sailed from San Francisco Bay under the Golden Bridge and to sea. We had one troop officer aboard who wore a captain's field artillery insignia. Well, after we were at sea, and so forth, why, of course, he ate in the officers' mess with us. He said he would cover any money that anybody wanted to bet that the war would be over by Christmas. Well, this was in July, and it was unheard of in normal conversations.

We got to Tinian, and we had about forty people come aboard, all in suntans. They wore no insignia on their cap or anything else, and they were involved only with the cargo that we had picked up at Port Chicago. There were Marines or could have been Army. They had somebody sitting there with big guns ready to go at the corner of every shipment that went out of there. Why, anything that was put on the trucks to haul away. When we were through, we discharged our regular cargo and came back.

On our way back, we heard the word about the A-bomb. Well, we kind of put two and two together, thinking that we possibly had something to do with it. Later, the newspapers said the SS *Indianapolis*, a heavy cruiser, took the A-bomb over there. But I've always thought that the events that I've enumerated indicate that we certainly had something to do with it, because we weren't in the normal shipping lanes between San Francisco and Pearl Harbor. History shows that we had already left Tinian, and that the *Indianapolis* did pull in there after us. It was a short time after that that the A-bomb was dropped.

On July 30, 1945, the Japanese submarine *I-58* sank the *Indianapolis* with two torpedoes. Due to a failure of communications and delay in rescue operations, many of the cruiser's crew perished.[6]

Stanley D. Smith, Class of 1944

Subsequent to World War II, Stanley Smith settled in Oregon. He has his own business in real estate.

I attended San Mateo Basic Training School on the west coast. It was about three months. It was the first information I had on ships. I was pretty green to the subject. They worked us pretty good, and after three months we went to a steamship company and asked for a berth on a ship. There were several films being circulated at that time to promote just such a thing, so that there would be an adequate supply of ship's officers in the merchant marine. They turned out ships pretty fast during World War II, once they got going. So that was it. I saw the films, and then others told me about the program. I can't remember the names of these films. I had to believe that they were produced by the government. I don't know who else would do it.

At San Mateo we had our first smattering of navigation. We had a little bit of seamanship—knots, ropes, line, I should say, cable splicing, etc. Ship construction came later. We had a little information on ship handling, maneuvering, steaming in convoy, that type of thing. I don't know whether it was by the individual instructor or part of the agenda: export ships, maintaining position, routes that you might be directed to be taking on. It was fairly extensive.

After three months of this, we were assigned to go to sea, and we went to a steamship company. It so happened that one of my classmates was already in the steamship office, and the two of us decided to ship out together. We shipped out twice both times to Noumea, New Caledonia, which was one of the first, early points where we off-loaded material. It was a minimum of six months at sea. So, we had six or seven months at sea. Noumea is the principal city of New Caledonia. New Caledonia is off the east coast of Australia.

What were you carrying, sir?

Except for the deck cargo, I have no idea. We had nothing to do with the loading of the ship.

The second trip was to Noumea, New Caledonia. We then started proceeding, as the war moved north. We were sent on various missions with our cargo, with some of our cargo north to some of the action areas. We went along for an extra six or eight weeks. I don't know the general cargo, but the deck cargo was what they called ducks and alligators. Ducks are jeeplike vehicles that would go on land and sea. The alligators were just a little bit larger. On the second voyage, we off-loaded these types of vehicles from Lunga Point, San Cristobal, where a major campaign had taken place. San Cristobal Island was near Guadalcanal, the first major campaign where the Marines went in and went ashore. That is where we off-loaded the ducks and alligators. They came day and night off of the ship: got a sling load of cargo, went back to shore.

So, it was a circular route that these ducks and alligators were taking, while your ship was off-loading?

Yes, on land as well as sea. I was a third mate. When we completed that assignment, we were in a bombing on that trip, too. We went into a port. The island was Mona Island. We were within bombing reach of the Japanese airport at Rabaul, and they attacked us one night. It was a night bombing. We were not hit, but we could hear people ashore who were hit, and that was pretty concerning. Some of the men that were hit were actually shouting. So you knew that they had been hit. It could have been you. I was a cadet-midshipman. In addition to my other duties, when an incident of this kind came about, we were loaders on 20mm machine guns. The Navy Armed Guard was on board to command those guns, but they needed loaders so we were assigned. The ship was the *Elwood Mead*. It was a Liberty ship. The engagement lasted about thirty minutes. We left within a couple of days, so we didn't see them come back. We returned to San Francisco, and then we went into the cadet office in San Francisco. They talked to us, interviewed us, and sent us back to the Academy.

So, they felt that you had enough sea time?

Yes, seven months. At Kings Point we had quite a number of courses including meteorology. We had one on U.S. Naval customs and traditions. We had one in advanced first aid. We had navigation and mathematics. We had ship handling, again, seamanship, small boat handling, quite a variety of exercises. I believe the courses were a wartime crash program of nine months. We graduated in December of '44. We were marching frequently. I was not a cadet-midshipman officer, so I was in the group that was marching. So, when they said march, we marched. And oddly enough, my father died just two weeks before I graduated, and they sent me back to San Mateo to prepare for my license in San Francisco rather than have it done here in New York.

I passed my exam for third mate, and the first job I had was on a Liberty ship. I was "second" on a third mate's license because of the shortage of people. There was an incident that we very fortunately got through. It was around the world from the west coast of the United States. I think it was out of San Francisco. The first stop was in Australia. Fremantle, Australia, near Perth. We took on fuel, water, etc., and I think within forty-eight hours we were on our way to India. That was our destination. So, it was up the Ganges River to Calcutta. We were there about two weeks, off-loaded our cargo, took on a load of hemp to bring back to the United States and three hundred monkeys. They were brought back onshore for experimentation purposes. We went through the Suez Canal, through the Mediterranean, past the Rock of Gibraltar, and the captain told me to set a great circle route to New York, which I did. We were diverted, however, to Savannah, Georgia. We made Savannah, Georgia, and that was the end of that voyage.

When we had moved south of Australia, we received word that a ship had been sunk just twenty-four hours ahead of us on the same general route. Knowing that, my skipper asked me, at sunset, to divert the ship ninety degrees right toward shoreline; we proceeded on that course for forty-five minutes, [and] reversed course. We came back, and by that time it was quite dark, and then we proceeded on. I believe to this day that we avoided being torpedoed, by that maneuver, by a Japanese submarine.

One more trip on my license and the war was over. We were loaded on that occasion for the invasion of Japan. We were loaded and on our way before the end of the war, and we went to the Philippines Islands. We were retained there because there was not anyone sure exactly what to do with us for a short time. We were in Leyte Gulf. The landings had already taken place. We were being held there, pending the invasion if the invasion did indeed take place. Of course, it did not take place. I am not sure we had full knowledge of our final destination until later. So we were not able to speculate at all on that.

We were at sea when we heard of the end of the war. Of course, VE day had already taken place. Then, we heard about the bomb, the bombing of Hiroshima and then Nagasaki. We didn't know what an atomic blast would do. It was all new to us, and we had that on our minds. We talked about it. But then Japan finally had to surrender, and we heard about it. We went back to the United States.

Joseph H. Lion, Class of 1946

Joseph Lion has made a career of marine engineering. His engagement in historic events continued after World War II. He was one of several engineers who constituted the original crew of the passenger ship SS *United States*. He sailed on the ship's maiden voyage when it clipped along at 36 knots. Later, he was a research and development engineer in 1957 at, as he states, "the height of nuclear submarines, before the missile boats came along."

I came to New York for my sea duty as an engine cadet. At that time, you could request what type of sea service you wanted, and I had said I wanted turboelectric, which would mean a tanker. So they put me on a Liberty ship, you know, government operations. It was heading to South America. When we got down to go through the canal, the DI there said, "Anyone for turboelectric duty, we got a tanker here waiting for you over on the Army dock." Three cadets were with me. One fellow never left his bunk. I mean, we didn't even drop the pilot, and he said, "I'll go take a wet [infantry] trench someplace." He just flat couldn't stand the ocean. So they put me and the other fellow on the SS *Mission San Gabriel*, which was one of the fourteen mission ships built with higher horsepower than all the other tankers. We never ran in convoy, with the exception of one time.

We'd always leave the canal. Normally, we'd go through the canal to Aruba or Curacao, the two big refueling centers from Maracaibo, and we'd pick up a load and go through the canal, and then they'd top us off, and we'd

*R & R at Eniwetok Atoll—
Spring '45,* by Robert Glenn
Smith. By permission of
Robert Glenn Smith.

*GI Laundromat Eniwetok
Atoll,* by Robert Glenn
Smith. By permission of
Robert Glenn Smith.

Liberty Boat Headed for White Sand and Clear Waters, by Robert Glenn Smith. By permission of Robert Glenn Smith.

head out. On the first trip, we went to Eniwetok and Kwajalein. On the next trip, we went to the Admiralty Islands, two degrees south of the equator in the western Pacific. That's where they had the big floating dry dock on the island of Manus. The dock was built here on the east coast and towed in ten sections by Moran Shipping Company through the canal and reassembled out there. It could lift two cruisers at one time. It was a huge thing, totally self-supporting. It was just like an open roadstead.

We came in there because they were going to assemble a convoy to the Philippines. It was the only time we went in convoy. It was probably late September 1944. There were fifty-seven ships. We had the *Mariposa* and two cruise ships that were being used as troopers. One was right in front of us. Most of them were all cargo ships and ammunition, and then the four tankers carrying aviation gas. They didn't want us to blow up in front of everybody so we were "tail-end Charlies," the last four ships in the column.

Well, down in Manus it was, as I say, two degrees below the equator, and the ships weren't air-conditioned, and we had blackout conditions. So every night you had to close all the portholes, anything that would show light, and the temperature of the ship would build up to 118, 120 degrees. Even sleeping quarters were hot, but not nearly that hot. In the engine spaces it would be that hot. We were working in fiddley and running on just natural ventilation. You had to wear gloves. If your hand touched the handrail it would burn; it would actually burn your hand, it was that hot. But that was very unusual conditions because we were getting no ventilation up there, at all.

We were in Ulithi on the twentieth day of December of '44, and two Jap midget submarines had gotten past the submarine net some way or other. I think they came in with another ship. There were five hospital ships in there at anchor at that time. The *Mercy* was the one nearest us when we anchored the next day. Patients were being loaded from a ship that came in from the Philippines onto the dock and prepped to take aboard the *Mercy*. They had a floating dock next to it, with doctors and nurses helping the injured off and putting them in baskets to get them up the side of the ship.

The Japs sighted this and cut loose with their torpedoes. The torpedoes were deep enough that they cleared the keel of the *Mercy* and blew up the dock. They killed almost every doctor and nurse on the ship. They had had to cannibalize the other four hospital ships to staff up the *Mercy*, which was about the saddest thing. We took aboard the personnel, which were mostly crew, because we were supposed to go back to Pearl Harbor. We didn't [go back], but we were supposed to. They were really shook up about it. That was about probably the most impressive thing that happened to me out there. These submarines attacked the hospital ship even though it was plainly marked, a beautiful white with a red cross on it and everything.

Fortunately we missed all that "fun." We were a very lucky ship. As I say, the only time we ever ran a convoy was between Manus and the Philippines. We didn't have to take too many precautions when we weren't in convoy. We would run a straight course to the Dateline, and at the Dateline we would run a zigzag course. They had different plots, like you could go 60 percent of your actual distance. We always used to run 85 percent, so we ran pretty straight. The captain was a young captain, and he wanted to get where he was going.

Another thing. I never paid any attention to it until we ran in convoy, and there were fifty-six other ships. I was up there looking around with the glasses, and I saw everybody had their lifeboats hanging right over the side. The only time ours ever left the cradles was during boat drill. I said: "Captain, that looks like a good idea. You just let the lifeboats go in the water."

He said, "Son," which was funny because he was maybe ten years older than me if he was that, "you know our tanker is highly compartmented." It had twenty-nine tanks, not including the engine room. And he said: "If we get torpedoed we're going to leave a huge hole in the water, and that lifeboat isn't going to help you a bit. The torpedoes are just going to hit a tank, and if it doesn't go off, we'll be afloat for hours before anything happens. We get in a bad storm, you're going to lose that lifeboat and you'll never have it. So they stay in the cradles. Either you'll have all the time in the world to launch that lifeboat, or you won't need it at all." So that was his attitude.

I was at sea for nine months and two weeks before I came back to Kings Point.

William E. Hooper, Ph.D., Class of 1945

Recognizing the value of education, Bill Hooper has pursued academic degrees in a big way. In addition to a Kings Point bachelor of science degree, he has four other degrees, including a doctorate in school administration. His career in that field has focused on supervising high school music programs. However, he also has an avid interest in the circus, as he states, "I was particularly interested in the tent systems of blocks and ropes, as it related to sailing ship rigging, and the strong circus march music."

Upon graduation from Kings Point, I shipped out as a junior third mate. The ship was a T2 tanker, the SS *Boundbrook*, Marine Transport Lines. I thought I was going to Europe, but they changed our orders and sent us through the Panama Canal, out into the Pacific. We carried diesel oil, pumped the oil into some smaller Navy frontline tankers, and back we went through the Panama Canal to Mexico and got another load for the Pacific.

About six months in, the third mate, who had been torpedoed twice and was an older man, just went all to pieces. We had no doctors on board, so the captain said, "Chain him out by the lifeboat." We would carry his food out on deck, and we would see to his needs as best as we could. I was promoted to third mate.

Out of all the degrees I have, Kings Point taught me to put my feet firmly on the ground, plan what I was going to do, try to stick to that plan, and have faith in myself. I think that carried me through so many other experiences. At sea, when I was standing on that wing in the rough weather, sometimes I felt like God himself was looking over my shoulder. I developed a sense of almost worship sometimes, late at night when I was out there, and I had all that time to think while I was on watch.

I grew up in a very strict home. I didn't drink and I didn't smoke. When the crew found out I didn't drink and smoke, some of them came to me and said: "When we go ashore, we always get too drunk, and they take all of our money to pay for the girls and pay for the drinks. What would you charge us to just come along and keep all of our money and you pay the bills?" I said, "I wouldn't charge you." So I actually did that one time for a group of the crew. They went to a place of not so great repute, had a bar downstairs, and whatever else they wanted upstairs, and I had to pay the bills. The bartender didn't love me, and the young ladies upstairs didn't love me either, because we set a price ahead of time, and I was the treasurer. I didn't know if I was going to get out of there with my life. They kept trying to give me something to drink, and I just sat there in the corner, which was an amusing experience for me.

Glenn Ohanesian, Class of 1945

Glenn Ohanesian saw service in the Korean War as well as in the Second World War. In the Korean War, he was a Navy navigator aboard the USS *Monrovia* (APA31), 1950–52. He earned an MBA in 1969 and worked in management positions for New York Telephone from 1952 to his retirement in 1985.

My first trip was from San Francisco on the *James King*. We went to Honolulu, to Saipan, Tinian, and then we went up to the Okinawan invasion. We were sitting off of Yontan air field up there, I'm sure within two or three weeks of when the first troops went ashore. We had some very tough periods with kamikaze air raids during the time we were up there, which was roughly three weeks. A lot of air activity. This would have been April of '45, right around the time Roosevelt died.

I remember one incident, must have been maybe eleven or twelve at night, a moonlit night. One of the Japanese suicide planes was using the runway on Yontan field as a guide. He lined himself up, and he flew down between the columns of ships, between my ship and another. And he was flying at bridge height so nobody could shoot at him. He was so close as he went down, I could see the moonlight reflecting on his gloves and his helmet as he flew by. But we didn't suffer any damage. What we did was act as a floating warehouse until they emptied it. Then we came home.

Charles M. Renick, Class of 1947

I made three trips on the *Brazil* to Europe, and then they put me on a brand new T2 tanker *Mattabesset*. We sailed from a shipyard in Chester, Pennsylvania, down to Texas. Loaded aviation gas right down as much as it could possibly take, went through the Panama Canal, and took P-38s, which were the pursuit planes, to Manila, to the theater out there. So, we went across the Pacific. Most tankers were named after Civil War battles. Liberty ships and all the other ships of the war, they were really hard pressed to come up with names for them. They were building them so fast.

Well, they were fighting in Manila, and the *Mattabesset* was delayed until the city was secured. We came in Manila Bay, and it was a very impressive sight because I think half the Pacific fleet and hundreds and hundreds of merchant ships were there. I remember that we were quite a ways off the beach. We went in to visit Manila, and I was in charge of one of the lifeboats that we got in to take some of the crew in for a little recreation. One of the skippers of one of the Liberty ships who was in the harbor had asked me to take him back to his ship. I said "sure," and I put him in. He could not find his ship. We spent the whole afternoon. It was getting dark, and I finally had to take him back to our ship. I don't know how he checked his ship, that is how many ships there were.

I had one story I think is rather humorous. We were sitting in Manila; we sat in Manila Harbor for a couple of months because they didn't have anyplace to put our cargo, and things were moving so fast. They sent many more supplies than they had time to consume, and we were serving almost as a warehouse or a tanker. The *Brazil* came steaming into the harbor, and this was quite impressive because a big old-fashioned ship was impressive looking. When they previously had taken me off the *Brazil*, they took me off very quickly, and my laundry was still at the laundry and I didn't get it back. I was not the best of a packer, and I left in my closet, in my quarters, my bathrobe and my bedroom slippers. As the *Brazil* came in the harbor it had a flashing light and it was blinking away, blinking away. All the communication, in fact, during the war was by blinker light.

I noticed they were blinking at my ship, and I was reading the signal. And of course everybody else in the harbor was reading the signal: "Do you have a Cadet Renick aboard?" The signalman up there on our ship signaled back "yes," and he [on the *Brazil*] said, "We have his bathrobe, we have his slippers, we have his laundry." So, every time the signal went, I was slinking down farther and farther. It is funny now, but it was very embarrassing then. Everybody in the harbor in Manila knew that I had forgotten my laundry.

Where were you when you heard of the end of the war, that is the victory—VJ Day?

I was out in the Pacific aboard ship, and we got the message. Naturally, there was a lot of jubilation. But we got one other message out of the Pacific that was a very significant message that I was involved in personally. We were out in the Pacific when they dropped the first atomic bomb. They had a radio up in the chart room which was hooked up to the speakers down in the mess halls and the officers' board room so they could hear, and my job was to try to keep some music going on this, but usually all you could get was Japanese jabbering.

I was going through the dial, and I came across a news broadcast, but it was so static that I could barely hear it. I had to put my ear up against the speaker, and they were announcing that they just dropped a bomb that was the equivalent of ten thousand tons of TNT. So I am the first one on the ship to know about the atomic bomb. We didn't call it the atomic bomb then, but I was going down telling everybody they dropped a bomb on Japan that was ten thousand tons. "Now, how did they drop a ten-thousand-ton bomb, you know?" And I said, "Well, they said they dropped it from an airplane." And you know, the ridiculousness of this, and I got pooh-poohed. I had the greatest story of the century, and no one believed me until two days later when they heard it over another broadcast.

10

WEATHER

Weather has been an unpredictable partner in voyaging since time immemorial, and the merchant mariners had special concerns aboard the Liberty ships. Although basically sturdy in design, Liberty ships possessed a flaw in construction that was enlarged by foul weather and by pitching and rolling in heavy seas. The Liberties were known to develop cracks, usually forward of the wheelhouse and engine room, either near the square hatch covers that were unstrengthened or the uppermost band of plating that circled the hull below the main deck. The cracks were caused by stress concentrations at the points noted and allowed to propagate due to the welded construction. In time, the cracking problem was solved. Crack arrestors, consisting of steel reinforcing straps, were riveted on the main deck. Also, hatch corners were reinforced, and bars were added to the gunwales.[1]

Karl J. Aarseth, Class of 1943

While ferrying troops home after the end of hostilities, Karl Aarseth encountered a North Atlantic storm that he remembers vividly.

We sailed to Barry Docks in Wales. We needed ballast cargo. We loaded PX supplies, Coca-Cola, chewing gum, etc., in trucks and vehicles, trying to get 1,500 tons in the lower hold of the ship for ballast. There was also a dismantled radio tower. I said, "Why not leave that in England?" Oh, no, no. We would have to pay duty on it. We finally did get our 1,500 tons.

In the North Atlantic, we ran into the worst storm I've ever been in in all my life. The ship was small and with no cargo. We heard that an aircraft carrier had turned back because of damage to the flight deck. Also, a French warship had a 1,500-ton turret damaged. We were losing headway and going back lightly. The fires went down the starboard boiler, but as water went down the stack, it was hopeless. We had GIs being shipped home. We took anybody we could get aboard. We had nine or ten GIs, and they had to sleep in the gunner's quarters, seasick all the time. One of the GIs slept between the boilers in the engine room. He was so seasick he was getting dehydrated. Finally, like all things pass, I got to Boston. The ship had several cracks all over it, just ahead of the housing for number-three hatch, from the storm. They were going to put the ship in lay-up. This was the vessel that had made at least three trips to Russia, four maybe, and the Normandy invasion. They were doing away with it. We went down there and turned her over to the corporation. I knew the war was over for me.

Henry H. Evans, Class of 1944

Henry Evans remembers vividly his experience with foul weather.

Four cadets from Pass Christian, two engine and two deck, myself included, were sent to a ship in Brown's Shipyard in Houston, Texas, the *William H. Crawford*. It was a new Liberty ship, operated by the Lykes Brothers Steamship Company. We loaded what seemed like two trainloads of cargo in Houston bound for the Persian Gulf. We loaded airplane parts, airplane equipment, and Sherman tanks. We had a full vector cargo two tiers high of crated military equipment on top of the deck. We had ammunition in number-one hold. I can't say for sure, but I would say we were overloaded and somewhat top-heavy.

We left Houston and went to Guantanamo Bay, Cuba. We made up a convoy there for the Panama Canal. At that point, the Persian Gulf ships were going through the canal across the Pacific. We couldn't get through the Mediterranean because the Suez was blocked. The South African movement was dangerous, so we took the long way on the ride out. We sighted some submarines, German U-boats. They called that the "Picket Fence" along the northern coast of South America and over to Central America. There were so many masts sticking out of the low water from all the ships that had been sunk.

We had one submarine come up in the convoy. He was confused, too. He was between ships in a closed convoy, and he didn't know what to do either. (*Laughter*) He submerged and, of course, the escorts were dropping depth charges. But whether they got him or not, I don't know. That was the first enemy action we had seen at that time.

Across the Pacific, we ran alone. The escorts carried us within sight of the canal, and as soon as we were out of sight of the canal, they turned us loose. In the Pacific, we thought we were subject to the greatest danger. Not submarines, in particular, because of the surface commerce raiders. But we didn't encounter anything.

We didn't get to the Persian Gulf, first. We had been at sea about thirty days in the Pacific, some latitude almost perpendicular to Tasmania, south of Australia. We were in thirty-foot seas. The seas picked the ship up, a wave on each end, dropped us down on a wave in the center, and broke us in two. The two ends hung together. It was like a stick. It broke in halves, and flooded the number-three hold and broke all the fuel lines and water line connections for all of the ship, and put the fires out. There were three forward holds, and the split occurred in the after-most part of the third hold near the bulkhead between the third hold and the engine room. My emergency station thought we had been torpedoed. It sounded like we had been torpedoed. Our emergency station was in the engine room with the chief engineer, so we went down, and between him and all of the engineers that came down, and the crew that was in the engine room at the time, we got all the valves closed on the forward bulkhead and started taking fuel from the sediment tank to get the fires going. We had a retired skipper who was about seventy-five years old, and he had come back to the war, an old sailing boat skipper. He called the engine room and gave a set of instructions of what to do.

At that time, the ship flexed and opened up and took on more water. It took us thirty-six hours to get it back into Hobart. The only thing holding the ship together was the double bottom. The heavy seas continued for a long time after the spilt. It was a hurricane. We didn't know if we were going to make it. We had General Quarters and had "abandon ship." People were with the lifeboats, but we were in the engine room trying to get things going, so we never did get onto the lifeboats. We stayed on the General Quarters until we got the thing back to port.

We went into the shipyard in Hobart and unloaded the forward part of the ship and brought the bow up. The shipyard closed the crack up, welded it back. They worked on both sides of the ship and put a forty-foot-long, one-inch by four-foot plate on each side after it was welded back together. We loaded everything we had left to load that we hadn't lost. We lost all the forward deck cargo.

We went on from there to the Persian Gulf. We off-loaded at Basra, in Iraq, and then came back to Abadan in Iran to fuel. We were there for about thirty days. We had some steel, but there was no ammunition coming back from Iran. All that was unloaded and then sent across the Russian border. We came back to Bombay, India, unloaded the steel, and went in ballast from Bombay to Cape Town, South Africa. From Cape Town, we were supposed to fuel and take on stores. By the time we got there, there had been so many ships in and out, they had no stores to give us. So we ate chicken and rice from Cape Town to Bahia, Brazil. When the pilot boat met us at Bahia, Brazil, he brought fresh fruit and South American steaks and ice cream and fresh milk, the whole works. (*Laughter*) We had a good landing at Bahia, Brazil.

We had about fifty people in the crew. They were shorthanded. I think it was fifty-six, originally, but we lost several along the way. They got sick.

We went around to what at that time was Dutch Guiana. We went way in, on a river to a bauxite plant. We loaded as much aluminum as they would allow going down the river without dragging. We went from there to Trinidad and topped off the bauxite. From there we came back to New York.

After we laid in the Hudson River off from Grant's Tomb for three days, they let us ashore. My total amount of time at sea was about eight months. I reported to the Academy and resumed my studies at Kings Point. I had a steam sea project and a diesel sea project. I had a lot of time to do it. In fact, they kept my sea project because they wanted to use it for training as a model. I continued my studies for the third assistant engineer's license at Kings Point and graduated in July of '44.

See chapter 6, "The Murmansk Run," for Henry Evans's next trip.

John J. Burke, Class of 1945

What was your feeling about the construction and the seaworthiness of the Liberty ship?

Great. You can see how many of those ships came back to the boneyards after they had gone on so long. One ship in particular was the *Jeremiah O'Brien*. I was on her in a typhoon off Okinawa, with Captain Jahns. When the trip finished, we found footprints on the walls of the galley where she had taken such a list that the crew had put their feet on the wall. We split up on the side gunwale,[2] which was normal for a Liberty, but she rode on. She could take anything. She was an old ship—I think she was built about 1943. She was a good ship. She could do a job without spending the time in port, and she could hold an excellent load.

After many years in the West Coast Reserve Fleet, the SS *Jeremiah O'Brien* was refurbished, and, still seaworthy, she operates as a museum in San Francisco Harbor.

11

THE PHILIPPINES

*During their occupation of the Philippines, the Japanese army
exercised iron-handed control over the civilian population. Japanese atrocities convinced many Filipinos that they had to fight
back with a vengeance. Pedro Beltran's interview sheds light on
the rapid transition of Filipinos from ordinary citizens into very
effective guerrilla forces.*

Pedro N. Beltran, Class of 1950

Born in Lubao, Pampanga, Philippines, Pedro Beltran describes his role
as a member of the Filipino guerrilla movement. Soft-spoken and genial,
Pete Beltran's actions during the war speak loudly concerning his com-
mitment to Philippine freedom.

**Will you please tell us some of your experiences during World War II
when the Japanese occupied the Philippines?**

I was a senior high school student when World War II broke out. As the
Philippines was under the United States, the Japanese lost no time invading the Philippines in accordance with their Japanese plan of an Asia Co-
prosperity Sphere. People from the cities and towns evacuated their homes
and fled to the barrios and villages. In the village where I lived, I saw several
Japanese soldiers coming. I thought they were nice people. I sort of greeted
them in a friendly manner. But they searched and boxed and slapped me
several times. I thought they'd kill me. They raided all the vacant houses;
they took all the foodstuffs available. Some women who were not able to
evacuate were raped. It was horrible. They told me not to escape and just
carry the foodstuff to the nearby town where they were camped. On our
journey to the town, I saw a few dead soldiers in advanced state of decom-
position on the road.

From 1942 to 1943, schools were closed. The schools that managed to open were required to teach Nippongo, the Japanese language. I had frequent bad experiences with Japanese soldiers because I did not bow very well, which is their style of saluting. I joined the Hukbalahap guerrillas operating in the lowlands sometime in April 1943 at Company B under the command of Captain Leonardo Fernando. Hukbalahap means People's Anti-Japanese Army. I participated in several encounters, such as the battle of Del Carmen and Calangyan, Florida Blanca. We also engaged in San Vincente, Lubao and Balite, Arayat, Pampanga, and the battle of Madama, Hermosa, Bataan. In 1944, I was designated as supply officer with the rank of second lieutenant. I was honorably discharged from active duty on December 5, 1945. The members of the Hukbalahap were mostly farmers, but the leaders came from the Socialist Party of the Philippines. Village or barrio people were organized to monitor Japanese troop movements so that evacuees could avoid Japanese raids. Japanese collaborators or civilian spies for the Japanese were investigated and, if confirmed as spies, they just disappeared and were killed. Crimes, rapes, and other criminal activities disappeared, and a sense of peace and discipline prevailed.

In a relatively short period, I was ordered to organize my own company, and I recruited young boys of high school age. To acquire more guns and firearms, we raided suspected gun owners, especially those who acquired firearms from soldiers who were in the Bataan death march.

The American liberation force that landed in Pangasinan in early 1945 arrived in Porac, Pampanga. We had already occupied and liberated the town from the Japanese forces. We caught a few Japanese soldiers whom we turned over to the Americans. From their uniform patches, the American forces belonged to the Thirty-fifth Division of the Sixth Army. An officer, whose family name was Moore, asked me to join them in their campaign to Manila to free the American prisoners at the Sto. Tomas University. He further told me that when we got to Manila, they would arrange for me to fly to the United States, have my physicals, and be one of them. I was almost tempted to accept the offer. But the Huks might not have favored the idea of my leaving them.

As soon as Pampanga province was liberated, the other group or faction of guerillas known as USAFFE units came down from the mountains. It stands for U.S. Army Forces in the Far East. Their members were recruited from the civilian sector, but some of their leaders or officers were ex-Philippine army officers. This group stayed most of the time in the mountains of Bataan and Pampanga, while the Huks were operating in the low-lands. The two groups were not on good terms. They even fought each other during the Japanese invasion. When their relations became very serious, I decided to go to Manila in order to resume my studies.

A competitive test was given in Manila around October 1946 for cadet-ship in the U.S. Merchant Marine Academy. I only had a vague notion of what "merchant marine" meant. In my mind and familiarity with U.S. Marines, I only entertained the idea of a military profession. But with the opportunity of going to the United States, I decided to take the exam. The Philippine government announced in the papers that the top one hundred qualifiers would be initially selected. We were more than 1,500 who took the exams. A second test would be given to determine the highest fifty who would be sent to the Academy. Due to time constraints, the second quali-fying exams were canceled. Classes in the basic school in San Mateo were scheduled in the first week of February 1947. The fifty who qualified had to obtain the necessary travel documents and travel by sea, which would take two weeks across the Pacific. So only the top fifty out of the initial one hundred qualifiers were picked. I was number forty-eight on the list.

The first group of fifty cadets boarded the SS *Marine Lynx*. It was a gray painted ship probably used before as a transport carrier. I never had any experience with sea travel. We had a sumptuous dinner when we left Manila, January 7, 1947. When we crossed the rough China Sea for Hong Kong, it was a most uncomfortable experience. The next morning, many of us were hanging on the ship's railing in an involuntary effort to give up the excellent food we had the previous night.

The ship proceeded to Shanghai. The Shanghai situation was worse than what I saw in Hong Kong, and this probably led to the collapse of the na-tionalist government.

Upon debarking in San Francisco, we proceeded to the cadet basic school in San Mateo. From six in the morning to ten in the evening, we went through a continuing series of indoctrination, orientation, training films, drawing supplies and personal necessities, and close order drill. Conditioned to more than three years of deprivation, the facilities and re-sources bordered on the fantastic. We were provided with everything plus a monthly allowance of $65, which was no mean amount in 1947.

After six months of basic training in San Mateo, we boarded a train for the three-day trip to New York and to our final destination at Kings Point. I was assigned to a room with two Americans, Paul L. Krinsky and John

MacKechnie. Hazing was expressly prohibited in Kings Point. Our class rates system was more humane and effective in instilling cadet discipline and drew the line between plebes and upperclassmen. There was mutual respect for human rights and the dignity of individuals. We completed our fourth-class or plebe training at Kings Point. I had a full year of basic training.

I reported to the district supervisor/commander of the New York Maritime Office. He gave me and the other Filipino engine cadets travel and subsistence tickets to go by train to San Francisco for our ship assignment, the SS *President Pierce*. We were very excited because the ship was scheduled to go to Manila, and we were looking forward to seeing our families after a year. We first docked in Yokohama, Japan, to unload army cargoes. While working on deck in Yokohama, a Japanese tried to talk to me in Filipino. I immediately concluded that he was probably one of the Japanese occupation forces in the Philippines. I got my leather stick and whipped the Japanese several times until I got tired. Afterwards, I went back to my cabin and sort of cried and felt sorry for what I did. Then the ship's captain and chief mate came to my room to give me a small glass of whiskey to feel better. They heard beforehand that I suffered during the Japanese occupation in the Philippines. I saw all kinds of ruthless punishment by the Japanese.

How did your war experiences, and your subsequent education at Kings Point, shape your outlook toward the rest of your career?

I have given you a compelling account of my life, times, the people and circumstances that helped develop my attitude and thinking. The sea training was an opportunity to work on shipboard, get along with other seamen, see foreign countries, and meet different people with varied cultures. What I also learned from my war experiences is the ability to bear hardships and to be of service to others.

After graduation, we all returned to Manila on board the SS *President Cleveland*.

Mr. Beltran joined the Philippine navy and later entered civilian employment.

12

PRISONERS OF WAR

The ordeals of merchant mariners caught in the Japanese occupation are grim reminders of the inhumane treatment that existed in prisoner of war camps. The odd situation of a Kings Pointer held in an Allied jail was yet another twist of fate that merchant mariners encountered in the war.

William T. Mitchell, Class of 1946

Recipient of two Purple Hearts, Bill Mitchell has made the most of his experiences. His ordeal during World War II did not deter him from moving forward in a maritime career. After graduating from Kings Point, Bill worked his way up the ranks to second engineer. He later married and went to work ashore. Mitchell states, "I went to work, took the examination and passed in San Francisco for the fire department, and I spent thirty years there." In retirement, he moved into the mountains nearby, where he served for twelve years as a volunteer fireman.

We went up through the Coral Sea, along Borneo, the Makassar Straits, and up in the Manila Bay. We arrived there the day after Thanksgiving of 1941. From there, when we checked in with all the people we wanted to unload from, they were kind of confused, because we weren't in our right place. To get the thing [cargo], they would have to remove the deck load of lumber that we had on board, and everything else. Anyway, they delayed things.

In the meanwhile, on December 8, the Japs attacked Pearl Harbor. I think they were behind the Date Line. It was December 7, but they hit us at the same time on December 8. They had different targets in the Philippines with their power [bombs]. The Japanese couldn't get off of Formosa until the fog lifted, and that determined the time that the planes would come in.

They would come in with fleets of twenty to fifty bombers. In the beginning, it was always high-level bombing, and they were always very accurate. If you were a target, not necessarily the main target, if the planes were coming in formation, the guy that was over you would drop the bombs on you. We were very fortunate, because in the interval between bombs, we were missed. They were near misses, causing all kinds of damage down in the engine room and other parts of the ship, breaking things loose and stuff like that. We weren't hit at that time.

We were told to anchor under the guns. At that time, they had what looked like five anti-aircraft guns. Since then I've found out that they had more. They hit them with the high-level bombers, and after they silenced the anti-aircraft guns, they came in with the dive bombers. The dive bombers had no trouble. They hit us and set us on fire. There were no [Allied] planes. And then they strafed. They strafed the lifeboats that we were hanging out until they were unusable. They also set a fantastic fire on our ship, the *Capillo*, and she burned in two places. The steam smothering system was ruptured, and the fire pumps carried away on account of all of the shaking up that the ship got.

There was forty-six crewmembers, from the captain on down. We abandoned ship and went to Corregidor. The provost marshal did not want merchant men on the island, and they said that they were going to get us off that evening. The MPs put us on a ship. Then the Navy came on board at the back end and took off the engineers that could operate steam. They wanted some guys to work there. They included me, a cadet, along with the engineers. In the morning, we'd get back and we were exhausted, so we'd eat wherever we could. It was pretty confusing. Then we'd just have to flake out, maybe on the side of the road. Then we'd get picked up by the MPs again. We'd end up in front of the provost marshals. By this time, he was pretty provoked at us, and he put us back on another boat that night to go to Manila. The Navy came on the back gangway and took us off again, so we didn't know how we stood. We helped them. All the fellows were that good. And this went on for four days from the night of December 26, 1941.

This marshal told the MPs not to leave us and not to release us to the Navy. They sent us to Manila. When we got in there, well, we were exhausted. I went to a hotel with all the rest of the fellows. All the help had left the hotel, and I just grabbed a room. There was a bed there with a sheet on top. That was all right. I was able to sleep there. I was not able to get my books for my sea project, though, and at the time, I thought: "This won't be long. I'll be back in the States very shortly, within a month or two." As it turned out, they were damaged in the bombing. I wasn't in that area of the ship, and my room was banged up bad. I wouldn't have been able to get them anyway.

We were in Manila on the night of January 1, 1942. At this time, Manila had been declared an open city, and the Japanese soldiers came in on bicycles. These guys were pretty good. First they sent our own people around to get everybody to come downstairs, but the guys didn't get me and wake me up. They sent two soldiers up there, and they found me. It was like one of these hospital beds that are high, and there was no sheet. This one soldier couldn't wake me up either. Evidently, I'm a sound sleeper. So he grabbed me by the foot and rolled me off the bed. The other guy is standing there with his gun and bayonet looking at me. He didn't speak English, but he wanted me to get out there and go downstairs. I said, "I'm going to put some clothes on." I had shorts, pants, and stuff like that. I got dressed. They were reasonable enough that they allowed me to do that. Then they took us downstairs. From there, we went to the University of Santo Thomas. I was there for a year and a half.

There was a plaque that said it was the oldest school under the American flag.

The conditions were very poor. Santo Thomas was a day school. And as a result, there was no hot water and no showers. There were conventional wash basins and conventional heads, but outside of that there were no other facilities. We had to sleep on the floor.

There were also no cooking facilities in the college. They had told us to take a brown paper bag with a certain amount of food from the hotel, and when that ran out, we were out of food. We had no way of getting food anywhere, so it's kind of funny, but we improvised. We took on, let's say, a hot dog stand that they had and volunteered to cook for the prisoners. Nobody else wanted to do it, really. The cooks didn't want to do it either. So it was the crews of the engine rooms and the deckies down in there. We were mostly making up soup. We got sufficient food, because we were able to kind of help ourselves augment our diets quite a bit. We were there for about a month until we finally put out a meal that got us fired.

At this particular time, they were bringing in supplies. They would give you so many cardboard boxes of food, and you looked through them, and then you tried to make up a soup. It was American food at that time, mostly canned beans and chowders, stuff like that. Then they gave us some cans of pilchards in tomato sauce. Now pilchards, in case anybody isn't familiar, are big sardines. They said, "Put everything in the soup." We said we didn't think the pilchard should go in. But we put them in, and it came out looking very, very vile. The skins came off the pilchards and floated to the top, and when you picked it up to ladle it out, well, the skin of the pilchards would be there.

There was such an uproar that they immediately made us captains of the heads. Everybody had diarrhea in one form or another, and the lines were horribly long. They figured out that they had to save paper. So one guy's job was to sit outside the head, and when you passed, he gave you four sheets of paper, and that was what you got.

When the American food ran out, we were always eating a type of soup. It had native vegetables, not American vegetables. To this day I can't recall what they were. Occasionally we would have rice or corn. And that was the extent of things. There was a certain amount of fresh fruit that came in, but I don't recall that it was available.

I would estimate that at one time there were as many as seven thousand people in there. The *Capillo* was not the only ship with sailors in there; there were others there, too. People tried, in the worst ways, to see what they could do to help everyone.

After we were there a year and a half, the Japs decided that there was a certain element that they had to be careful of that they could not control by threatening, and I was included in that group. They took people between a certain age group that were not married, that did not have any relatives on the islands or in the camp, who they could use to threaten the people. I was probably around twenty years of age. About six hundred of us were put into a separate camp. There were thirteen naval nurses that were caught in Davao in the southern island, and they were sent down with us. Those were the only women.

We were sent to the University of the Philippines Agricultural School at Los Banos. It had been in use for a long time. They were developing trees down there, different plants. They had coffee beans growing there that we could use, and we did have coffee. Down there the food may have been a little bit better.

There were six hundred able-bodied guys there, and the Japs finally found out that we were more than taking care of ourselves and taking care of the jobs as they needed to be taken care of. We had to revamp the septic system by digging big latrines on the side of the hill where one would overflow into the other. These were just for the prisoners. You would be assigned different work jobs.

I had a hard job, making coconut milk. I got up around three thirty in the morning and would have to go to the kitchen, where they built a kitchen for us to make the coconut milk. I would actually work until about four o'clock the next day. We would work that long. Then you were on free time, and then you had dinner after that. You always had to roll up your bed. I would just sit down at the end of the bed, and there was a Dutch fellow on my right, and an English guy on my left. He was older, and he would eat early, so he could keep an eye on the line where they fed us. He would wake me up when the line got short, and I'd get up and eat. He was very faithful about that. He was always Mr. Schaefer, and I was always Mr. Mitchell. I never got past it.

At one point, the fellows there started up baseball teams, and did Olympic trials, and we were reduced to transplanting palm trees. That's how they would keep us busy.

We lost a tremendous amount of weight, and I was a pretty healthy fellow when I went in. The only way I could tell how much we had lost was by putting our fingers and our thumb together, and this would go around the waist. Toward the end there, the Japanese ran out of food, and they were actually going to shoot us the day before we got out.

In the meantime, the work we had done in the first camp was to establish fields, where we planted different foods. Then they came along and said, "You move over to the other side of the fence," and they took all the food away from us. So we were basically not too well off at all. We were down to field corn, and stuff like that.

There were some attempts to escape, and they were successful in all cases. In fact, even I had been outside the camp. You'd meet up with the guerrillas, and they would feed you. Sometimes they would give you more than you could eat, so that you'd have a guilty conscience. You'd stop, and then bring it back in. But they didn't want us. They said that we were too run down. They said "You'll be safer in one place, rather than roaming around out there" because we didn't know the language and stuff like that.

That's what we were basically saying. You don't come in and release 2,200 people without quite a bit of organization. We got out on February 23 of 1945. The Americans used paratroopers, guerrillas, amtracs, and other equipment, to come behind the lines, and rescue us. At this time, the

Japanese moved us from one side of the camp at Los Banos over the fence to another set of barracks that they had built. There was a large detachment of something like eight thousand Japanese soldiers within about eight miles of the camp. How they snuck in behind them, I don't know.

One of the things characteristic of the Japanese was that they insisted on morning calisthenics. And when the guerrillas attacked and the paratroopers dropped in at 0700 hrs, close to one hundred guards were caught doing their calisthenics and couldn't get to their guns. This was poor thinking on their part. But, as we were supposed to be shot in about two hours at roll call that morning (0900), we really didn't have too much sympathy for them.

The Americans knew that we were going to be shot. We were supposed to be shot the previous day at evening roll call, and they set up a figure-eight bombing with about twelve P38s. What they did is make a big figure eight, come down to attack, and then go back up. As some of them were flying, some of them were going back to reload, others were being reloaded, and some of them were coming back. And this spread out over about three hours back until roll call time. How they knew about it, I don't know, but they did.

The people, especially the guerrillas, were taking no prisoners, and I didn't see it. Now, some escaped, but they didn't take any prisoners that I know of. Most of the Japs that I came in contact with were fairly reasonable. You did what you were supposed to do, and you watched it. I was very surprised, but most of our mistreatment came from one member of the Kempetai, which is tough on its own people. That's their military police. It's like the Gestapo. We found out later that this guy, [Lt. Sakaadi] Konishi, who really gave us a bad time, was one who had escaped. He did not do his morning calisthenics. But he was later tried as a war criminal and was hung.

By the end, they had sent down women and children without families or people to take care of them. This increased the load up to 2,200 people in the camp, and this was the number liberated. They didn't lose any American forces or the prisoners, and they lost two guerrillas. It was a very successful operation. But two days afterwards, this guy Konishi rounded up those eight thousand troops and went down and attacked a neighboring village, wiping out the whole thing, women and children. I think it was pretty close to a thousand people that he killed, which was very sad. We didn't know about it until after.

I was met by my public relations officer, some people in San Francisco, and also Mr. Crossman. He was very influential. When they saw us, the first day we were there, they had a uniform for me. They met me at home, and the first thing they asked was, "Do you feel like you'd like to continue in the Cadet Corps?" I said, "I'd love to." Then they said "Fine," they'd give me a month off.

Roosevelt died right after that. That was kind of a shock. I didn't expect it at all. Anyway, we went on from there, and they treated me very well. After a month off, they sent me down to the Cadet Basic School in San Mateo, and they treated me very well. They said I should go through my indoctrination again. I was not used to studying anymore, and to be very frank with you, I was having a hard time with it. They put me into quite a physical regimen. It built me up quite a bit, and evidently I recovered pretty well. They had me running around the field, where I had only completed a slow walk the first time. I had unlimited time in the gymnasium, and also in the swimming pool, which was very good therapy, besides going to classes. Whatever the classes were at that time, I went to them all.

I finished at San Mateo in 1945. I was down there on VJ Day. I was glad that it was over because I had a couple of brothers and an awful lot of friends that were in different services. I had no hard feelings. Everybody [Japanese] that I was mad at was gone, as far as I was concerned. They had been wiped out.

In the prison camp, I learned that you had to face up to people, and that different people were capable of different things, including yourself. You had to be able to size them up. I had a lot of good help in prison camp too. I met a lot of nice people there. When I came back, there were a lot of good people in the Cadet Corps, like the trainers, and the medics that I was sent to because I had a tremendous amount of tooth damage. There was a certain tenacity, if you want to put it that way, among all of them. They all had a purpose, and they seemed to stay with it. I admired that and tried to stick with it.

I had to start all over. I was reassigned after going to the Basic School, and those people were very helpful. I was reassigned to another ship, the *Villanova Victory*, to complete my sea projects. It was supposed to be a short trip up to China and then back to the west coast, and then I was supposed to go back to the Academy to finish. But as it happened, the captain and port captain disagreed on so many things that they could never get together, and we were sent all over the Far East.

I came back to Kings Point, and then we went through the license preparation course. I was there from December to July of 1946, when I graduated as third assistant engineer, unlimited, unlimited tonnage.

In 1978, I came back to Kings Point and was presented with an award that I had earned when I was a cadet, which amounted to sixteen medals and decorations. I have also received two Purple Hearts and one POW medal. Then I have various assorted American naval medals from the Pacific. Also, because of the trips around the world, I have the Mariner's Medal, which is quite high up there. I also have an award for the sunken ship. I have all the Philippines medals that came through. There are about four of them. I also received a medal from Nationalist China.

Japanese aircraft bombed the SS *Capillo*, 5,135 gross tons, in Manila Bay on December 8, 1941. The ship was rendered useless, and U.S. Army forces had to sink the *Capillo* on December 11, 1941. Of the crew of thirty-six men, no one was killed or injured, but six of the crew died while held captive by the Japanese.[1]

Steve Antos, Class of 1944

During the war, Steve Antos served in the Atlantic and Mediterranean theaters of operations and made more than twenty Atlantic crossings. Following hostilities, he was employed in Sharon, Pennsylvania, by the Westinghouse Company in their Transformer Division for thirty-three years. He later reactivated his engineer's license, and for ten years he sailed on the Great Lakes, until retiring in 1989. He was an avid Major League baseball fan, especially of the Cleveland Indians. Musically inclined, he played the guitar, harmonica, and piano.

My first assignment as a cadet was on a Hog Islander built in 1919. It used to be the *Salvation Lass*. I will never forget. It started in 1944, when we arrived in Casablanca. We walked into a native quarters, inadvertently, and we were arrested. We were charged as prisoners of war and taken to jail. That was an experience. There was an injured British officer that they threw in there. He was bleeding from the mouth and the ears, and they paid no attention to him whatsoever. He was just laying there. We had to make some loud noises to bring the keeper's attention to the fact that there was an injured person in there at the time. Finally, they did come in. They dragged him out and closed the door quickly. The following morning, we were brought out and transported to another jail where there was a DPC, a disciplinary planning center, later on known as a concentration camp. This was an American-run facility, and I was an American citizen, but I was detained.

The men were in little two-by-two shacks, which they could hardly even stand up in. We could just barely make their faces out in the little screen in the window. We were subjected to probably fourteen to sixteen hours of work every day, pulling weeds or pulling nails out of the barracks they had taken down. Then we would have to sort the lumber. We were in there two days and two nights. We slept in tents, and believe you me, that sand gets mighty cold even in the middle of the summer. It gets cold.

Since I was a cadet, I had to be released by an officer from the ship that I had been assigned to. Our good chief steward came down, and through his efforts, we were released. There were three of us. There wasn't any reaction from the Americans operating the prison when we were let go. There was no chance to even ask why we were there. We were told that by the martial law we were prisoners of war with no charges, and if we behaved, why, things would go well for us. That's all we were let off with.

When we returned to the ship, she was already in anchor waiting to leave. On the Liberty launch transporting us back to our vessel, a fight had broken out. Somebody went overboard, and to my knowledge, they never came back out. We had to leave Casablanca because it had no facilities for water and oil.

I returned to the Merchant Marine Academy and finished training. I sat for my steam and diesel license in September 1944.

13

INDIAN OCEAN

The sea routes through the Indian Ocean were harrowing to those merchant mariners who braved submarine attacks and extreme heat to bring cargoes into port. The ports constituted a back door for delivering badly needed supplies to Russia and for military operations in southern Asia, such as the Burma campaign.

Jack R. Kersh, Class of 1944

Jack Kersh received his preliminary training at the Federal Training school at Pass Christian, Mississippi. After his sea training, he came to Kings Point. He graduated on November 10, 1944. After graduating from Kings Point, Mr. Kersh made supply runs in the Atlantic and Pacific theaters of the conflict in addition to the Indian Ocean.

When we got into the port of New York, they started loading cargo. We lost half of our unlicensed personnel, because the cargo said USSR. They knew that they'd most likely be going to Murmansk, and they were losing a lot more ships going to Murmansk that way than the other way.

When we got loaded and sailed out, we did not go with the Murmansk route. We went the long way to Russia. Before we left the United States, we were fitted with torpedo nets, the big old nets that you hang on the sides. Of course, they reduce your speed and all, but we got into a place where we used our nets. We went in convoy across the Atlantic and into the Mediterranean. Through the Mediterranean, we were under German air attack several times, especially off of Malta. I guess they were flying out of Italy. We arrived at the Suez Canal. As we entered, we raised our nets, and one of our nets was torn up. Apparently we were shot at with torpedoes in the Red Sea, but nothing happened. An agent came aboard and said, "How did you fare?" We said, "Maybe we lost two or three ships." He said: "See, you're lucky. The convoy ahead of you lost a third of its ships." We went on through the Suez Canal and got into the Red Sea, and they put us on our own. We went down through the Red Sea, the Indian Ocean, up the Persian Gulf, and then to a place in Iran called Khorramshahr. The Russians had truck drivers there. They'd come along the dock, eighteen-wheelers. The Russian drivers, they wouldn't speak to anybody, but they'd just drive everything off for Russia.

I was the deck cadet, and there was one engineering cadet aboard ship with me, and I worked with him quite a bit. One weekend we caught a ride into Basra in Iraq. I believe we went to stay at the YMCA in Basra, Iraq, for Saturday and Sunday, and then we went back to the ship. I was probably twenty years old. We discharged that cargo, then dropped back down to Abadan, Iran, loaded and came back.

Then we came on back to the States, and I was assigned to the Academy as a deck cadet. That was in the first part of 1944. I went through the Academy and graduated November 10, 1944.

James L. Risk, Class of 1942

After I came back from Russia the first trip, my following trip was to India. Went over taking P-38 aircraft on the deck, and also parts down below to India, into Karachi, for the Burma campaign. That was the equipment we were hauling at that particular point. Right across the Indian Ocean we were independent and had no convoy. However, across the Atlantic and then to Gibraltar down through the Mediterranean we were in convoy. But in the Indian Ocean, on the Red Sea and so forth, we had no convoy. We were independent.

When we got the P-38 aircraft on deck load into Karachi, the pier was up against a long peninsula of ground sticking out in the harbor, in the bay. We would off-load the aircraft onto the dock, and it was a very short run over to the pier. The ground on the peninsula made a rough landing field there. An hour after the aircraft hit the ground, it was up into combat because they needed them so desperately bad.

Peter Van der Linde, Class of 1944

We were on a voyage to India. We'd been to Bombay. It was the maiden voyage on the *Express*. This was now June 1942. I was twenty-three. We

3rd Mate—My Quarters. SS Fort Cumberland *1944,* by Robert Glenn Smith.
By permission of Robert Glenn Smith.

loaded a cargo of manganese in Bombay, and we were headed back for the
U.S. on our own. She was a fast ship. It was early [in the war], and there
were no convoys at that time. We did have a gun tub and 5-inch ammunition, but no gun. We were heading for the Mozambique Channel in East
Africa, where we were actually chased for awhile by a raider, believed to
be German. She would come up above the horizon, and you could see her.
We were zigzagging, of course, and we gave it full speed at that time. She'd
dropped down below the horizon and hid herself, and then a little later
she'd come up right abeam of us. She was a fast ship. We still kept ahead
of her.

That night about midnight, we were northeast of Madagascar in the
Indian Ocean. It was June 27, 1942. I was in my bunk, and two huge explosions occurred. One was in the engine room. This was a high-pressure

Gunners Practice. SS Fort Cumberland *1944*, by Robert Glenn Smith. By permission of Robert Glenn Smith.

Painting—Fort Cumberland '44, by Robert Glenn Smith. By permission of Robert Glenn Smith.

steamship, and apparently both boilers blew up, and a number of fellows down there didn't make it. A second torpedo went into the magazine, and the ammo all blew up. My job was to go immediately to the bridge and throw the codes over the side. I went to the bridge, and the captain handed me a steel box with holes through it so it would sink. I took it off the wing of the bridge and threw it in the water. I came back to the captain, and he gave me a briefcase that had the ship's money, $5,000, in it, and a pair of 10–50 binoculars, which I put around my neck. Then I went to my boat. We had just two lifeboats.

The ship went down so fast that by the time I got to my lifeboat that I was to be in charge of, it was gone. The ship was standing almost on her stern end, which had been washed into the water. Because we were moving so fast, the seas just came up and we were still going ahead and were taken right off the deck. So I went around to the other side of the boat deck, and we got that lifeboat away.

The ship went down in six minutes. A Japanese U-boat is what it turned out to be. It was pitch-dark and the monsoon season, very rough seas. I saw the submarine surface for a little while. She fired a couple of shells at the lifeboat, but they went way over us. It was too rough for them to aim, and then I saw it just submerge. We kept the boat there all night, looking for survivors and hoping to pick up people.

We sailed for over seven days toward East Africa. The first thing we did was heave up a standing lug sail, sort of a lateen-type rig. There were two of us aboard that could sail, so we changed off handling the tiller and the sails. We had forty-two people, with capacity for twenty-three or twenty-four. There was very little free board, which meant that the provisions were not too much and mostly consisted of pemmican in little cans. Pemmican was a Navy and military food, supposed to be very rich in proteins and things you need. The cans were little tiny cans, just a few ounces. And you would only take a little at a time. We had two water breakers in the boat. Unfortunately, during the voyage sailing toward Africa, one of our men drank a lot of salt water and just went out of his head. He didn't know what he was doing, but he opened the water breakers up and let all the freshwater run out. So we used the boat cover, which was in the boat. It had a lot of salt from spray in it, but luckily there were rain squalls because it was monsoon season. We held it out over us and caught water in it. We gradually tried to fill the water breakers up. We had maybe three ounces of water a day, something like that. The crew was in pretty bad shape because of the hot sun during the day. Since we had to leave the ship so quickly, most of them had just maybe underwear on. It was an extremely hot area. But at night it got cold, and we'd see them shivering there.

We didn't have a sextant in the boat, so luckily we wanted to go due west to get to Africa. We just took the North Star. As long as you kept the angle between you and the North Star about the same, you went right along a parallel of latitude, which we did. We sailed right into the Mozambique Territory, which was Portuguese East Africa at that time.

It was sort of a funny incident when we came in. The captain was a very strict disciplinarian. He had been in the German navy years and years before that, but had come to the States and become a skipper and was a good man. He looked through the binoculars at the beach, which was finally there, and he said to me, "Mr. Van der Linde, there's women on the beach, and I want no talking to them when we get there." So I told all the fellows, "Look, just line up when we get on the beach and keep cool." Then he handed me the binoculars, and I looked through, and there weren't any women on the beach. It was just great big black rocks out in the water.

There weren't any people on land. It was solid jungle. The boat turned over just as we got on the beach, and everybody got out safely. Then, of course, we started to think about how we were going to get out of there. There was nobody there. We did make a couple of little hikes into the jungle, but you just couldn't go anywhere. You needed a machete to get through. And we couldn't find any water. We finally found some stagnant brown water, which we took. We had matches, and we started a fire on the beach. We took that water, and we caught those little sand crabs, put them in the water, and sort of made a broth out of that. That's what really kept us going for four or five days on the beach.

After awhile, we could hear natives in the jungle. They signaled by tom-toms, but they never came near us. The captain told me to get one member of the crew that was in good physical shape and set out for a settlement to get help. Everybody was sitting around on the beach. So at four one morning, another ordinary seaman and myself started walking down the beach. We went southward and walked and walked, and it was quite an experience. One time, I almost went down in quicksand. I saw an old native lady, all by herself in a little village of grass huts. Nobody else was there. She actually pulled me out. Then she led us around another way so we could get around that.

We kept on going a second day. I met a man in the jungle, and he just stood there. I had my license taped to me in case we were sunk, and on the license it had a picture of a steamship. So I put that in front of him, and I said "Bang!" and "Sank," and all that kind of thing. I think he understood roughly. He was with two of his sons, and he said something to them, and then we followed them. They took us to a village, and I'll never forget, they brought out half coconut shells filled with ice-cold water. We stayed there and waited for awhile, and they brought in a Portuguese administrator. He and two Mozambique soldiers went back with us, and we finally arrived back where the fellows were on the beach. Then those soldiers shot a springbok, like a deer, and they put it on a spit. I remember all night roasting this thing over a big fire on the beach.

The next morning, we all went to this little village on an old bus along a sandy road. That thing couldn't make any of the hills, and all the crew would have to get out and push. But we finally got out to a little town, and they had a hospital with about four or five beds in it. We settled in the hospital for about forty-eight hours. It's the only hospital I've ever seen where they served beer. Then they took us to the biggest town in Mozambique. We stayed there for a couple of days. We got some clothes, and then we got on a train, which took us right through the Krueger National Park. They would stop when they'd see elephants or lions and things like that. So it was an interesting trip to Johannesburg.

Then we caught a ship back to the U.S. It was an old passenger ship, one of the old Eastern steamships. It was a terrible old thing, but it got us back safely, and then we just went right back to sea on another American Export Line ship. I just went all over the world, in every ocean.

The Japanese submarine *I-10* torpedoed the SS *Express* at 0030 hours on June 30, 1942. Torpedoes struck the ship, and it sank stern first within eight minutes. Eleven crewmen and two Navy Armed Guard were lost.[1]

14

NAVY

Many Kings Pointers volunteered for active Navy duty and served with distinction. Often going into harm's way during their Kings Point sea training, Kings Pointers had a solid basis for the trials they encountered aboard Navy vessels after graduation. A number of Kings Pointers, such as Rear Admiral Carl Seiberlich, chose a Navy for a lifetime career. Following this tradition today, upon graduation Kings Pointers receive a commission as ensign in the Navy Reserve, and many go on active duty.

Kenneth A. DeGhetto, Class of 1943

I got my license about October 6. I was nineteen, just about nineteen and six months old when I got my third assistant engineer's license, and I went into the Navy as an ensign. I was assigned to the USS *Cimarron*, which was a fleet oiler, AO22. It was the class oiler for that type of ship. We were very heavily armed. There were only two tankers that were left when I got on that ship in November 1943. And I became "A" division officer. We had about four 5-inch guns, two forward guns in turrets. Radar-controlled. The forward two guns were 5-inch guns in turrets. It was fire-control radar. And they were very heavily armed. We had, I think, twenty 20-millimeters, and eight 40-millimeters. When you were in the engine room, and they were firing those guns when we were under attack, you know, you thought the whole place was going to shake apart.

One other interesting thing. I was going to pick up the ship in San Francisco. So I took the train out to San Francisco, and I stayed in the YMCA. By the way, the *Cimarron* was the only ship that was not sunk that was on the Tokyo Doolittle raid. It was part of the task force on that raid. The Japanese had said they were going to sink every ship that was on that raid, and they did, except one. That was the *Cimarron*. I was not aboard on the Doolittle raid.

The ship had not yet arrived when I reached San Francisco. In the meantime, they asked me to, or I was assigned, now mind you, I'm nineteen and a half years old. Fortunately, I'd been to sea, and I think I grew up. And I'd lived away from home, because I was a handful when I was a kid. So it wasn't new to being away from home or anything like that. But they made me a shore patrol officer in Oakland from midnight to six in the morning. So being that I was young and real "smart," I would go over to Oakland, go to the all-night movie, show them my shore patrol badge, which I used to wear on my arm, sit in the back row. When it was six o'clock, I left. (*Laughter*) I was not about to get involved with any of the drunken sailors or anything. That's where I did my shore patrol duty, watching the late movie.

When the ship came in, I got aboard the ship. When I first got there, our base was Hawaii, in Pearl Harbor. Soon after, I was on my first of seven battle operations, where I wound up getting seven battle stars on my Pacific Ribbon. The first one was Kwajalein Island. And as we took bases, they became basically the place where we would pick up our fuel, from the merchant tankers that would come out to meet us. At the island just captured, the *Cimarron* traveled right with the fleet.

Now one of the interesting things, you talk about a Kings Point education, and the experience of recalling the old chief saying: "Don't tell me you know when somebody with experience like me asks you, 'Do you know what's wrong with it?' Say 'No,' because he may tell you something you don't [know]." I boarded the *Cimarron*, which was commissioned in 1939. It was a class Navy ship. It had a problem with the midship pump ever since it was built. Every now and then, the head would crack off. The piston head would crack. And being that I was "A" division officer, that came under my responsibility. Sure enough, when we got out to Hawaii to pump the fuel oil from one tank to another, it happened again. So I went down with the chief. We took the pump apart, and I said, you know, chief, all you have to do is make this adjustment and repair the pump. I solved the problem that they had not been able to solve. Very simply, the ring on the piston head would move, and eventually get snapped into the steam inlet port and open up. When it hit the port, of course, then it would crack the head off. My idea was to drill a hole through the ring into the piston head, make it big, put a pin in, and that ring would be able to still deflect, but it can't rotate. They never had the same problem again. I really gained a lot of respect from the enlisted men. I was able to solve that problem. And I relate that to my Kings Point experience.

For the record, could you describe some of the campaigns that you were in? I know you mentioned Kwajalein Island.

Yes, that was the first one, then the Truk operation. Basically we traveled right with the fleet, and if anything, we were under air attack only. I never had a surface action. We would fuel the fleet ships while under way, then stay off away from them while they were in bombarding the Islands. We would fuel the surface fleet. We would take two ships, the heavy ones on the starboard, and the destroyers and DEs on the port while at sea, under way. One of the lieutenants on deck and I became real friendly. He was a career enlisted man in the Navy. He was a chief, and when the war started, they made him a lieutenant. They just needed officers with experience, and he was one of the deck officers there. They had a system of transferring the hoses from our ship over to the ship we were going to fuel, and working with him, I helped him develop a better way to do it by having a heavy cord line go over versus a wire. I had mechanical drawing ability, having learned it in high school. So I drew all the drawings up, which he then submitted to the Navy, and eventually that's the way the tankers were all instructed to follow the revised fueling system. And when we needed more fuel, we'd come back to one of the nearest islands recently recaptured to take new supplies from a merchant vessel. Our ship, we carried a million gallons of aviation gas, thirty thousand barrels of diesel, and Bunker C for the carriers.

What battles were you in?

The Philippine operation, the Philippine liberation, and Iwo Jima, and Okinawa. At Okinawa, we were under pretty heavy suicide attacks quite a few times. We made four different trips there. We used to steam in between the islands, and the ships would come in and fuel. At night they would cover us with smoke. Fortunately, we weren't hit. One of the other tankers that was beside us got hit one day, and it's so many years ago, but at the same time, if I watch a wartime picture and see suicide planes coming in, I still get that little bit of thought. I was in the engine room most of the time, but occasionally I'd go up just to see how things were.

The operations in which our ship earned its battle stars were the Kwajalein Islands (part of the Marshall Islands); the Truk Island raid, which was a naval base for the Japanese; Eniwetok Atoll; the Marianas, which were Saipan, Guam and Tinian islands, all taken from the Japanese (no battle star was awarded for this raid); and the Iwo Jima operation. We returned to the States in October/November 1944 for repairs and then returned to Leyte Gulf shortly after the invasion and Okinawa. Other island areas where we traveled but did not participate in the takeover battles were Palau in the Solomon Islands and Ulithi Atoll in the Admiralty Islands. Ulithi was one of the major ports used by the U.S. fleet when stepping off on the Philippines and Iwo Jima operations. I recall one day when we were in Ulithi when a Japanese sub entered and torpedoed one of the ships in the harbor. Also, there were other places we stopped.

When I came back, some time in early '45, maybe May or June of '45, I came back after the Okinawa operation, and I was assigned to a new ship being built for the Navy, the USS *Taconic*, which was a communications command ship. I was a lieutenant jg and assistant engineering officer. I took the engineering crew up to Newport, Rhode Island, for training while the chief stayed down at the Brooklyn Navy Yard with the ship. At one time, we took the crew down to Philadelphia for firefighting experience, training for about two or three weeks. Then we came back up to Newport. While we were at Newport, the Japanese surrendered, and the war ended.

I had enough points to get out, but I felt I wanted to be a career naval officer. I had already married. Recapping, the USS *Cimarron*, my ship, came back in late October of 1944. The ship came back to San Pedro. I took the first fifteen-day leave. Since I had been in battles I had the priority, and I flew across the U.S. in a DC3. When I arrived, my parents had brought my girlfriend with them to LaGuardia Airport. We had been engaged when I was commissioned. In those days to do what married people did, you had to get married. So on the way home to Clifton, where my parents lived, I asked my fiancée, Helen, if she would marry me, and she said yes. I guess anybody could have given or gotten 1,000 to 1 odds that this marriage would last, but on November 15, 2004, we will celebrate our sixtieth anniversary.

George F. Koury, Class of 1943

First trained as a merchant mariner, George Koury had the unique experience of pursuing Japanese merchant ships in the Pacific.

The Navy was interested in seeing how well we could compete against the Naval Academy. So somehow, some way along the line, they picked me to go to submarine school. I went up to submarine school. If I recall correctly, there were about 172 in the class at submarine school. There were 171 Naval Academy graduates and me. This is in New London, Connecticut. Actually, some of the men that were there had come back from the USS *San Francisco* and had lost their ship. Some of them were lieutenant commanders, and lieutenants, and jgs, but the majority of them were kids just out of the Naval Academy who had just graduated. The class of '44 was graduating in '43. They were a great bunch of men. I was the maverick in the group.

And what were some of your experiences in the training that reflected the attitudes toward this one Kings Pointer?

Well, part of our training was going to sea on submarines. Of course, they were archaic submarines, the old O class, and they had the *Cutlass* and the *Cuttlefish* there. The *Cutlass* and the *Cuttlefish* were a little more modern. We'd get out on the Sound, and they were teaching OOD [officer of the deck] training, and of course I had a lot of training having been to sea before. They would take a box in man-overboard drills, and heave it over the side, starboard side, port side. I had various ways of picking it right up on the submarine. Either you made an end around, or you backed out on a Y, and picked it up. The first time they threw it over, I said, "Hard right," and nothing happened. "Hard right" again. Nothing happened. So I told the helmsman, "I said I want to go that way." When I got back, I had a little note in my box. If you had two of these you had to leave the submarine school, and that was it. A little note in my box to go see the officer in charge. So I went over there, and he looked at me, and he said, "Mr. Koury, in the U.S. Navy, we don't use 'hard right,' or 'hard left.' It's right rudder, or left rudder, right 15 degrees rudder."

How long was your training at New London?

It was three months. I learned a little bit about the propulsion, the diesel engines, and to take care of the battery. Diesel-powered with battery propulsion. In effect, it was mostly a hazing operation. I mean, you'd go out to sea and you'd be the diving officer, and when you'd say "flood," they'd pump, and when you'd say "pump," they'd flood, just to see how rattled you would get under the circumstances.

So they were as much interested in your temperament, or stability of temperament because of the rigors of undersea warfare patrolling.

That's correct. They also screened you very well for claustrophobic tendencies. You made ascents in the diving tower, and they'd put you in a small compartment with pressure of fifty pounds per square inch, where you were almost toe to toe, and shoulder to shoulder. But it was a great experience. The men were outstanding. They were no different from the kids that I went with here [Kings Point]. They were just darn good, wholesome American boys.

Because of my standing in the class, I had my choice of duty. My first choice was Southwest Pacific; my second choice was Pearl Harbor. I got the first one. I had ten days leave, Christmastime. So I went home. I received a telegram changing my orders to the submarine USS *Barbero* (SS-317). I came aboard as the junior officer. On that submarine there were nine officers. There were two mustangs, six Naval Academy, and me. The *Barbero* was a thick skin. In the fleet there were two types: the thin skins and the thick skins. Initially, before '43, they were building them to test depths of 325 feet. Thick skins, the test depths were 475 feet.

The *Barbaro* left New London stopping in Key West for additional training and then through the Panama Canal to Pearl Harbor. There she was assigned her first patrol area. Intelligence suspected that the Manila-based Japanese fleet would transit San Bernardino Straits to engage the Seventh Fleet. We were assigned the duty of remaining in a one-mile-diameter circle at the eastern exit to San Bernardino Straits and report when the Japanese fleet was seen transiting the Straits. We were not permitted to fire at any targets. Our job was to remain unseen by the enemy and report their makeup, of course, and speed in the hopes that we may trap them.

We sat in this one-mile circle for ninety days, surfaced at night, submerged during daylight. We made no contacts with the Japanese fleet. We were relieved on station by a sister submarine. Shortly thereafter, the Japanese fleet did come through San Bernardino Straits, and the Battle of Leyte Gulf was the result. We were ordered to Perth, Australia, for refit.

The *Barbero* left on her second war patrol transiting Lombok Straits for entry into the South China Sea. Lombok Straits was protected by shore batteries, Japanese aircraft, and three destroyers, Shake, Rattle, and Roll. Submarines operating from Perth normally transit these straits at night on the surface. Since we had the advantage of radar and the Japanese did not, the submarines managed to stay ahead of the shore-battery firing and keep away from the destroyers.

The Americans were not as skilled in operating wolf packs as were the

Germans, but the submarine force was attempting to use and develop tactics for wolf pack operations. The *Barbero* in her second patrol had been joined by *Redfin* and *Haddo* as a wolf pack.

Barbero, en route to the patrol area off Manila, made contact with a medium size "transport." We made a submerged approach and fired two torpedoes. Neither hit. It appeared that our TCD (which helped decide on the target's course and speed and set the spread of the torpedoes) seemed to be faulty. We headed for an optimum attack course and fired a torpedo with a zero gyro angle. It hit, and all indications were that the target was destroyed. We encountered many floating mines on our way to the patrol zone and exploded many by 20mm fire.

We made radio contact with our wolf pack and attempted to retain it. We were intermittently successful.

At first light one morning, we picked up a convoy of what we believed were four large targets escorted by four escorts. We kept them in sight on the horizon and continued to plot their maneuvers. We attempted unsuccessfully throughout the day to contact *Redfin* or *Haddo*.

Finally our captain, Cdr. I. S. Hartman, decided that we should do something so that this convoy did not escape. He maneuvered *Barbero* on the surface to become the third ship in the column. We ran for approximately two hours in this position still trying to reach *Redfin* or *Haddo*. Suddenly someone in the convoy decided that there was one ship too many. They fired a star shell and discovered us. *Barbero* moved away from the convoy, and in the dark night ran toward the horizon on its 21–22 knots with two escorts chasing. *Barbero* made a 180 and on the surface destroyed the largest ship of the group. In the meantime, the convoy had scattered and its escorts blocked our interception on the surface, and we could not close the range submerged.

Our guardian angel was looking after us since we later discovered that *Redfin* had made a submerged attack on this same convoy, fired six torpedoes in a spread to hit all ships in column (we were number three), and missed with all torpedoes.

We needed a reload of torpedoes and were directed to obtain them from a tender in New Guinea. On the way there, I was the OOD [officer of the deck] at first light, and I had a contact with a squadron of American B-26 aircraft. I fired a recognition flare. The planes turned and headed right for us. I immediately dove *Barbero* to one hundred feet. A spray of bullets was heard on the surface, and a few bombs were dropped. When we arrived on the tender, the captain and I visited the commanding general. He reported that we were firing at him. We informed him that those were recognition flares. "Oh," he said, "Is that what they were?"

We returned to the patrol area. One evening after receiving a top-secret message, we found ourselves approximately twenty miles away from the suspected target. On the surface in very shallow waters, we made a surface attack and put two torpedoes into a medium-size merchant ship. The increasing shallowness precluded the pursuit.

We were ordered back to Perth. Once again, we must transit Lombok Straits. The night orders stated to stay on the surface until first light, do not enter the straits, submerge and wait till night to transit on the surface. We had a nondirectional SD radar, which was to tell us when there were aircraft in its range. It picked up a flight before first light, and, before we could take any action, dove and bombed us close aboard. We dove. The destroyers picked us up and proceeded to work us over. They continued the attack for over thirty hours. We were forced down to seven hundred feet, far below our test depth. Our soft patches were leaking, and our pump room and our bilges were flooded. Shake, Rattle and Roll were still there and working us over. Finally the engineer came to the conning tower and reported to the captain that he did not have much "can" [storage battery] left. The captain stated that he wanted to take a periscope "look around" to see what we must do, and ordered one hundred feet and level off with the expectation that we would ease up to periscope (sixty-five feet) depth. We started to come up, but could not take the angle off the boat with all that water in our bilges and pump room. We kept coming up and broached in close proximity to a destroyer. They hit us with everything. Finally, the engineer reported to the captain that unless we surfaced we may not have enough power to do so.

Our captain was thirty-five years of age, and I was twenty-two. I believe that the average age of our crew could not have been over twenty-four. The captain looked at me and said: "We cannot live forever. If we must go, we'll take someone with us. Battle surface." We had pumped out a great deal of the water. We had a 5-inch 25 gun, twin 40mm, two 20mm, and some small arms. The gun access trunk was about the size of this table. The entire 5-inch gun crew would jam into this trunk. As soon as the ship broached the water, the crew would open the access door, man and fire the 5-inch gun with water up to their chests. They were very efficient. As soon as we could look in the periscope, we were surrounded by the heaviest rain squall. Visibility was nil. One of our reduction gears plus other things were damaged. We locked the damaged gear and put all our diesels on the other shaft and escaped to Perth. Tokyo Rose had reported us sunk.

It had been a good patrol. It lasted 65 days. We had, by our count, sunk four ships and severely damaged a fifth. Perth could not repair us, Pearl Harbor did not have the facilities for which *Barbero*'s next patrol was intended, so back we went to the Portsmouth Naval Shipyard, Kittery, Maine. We were undergoing conversion to a radar picket boat. During the time we were in the shipyard, Germany surrendered. The qualified submarine officers, of whom I belonged, and some of the crew boarded and sailed German U-boats into American ports. We appreciated our boats when we saw how Spartan the German submariners lived, no air-conditioning, no corking for the interior, etc. Their snorkel and torpedoes were very interesting.

The fleet was losing destroyers. Kamikazes were getting through to the main body. The destroyers in the picket lines were being attacked and often sunk. The theory was proposed that submarines be used instead of destroyers. They had already known how to form a picket line to rescue downed aviators. They would form this picket line submerged except for the conning tower and have a CAP (Combat Air Patrol) for their operations. After an air strike, the friendlies would pass over the submarine picket and trigger the IFF [Identification, Friend or Foe].[1] When a "skunk" appeared, the submarine would vector the CAP to intercept. If the kamikaze got past the CAP and headed for the submarine, the submarine would dive and the kamikaze would strike the water and be destroyed without any damage to any ship.

In Portsmouth, they loaded us with many black boxes. Hopefully we learned enough about them to be able to operate properly. *Barbero* was headed for the Sea of Japan as a submarine picket boat when the atomic bombs were dropped and the war ended. *Barbero* was later converted to the first missile submarine.

I stayed in submarines most of my career.

Launched on December 12, 1943, the USS *Barbero* was engaged in war operations from August 9, 1944, to January 2, 1945. She received war credit for sinking four Japanese ships, but the postwar Joint Army-Navy

Assessment Committee gave official credit for sinking three merchant ships totaling 9,126 tons during her patrol in the Java and South China Seas.[2]

Captain Francis J. Ford Jr. USNR (Ret.), Class of 1939

Captain Ford traveled in war zones throughout the conflict and endured the threats of German submarines and Japanese kamikaze attacks.

I was on the USS *Harris*, a passenger transport easily converted to troop carrier. Subsequently, I was prepared for the invasion of Saipan, where I acted as assistant ops officer, and the Army and Marine Corps fought there. We had originally been intending to reinforce the invading of Guam, but that was canceled. We landed our troops on Saipan. Subsequently, as we transferred staff when we were afloat, we went in the invasion of Leyte Gulf. That was the opening chapter of the loss of the war for the Japanese. There was a carrier battle, which is still in controversy. We suffered under kamikaze attacks, which were most demoralizing. They went for the center of the ship in order to kill off those who understood the operation of it.

And you witnessed these kamikaze attacks?

My brother and I, he was on another ship. We still argue over who shot down one of the kamikazes, and, really, that weapon was demoralizing. They spread gasoline—it was a terrible thing. On this occasion, if the kamikaze had one bomb, you can tell a pattern with bombs, we knew he would have another one, but, fortunately, he came down and winged over and scooted across the water into the side of another ship. They were lowering boats, and about four to six men in the boats were killed, and they found the Jap pilot's head in between. We went on to the Surigao Straits. There were constant kamikaze attacks.

What type of ship were you on?

C-3 cargo, carrying troops, a regiment of troops. We had seven to eight ships in our division, for which we were responsible to land so many. And kamikaze attacks, I remember one, coming off Panay. The commodore and I were standing on the bridge, under kamikaze attack, and on one attack plane, we saw him coming in from about six thousand feet. We knew what happened when they hit. The commodore looked at me, and I looked at him. We thought we were going to be hit, but he hit another ship. The kamikaze attacks were so devastating that the battleship commander coming into San Bernardino Straits wired that the issue was very much in doubt and recommended canceling the invasion. But here you had ships for two thousand miles coming on time elements with troops, supplies, ammunition, and so forth; you couldn't stop an outfit, an invasion force, by just canceling. First of all, an invasion was so complicated that, overall, to try to stop the movements, you would never get everyone to stop.

So it had to keep going forward.

Right. And we were successful.

Rear Admiral Carl J. Seiberlich, Class of 1943

Making a career of the Navy, Carl Seiberlich was the first Academy graduate to become an admiral. Admiral Seiberlich had primary responsibility for surveillance, reconnaissance, and antisubmarine warfare during the Cuban missile crisis of 1962. Seiberlich was chosen to command the USS *Hornet* (CVS-12) when the aircraft carrier picked out of the sea the crew of Apollo 11, including Neil Armstrong, first man on the moon. His ship also retrieved the crew of space mission Apollo 12.[3]

A few weeks after the Academy's dedication on September 30 [1943], I sat for my license. You took a commission in the MMR (Merchant Marine Reserve), and if you sailed, you could remain on inactive duty. If you stayed ashore for thirty-one days, you were called back to duty on the thirty-first day. I had really reached a conclusion that the merchant marine was not the place to be. I wanted to be some place where I could shoot back. So I went to the Navy and told them I would come on active duty if they put me in combat. It turned out, I was among the first to go into combat.

I applied for active duty in late October, and then I had to go take a physical with a lot of others. I was assigned to the USS *Mayo*, a destroyer, in December 1943. That's a *Mayo* 21 class. They were the first ships with an engineering plant where you had fire room, engine room, fire room, engine room. These were what they called the split plan, and they did that for damage-control reasons. If one was knocked out, the other would be available.

In 1934, this slide was put up at the general board of the Navy, and it was saying there will never be another submarine war because the sub-

marines were outlawed by the Versailles Treaty. So they voted not to put
any money in ASW [antisubmarine warfare], and the British were working
on an active sonar called ASDIC. So when the submarine war got perking
in early '41, they hurried back and they went to Key West and started the
Fleet Sonar School. He told me, "When you go into a major submarine war
with four qualified captains and no flag officers, they put one at eastern
sea frontier, one at western sea frontier, the Pentagon, and at Key West."
You know, we didn't have the equipment, and that's why all these ships got
sunk. If you took the number of merchant officers on board on December 7,
'41, 50 percent of that number was killed in the first year. Of course, you have
to understand that they added a lot during that time. As a matter of fact, the
highest attrition was experienced in the merchant marine until the Marines
at Okinawa caught up with them. So the Marines had the highest attrition
rate, and then the merchant marine second, and then the other services.

I was the navigator on the *Mayo* in the Atlantic and the Mediterranean.
The more MMR [Merchant Marine Reserve] badges that I saw on the uniforms of the people in the audience, the better the convoy went. We were
not allowed to wear our MMR insignias on active duty. It was only a reserve insignia. Actually, that badge was invented so officers would wear
the merchant uniform on active duty for training and put the badge on. I
said to the escort commander—I was a navigator for him as well as for the
ship—that I would like permission to wear my MMR badge when I'm briefing the convoy captains so they know I am one of them. I put it on before
I went in and took it off when I came out.

One of the most trying experiences that I ever had was when the early
escort commander called me in and said, "They have a secret thing called
Loran, and they are going to put one on each escort commander ship." We
were in the Brooklyn Navy Yard at the time. There was a three-day course
that you could add and take it. So I went down and took the course. While
I was gone, they put the Loran in, and we sailed with the convoy. There
were seventy ships, one destroyer, and nine DEs, so there were ten escorts.
Actually, we started out with five escorts, and then as the war went along,
they kept building more ships, particularly the destroyer escorts. As the
war progressed, there was more air protection and more escorts.

In any event, on this particular deal, we couldn't get any celestial obser-
vations. The weather was terrible. As we went along, I tried to take some
depth indications, but those charts were not all that accurate out in the
middle of the ocean. So here is this seventy-ship convoy with nine escorts.

Everybody is within five miles south of where we are. As we keep going across, the escort commander said, "You really know how to operate this thing?" I said, "Yes sir, I am doing the best I can with it." I was just absolutely ready to have a heart attack. But he stuck with me, and after a while all the other ships' positions were thirty-two miles south of mine. We hit Gibraltar right on the money. When we got into North Africa, some of my Kings Point friends were in the convoy, and they said: "Boy, we thought you were really screwed up. Everybody else had a position." I said, "The problem with you fellows is you didn't pay attention to dead reckoning." I didn't tell them that we had Loran because that was secret.

Our destroyer was about two thousand yards due ahead of the convoy. We were actually leading as the command destroyer. Everyday at noontime, every ship put up what they think their position was, and these were all recorded. We used signal flags up on the mast to recognize each other's position. Or what we thought the position was. If the escort commander made the decision, he could have stuck with them, and we would have changed course to get to Gibraltar.

It was very interesting, briefing the convoy before we sailed. A lot of people think that the convoy commodore really called the show. The answer was that he worked with the merchant ships and kept it all together, but the escort commander made the decisions.

Where do you think the most technological advances affecting the submarine war in the Atlantic happened more than anywhere else? The answer was the aircraft searchlight. What would happen is, you would be attacked by U-boats, and then they would go out on a wing [of the convoy] and come to the surface and get ahead of you and attack you the next day. Once they got illuminated by the searchlight—not that the airplane could hit it very well—the U-boats submerged, and then they couldn't catch up with us. So the searchlight made all the difference in the world. I operated on the theory that the most important thing was to get the ships to convoy where they were going. So the searchlight made all the difference in the world. Whether you sank the submarine or fended the submarine off, it didn't make that much difference.

We had submarine alerts all the time. They fired torpedoes at us and the whole ball of wax. We had numerous attacks. I remember one night we were under attack, and the U-boat was in the middle of the convoy. We went down at night in the opposite direction of the ships, dropping depth charges and rocking the merchant vessels. But we drove him down.

See, the submarine would go down once under depth charge attack. It was not just sinking, although you hoped you could. Having U-boats shooting torpedoes around, you would depth-charge the U-boat, and then you would go out 1,500 yards to make a turn to come back, and he would shoot his torpedo at you when you were making the turn. It was their survival, you know, in case you were going to come back and nail them again. The main thing was to drive him down so that he couldn't fire torpedoes, and then the convoy would get ahead of him. Then the aircraft kept them off the surface. So instead of dealing with them every day, you only dealt with them once, and then they were behind you.

We lost an old British ship crewed by Indians and some British officers in late fall of '44. I was twenty-one. It was back when we only had five escorts. They fell behind, and they got torpedoed. We went back to pick them up. They had only been in the water for probably thirty or forty minutes, but forty-five of the crew died of hypothermia. We were stacking the bodies on deck, and they took the ones they thought they had a chance to revive below. A doctor was down there.

We had a convoy with the French aircraft carrier the *Bearn*, which they [the Allies] had taken. It was down in the Caribbean, and they brought it up to New York. We were in dry dock in New York at the time, and the British battleship that had been shot up by the French off of North Africa came in. The crew of the French carrier and the British battleship met out on the pier and started the biggest fight I have ever seen. I stood up on the bridge of the *Mayo* in dry dock and watched these people. The Marines came down and stuffed everybody back on the British battleship. It was the *Prince George* or something like that.

It left New York, and they got the *Bearn* repaired, and then we took her into convoy in February '45. She lost steering control and hit a U.S. merchant ship, full of army troops. They were sleeping in the hold in bunks. It split the ship open, and forty or fifty of them ended up in the water. It was really rough. We were four hundred to five hundred miles off Boston in a great circle to Europe. We tried to pull them aboard. You'd throw them a rope, and they'd get bashed up against the side of the ship. We rescued four or five of them, and then there were the others we couldn't. A couple of the other escorts tried to do it. So these people were in the water in the cold. The water was sweeping over the deck of the destroyer, and our guys did a great job. We secured our guys with rope lines. I was on the bridge, of course, being the navigator. But it was terrible to see. There was one fellow that I talked to who had been asleep in his bunk, and the next thing he knows he is in the water. The ship just split open, and water washed in the hole and swept him right out. That was a "toughy" to take because they were our guys, you know.

Then we came back to the States. The squadron, which had been split up from convoys, was brought all together. It was either February or March of '45. We went through the canal up to Pearl, and I applied for flight training. On the way through, we joined a carrier force. We hit Wake Island on the way by. We watched airplanes strike and shore bombardment, and then we fired. Any carrier force going out to the Western Pacific would stop by Wake. What we were trying to do is destroy the water supply. They would put their hospital right up against the water supply, and the hospital got destroyed. Whether we did it with our shells or the bombers did it, I don't know. The Japanese were using them more or less as a hostage because by international rules there couldn't be an attack on the hospital. So they had a treaty through the International Red Cross and sent a hospital ship to Wake to take off the Japanese who were hurt in this attack and take them back to Japan.

We went on out to the war, and we were involved in escorting ships up to Okinawa. We did radar picket duty up there. In July of '45, up off the coast of Japan, we were told there was no opposition. Except they were saving ten thousand kamikazes for the invasion. People criticized President Truman. And I will tell you, if you had been up off the coast, and the intelligence was saying we are now able to jam your radar and jam your voice, and you won't have the fighter support that you had in Okinawa. It was a tough deal.

We would be on station for ten days. Then we would go back to Bombay to get refueled, and on two occasions the ship to relieve us got hit by kamikazes. We just had to do the best we could. Those Baka bombs were pretty bad, so it was a tough go. The U.S. had 32 ships sunk and 323 ships damaged at Okinawa. It was in the final stages of "mop up." The kamikazes were coming from other nearby islands.

The Baka bomb was towed underneath by what we call a Betty Bomber, which is a twin-engine bomber. They lit the rocket off it. The thing made about six hundred miles an hour, and the individual in there was folded in. So if you got a radar contact of the speed of a Betty Bomber, then the first thing was to try to get one of the fighters to take it on. Then you would look with your glasses and see the flash when they lit off the rocket. To try and stop it, you turned toward it and accelerated to 12 knots, and they get settled on you. Then you started speeding up to 36 knots right at it. He was locked into a different pattern, and so you could alter your course or speed, because after a while at 600 knots he wasn't that maneuverable. But we were fortunate in that it was always headed for some other ship. They were pretty dangerous.

We got up off the coast of Japan. Our radars were going to get jammed, and then Curtis LeMay made the big firebomb attack on Tokyo and burned the whole place down. There were 170,000 people killed, and they didn't quit. Then, of course, it was the first atom bomb and then the second. I have to give President Truman credit, because he told them that there was a third under construction, which is why the emperor stepped in. President Truman said [in effect], "I am going to keep dropping these things until you shrink." And it scared him into it.

There was a message sent out that said: "Cease-fire executed with Japs. If Jap aircraft should approach your ship, shoot the bastard down in a friendly manner." Part of the time we were up off the coast, and then the *Indianapolis* got sunk, and we were sent down to look for the survivors. We didn't find any, but the *Benson*, which was a ship in our squadron commanded by the former secretary of the Navy, Grant Klater, picked up quite a few of them. Then we got ordered to go back to Japan. I was the officer of the deck, and we picked up a sonar contact. I immediately called the captain and headed toward an attack, because I didn't want them to be in a position to fire at us. I remember when the captain came out on the bridge, the depth charge was starting to go. I said, "Captain, I gave an order to attack." He said that that was the right thing to do. I wanted to sink the submarine, but we drove him down.

I remember one thing that got me as scared as I ever was. We were anchored at Okinawa between pickets, and a kamikaze came in to go to the battleship *Pennsylvania*. They started firing 14-inch shells into the water, making big splashes. The kamikaze guy made a turn, and we got in between the ship and these 14-inch shells. You would hear things going over the top of the ship. It was no fun to be there. He hit the *Pennsylvania*, but it was superficial damage.

We were ordered to go into the bay, and we were in the second destroyer squadron in behind Arleigh Burke's squadron. We were the Atlantic Squadron. Being the navigator, I had my own binoculars, and I watched the whole thing. I was the officer of the deck when we took the ship in.

They said a Japanese naval officer would come aboard with a chart of the minefield. The Japanese naval officer came aboard, and he saluted the captain and put the chart down on the table. The captain is on one side, and I am on the other. The captain said to me, "Do you think we can trust this fellow?" Without looking up, he said, "I am a graduate of the University of California in Berkeley." I said, "Berkeley, oh my god, Captain, we are in serious trouble." But the truth of the matter is I could take a bearing on this, you know, and do this. I tell you, it was all business. He spoke good English. I only talked to him about the piloting and the charts and the mines. He was the enemy. We didn't talk about anything other than taking the ship in.

Since we were early in, we stole somebody else's anchorage, one thousand yards from where the *Missouri* was. So I watched the whole thing. I watched the boats come out and all that. Then they had a flyover. I have never seen so many airplanes in my life. I bet there must have been five hundred to six hundred airplanes that flew over. Then we were ordered to go into Yokohama Cove to meet a station ship in there. So we went in, and right after we anchored, a PBY came in and landed, hit a log, and sank. I was the officer of the deck, and I sent a whale boat over to pick them up. They came back aboard and were all standing on the wing. As it was sinking, the captain said to me, "Well, I'm in a lot of trouble." I said, "What do you mean?" He said, "Before I left, the commanding officer said don't land inside the cove." I said, "Well, he is going to notice you losing an airplane."

We had a chief supply clerk. He maneuvered everything he could think of. He decided that we were going to have a rifle for everybody on the ship. So he got this truck from some place, went over to the warehouse, which the Japanese were guarding, and got a rifle for everybody and brought them back to ship. I still have my rifle at home. Then we were told we were going to support the landings in the northern islands. So the communications officer, a fellow named Charlie Yates, who was a great golf champion before World War II, and myself were told to go up to Tokyo to MacArthur's headquarters and get all the charts and the communication stuff for landings up in Hokkaido. We went down to the train station, and there were hundreds of Japanese people standing down there, and every one of them had one of these white masks on. Charlie Yates was smarter than I because he took me by the arm up to the front. When the train came in, he held up his stripes and rapped on the engine, and the engineer let us in. We rode up to Tokyo in the cab of the engine. On both sides of the tracks, they leveled everything. They had left tracks and the fort because they wanted to use it, and they definitely did that. But as far as the eye could see, there were safes. All these buildings burned down in the bombing, and there were safes all over the place.

We got up to Tokyo and took care of our business. I went into a store with my occupation scrip and bought a little statue. I still have it. Then we rode the train back, got under way, went down to the Philippines and picked up the Twenty-eighth Infantry Division. We escorted them up to Hokkaido. This was the occupying force. We were there to offer gunfire support. We really reached the conclusion that Japan had been subdued in Tokyo Bay, but we weren't taking any chances. I went ashore on shore patrol the first day we were there. In fact, I ate army K-rations. I was glad I was in the Navy. There was no one on the streets. All the stores were closed, and you could see people peeking out their windows. The second day, they came out and sat on the porches. The third day, they opened the stores, and the soldiers went in with occupation scrip and really bought stuff. They had a lot of skis and stuff because Hokkaido is a big ski resort. The fourth day, they doubled the prices of everything because they found out we weren't going to steal it. Then we went back to Tokyo Bay, got the squadron together, and sailed for Charleston, South Carolina, to go out of commission.

William G. Holby, Class of 1944

With my background, the Navy assigned me to auxiliaries, which in my case happened to be an ammunition ship. I sailed on a Victory. It was one of ten Victories that were directly commissioned by the Navy to carry ammunition. They were not well prepared for ammunition; the holds were lined with wood everywhere for this task. The name of the ship was the USS Lakewood Victory, AK236. I was assigned as a watch officer and did navigating duties. I was an ensign in the Navy, and after a year and a half I became a lieutenant jg. But I did navigation duties mostly and was a division officer, and then we sailed across the Pacific. We loaded ammunition in the San Francisco area, Port Chicago, and took part in two invasions.

The first, most notable, was Iwo Jima and then Okinawa. And then we were pretty well empty as far as our ammunition was considered. So we went down to the New Hebrides in the South Pacific and cleaned out their naval magazine, which consisted of mostly smoke pots which they put on the deck, fortunately, because when we were up in the Philippines, we had a fire among the smoke pots, and this was another memorable experience, having a fire that's not actually rapid combustion. It was the smoking, but they were intensely hot, of course.

A smoke pot is a device; it's a canister. It's as big as a five-gallon bucket. You throw it into the water, and the water activates it, and it starts it smoking. It throws up a smoke screen around a ship as a defensive measure. So we had a gigantic smoke screen in Leyte Gulf at that time. So the tactic was to work our way toward the smoking ones, throwing all of them overboard on the way up.

Among the heroes of that occasion were two boatloads of men from the *Bucyrus Victory*, which was just in the next anchorage. They were an ammunition ship, and they volunteered. They came over and helped us do this job. So we got the deck cleaned off, and I don't know how long we were. It took an hour or two to do that. But they finally got everything under control without any casualties. They kept water running across the deck to cool the deck off because there was live ammunition underneath. This was in Leyte Gulf in the Philippines. This was in preparation for the final drive to Japan, which was interrupted by the Hiroshima bombing. So among all this, I attribute training here that saw me through a lot and permitted me to do my job, really. They sent me to several schools.

When I first docked in San Francisco, that was Treasure Island, that was a training center. "Pre-commissioning training center," they called it, where crews were assembled for ships. I went through a navigational course that they had, but it didn't improve on anything that I already learned here [Kings Point].

Those are the lively experiences, you might say, that I had, and it just shows the training prepares a person for what you'll inevitably meet at sea, and that's what they gave me here.

Paul L. Milligan Jr., Class of 1944

I accepted a naval commission. I was never really sorry for that, but in all deference to the merchant marine, I loved that too. I loved the people there. I owe the Academy a great deal of my success in life later. First of all, I think it made you a gentleman if you weren't one, and it certainly gave you discipline, that if you were to go in the Navy, you didn't have a problem. I saw people come into the Navy, let's say from the ninety-day-wonder school, that had no idea what discipline was all about.

I was assigned, got my Navy assignment to the west coast on an attack transport, brand-new again, another new ship. It was called the USS *McGaughin*, APA 199. McGaughin County, Kentucky, I think was the origin of that name. It was commanded by a very famous guy by the name of Myron C. Grable. He was the skipper of the *Oceanographer*, and at that time he was one of the pioneers in charting the Pacific. I don't know why he was then assigned to an attack transport because he had a wonderful mind. He was an Annapolis graduate, full commander at that time, and after made full captain, a real taskmaster and a wonderful captain to serve under.

I went on there as a dual role. I went on there as assistant navigator. I went on their Naval Intelligence, and we went off to the Pacific and stayed in the Pacific. Went to Guadalcanal, Leyte Gulf, with the First Marines for invasions. Some of them were the first waves. Some of them were the second. Okinawa was the first wave. I think that was the last big naval engagement of the war. And one of the bloodiest as far as the Navy was concerned. But it was a great experience. I loved the Navy too because I liked the discipline. I'm a disciplined person.

Several times we returned to Honolulu to pick up troops or bring troops back, a very pleasant experience, sometimes very difficult. On the Okinawa invasion, I was able to volunteer as a beach master, and that really was a thrilling thing. Got through that unscathed. The ship was struck once by a kamikaze plane, just the wing of it. That was Easter Sunday, as I recall. There were a lot of kamikazes in the area at that time, and there were quite a few ships, both large Navy ships and ships the size of ours. Ours was about the size of a C-3, as I recall. There were guns everywhere. Everybody was manning a 40-millimeter or a 5-inch gun, or whatever you had on there, shooting it seemed like indiscriminately, but not necessarily. I think they certainly were. But these planes would keep coming in, and you would be shooting at them as they came in. They were coming in so low, you were almost going to take the mast off the ship not too far from you. One of them did come in, and one of our gunners evidently nailed him fine. As he came in, he just passed over. The wing tip hit the bridge stanchion and broke it. I was standing there, but I didn't get hurt. That was really the only damage, if you could even call it damage, to that particular ship.

The day the Marines went into Okinawa, it was almost calm. It looked like they weren't expecting us at all, almost walked up the beach. The next day all hell broke loose. They were expecting us and just sucked us right in on the beach, and then all of a sudden they came in with what seemed like hundreds of planes. I think it was really because they sunk a lot of ships. The gunners on all the ships downed an awful lot of kamikaze planes. It was kind of frightening to see those guys come in because they just never stopped. They picked their target and went in.

We got through that and then went back into the beach and collected the wounded because we had a full complement of surgeons and nurses aboard, and that was the reason for it. We had the complement going in, and then we were to stand off. Go take the troops in, stand off, and wait for the casualty list and go back in with the small boats and bring them back, and do the surgery that we could there—really triage, this stuff. We had operating rooms, two or three of them on the ship. Anything that we couldn't handle was then transferred to hospital ships. Two or three of them were sitting out there, really big stuff.

I'm not sure where we went from there, but we ended up in Yokahama as soon as the war was over. We went back to Seattle and decommissioned the ship. There were only two officers left on the ship on decommissioning. I was one of them. I was at that time lieutenant jg. So that was interesting too. You felt like you had some authority at that time because I think the ship's complement for the APA, including the doctors and all that sort of thing, was probably somewhere in the neighborhood of a thousand, somewhere between eight hundred and a thousand people. All of a sudden, there's just a few of you there on the ship handling the decommission. It was kind of sad in a way. After decommissioning, I was discharged in California. I stayed out there and got married. Married a Navy girl.

I always look back to the Academy and this system you have here of conditioning you to be able to take on the tasks that have to be done, and go ahead and do them.

Two merchant mariners performed Navy duty that spanned the entire war: Wendell Slayton and Robert Davis.

LCDR Wendell D. Slayton, USN (Ret.), Class of 1940

Prior to coming to the Academy, Wendell Slayton graduated from the Massachusetts Nautical School and trained aboard the steam-powered bark USS *Ranger*, which eventually was made the U.S. Merchant Marine Academy's training ship under the name *Emery Rice*. He subsequently enrolled in the U.S. Maritime Commission's Cadet program. Later, he volunteered for Navy duty.

They wanted to know the earliest date I could report to the Philadelphia Navy Yard. I told them the earliest date I could report was December 1, 1940. By the time I got back to New York, I received a letter that stated I should report to the Twelfth Naval District in San Francisco on December 1 instead of Philadelphia. The assignment was to a ship called the *City of San Francisco* with the Baltimore Mail Lines. Later the ship was renamed the USS *William P. Biddoe*, the AP15, and later the APA8. She was commissioned at Mare Island Navy Yard. The first shakedown cruise was from San Diego, California, with a Marine team. We sailed by way of Honolulu to Pago Pago, Samoa, to set up a new Marine base in Samoa. This was April 1941. After that shakedown cruise, we loaded troops again in San Diego, proceeded around through the Panama Canal to the east coast, Charleston, South Carolina, loaded on more troops and took those Marine troops to Iceland. One more reinforcement trip to Iceland on that trip, and then we turned back to Norfolk, Virginia. Then for about a year or so we operated as a training center for landing boat crews.

During any of these trips were there any submarine sightings or hostile action?

I can't think of any; we had a pretty heavy escort, battleships, destroyers, and everything else at that time. It was classified as an expeditionary force at that time.

So you were a part of a military operation before December 1941?

Yes.

In late 1942, I was transferred to New York to the USS *Lakehurst*. That was formerly a freight car transport with Sea Train, New Jersey. When I got aboard that ship, she was about half loaded for the North African landings we made. Not in the Mediterranean but on the Atlantic border of Safi, south of Morocco, south of Casablanca. We went in there mainly because we had about sixty medium tanks, ten thousand gallons of gasoline in portable five-gallon cans for General Patton's Second Armored Division. We made one more reinforcement run to Casablanca, two more supply runs to Oran. We were supposed to come back to get a fast convoy at Gibraltar to come back to the States and load up for a Sicily run.

I received ten days delayed orders, then was assigned to another conversion, which was the USS *Clay*. I put that ship in commission in 1943 and then headed for Norfolk, Virginia, and the South Pacific. The first run was to the Admiralty Islands, then back to San Diego, California, where we loaded the Marine troops. Then we took those troops to the island of Saipan and the Marianas for those landings there. There were numerous other reinforcement runs.

We eventually ended up with Army personnel going down to the Leyte Gulf landings and Luzon, this in 1944, General MacArthur's landings. That was the last. We had one more run on the Okinawa landings. After the Okinawa landings, we took on the American Division there, and we went back down to Cebu in the Philippines. Three days after the Japanese peace treaties were signed, we went into Yokohama, Japan. We returned to the Philippines and took on another load. Three weeks after the peace treaty, we went into the northern island of Honshu. We went from there to Tientsin, China, and picked up some troops for transport to the United States for discharge. That was a final run.

Captain Robert H. Davis, USNR (Ret.), Class of 1940

Ordered into the Navy at age nineteen, Davis was promoted to the rank of lieutenant commander at the age of twenty-three. Later, in civilian life, he was an administrator in three different financial companies in the Baltimore and Philadelphia areas, finally retiring in 1987 as president of Commercial Credit Supply Corporation.

I graduated from Pennsylvania Maritime Academy in May of 1940 and then subsequently served as a cadet officer aboard the *Lidonia*, surveying the northern entrances to Cape Cod Canal. I was ordered into the Navy. In fact, I tried to remain in the merchant service but couldn't. At that time I was nineteen years old and got a waiver on age as an ensign. I was ordered to the first AKA known as the USS *Arcturus* in the Philadelphia Navy Yard. The AKA was an attack cargo vessel typically in the amphibious force. I stayed aboard that vessel as communications officer and watch stander for several years.

During my stay on the *Arcturus*, I participated in the occupation of Iceland. Then I was assigned to a commodore's staff as a staff communicator. That was in the year 1941, and we had a convoy come out loaded with Marines to replace the British in Iceland, because the British and the Icelanders were not getting along too well. I think our participation was inevitable, and we wanted to get a foot in Iceland as a base for aircraft for air defense for the convoys.

After reporting to Commodore Gray, commander of Transport Division Five, I participated in the landing of North Africa. Having been assigned as an aide to Major General Lucian K. Truscott of the Army, who made quite a name for himself in North Africa, I was there to interpret Navy expressions—Navy lingo, so to speak—for the general. From there, we went out to the South Pacific, and I was detached from the commodore's staff and was ordered to a rear admiral's staff, whose title was commander of landing craft, South Pacific Force. With Admiral George Fort, I participated in two landings in Guadalcanal, one landing in Munda, one landing in Bougainville, and one in Okinawa. They were all very difficult operations.

In Okinawa, I was detached from the admiral's staff and had been assigned as an exec of an APA. That's an attack transport, the USS *Freestone*. I was second in command of the *Freestone*. Incidentally, I was two years in the Pacific without touching the United States. When VJ Day came, I was ordered to command the *Freestone*. I declined because I had enough points to get out of the service then. I elected to go home, which made the present commanding officer unhappy because he had to stay. Upon returning to the United States, I entered civilian life.

I remained active in the Naval Reserve, having commanded a naval transportation service division in Philadelphia. Subsequently, by change of my civilian occupation and moving to the city of Baltimore, I assumed command down there of a shipping operation and was promoted to captain. Incidentally, I was alleged to be the youngest lieutenant commander in the Navy during World War II, having been promoted to that rank at the age of twenty-three.

15

THE END OF THE WAR

*Personal recollections of the end of an armed conflict are often
vivid, much like memories of a war's commencement. As described in the following interviews, the sudden realization of the
lifting of danger and the onrush of pent-up feelings worked on
human psyches in dramatic ways. The reactions depicted were,
no doubt, multiplied thousands of times by other combatants in
other regions of the conflict.*

Eliot H. Lumbard, Class of 1945

I was third mate. We were in convoy, to Gibraltar, then alone, because by
now the Mediterranean was our lake. This was in the spring of '45. Got to
Brindisi, and went immediately up to Bari, and just shortly before we got
there several ships in the harbor had exploded. I think it was an air raid,
and ammunition atomized, literally. We went into that same dock, again.
The hostility with the British, I remember, was just unnecessary. But our
cargo, five-hundred-pound bombs, was destined for the Air Force north of
Bari. There were a lot of principal types of targets.

I was there about forty days. It was a very tough time. The captain had
a heart attack. We had a replacement captain come out; he was drunk all
the time. We discharged the cargo, and then suddenly it seemed like the
world war was going to end in Europe. So we were beginning to organize
for Japan. They reloaded all the ammunition, which included, again, about
six or seven thousand tons of five-hundred-pound bombs and machine
gun bullets and aircraft. On top of that, there were thirty tons of green beer,
made by the Schlitz Brewing Company in Philadelphia, Army-type cans,
so-called, for recreation.

We'd been so long at the dock that a tremendous amount of weeds had
grown on the bottom of the ship and nobody knew it. We went out of the

port, and we had to go through minefields. We made our turn, thinking we were going one speed when we were going another, and we turned right into the minefield too early. The captain was dead drunk; he was no use. I was on watch, actually, and had no help, and I got us out of there okay, but it was scary as hell.

We went down to Brindisi, and while in Brindisi everyone else had gone off the ship and I was alone. Suddenly everybody in the harbor knew; the place was packed with ships, started firing every rocket they had, guns in the air, 20mm guns, just total wanton chaos.

But what panicked me was these flares were coming down on the ship, and we had canvas covers on the holds. They were the hatch covers. The top was canvas. They were wooden sections and then a canvas watertight cover. There were no metal hatch covers, as nowadays. And the ship was about four hundred–plus feet long. I was the only person, and I was running around, terrified, like a madman. Threw a bucket of sand or whatever and shoveled, trying to get this stuff over the side. I can tell you, there was little joy in my heart, even though that war had ended.

Also, I had learned our orders, which were that we were to sail through the Dutch East Indies the shortest way to Okinawa, our ultimate destination, and that meant there were no navigational ways there, no lighthouses, no nothing, black. I never sailed on a ship with radar. We had no aid, nothing. There were no radio bearings, and it was an ammunition ship. I've got to tell you, it was a terrifying prospect.

In any event, we sailed. We went down through the Red Sea; it was in August 1945. The sea water was 96 degrees under the sun. The engine room was 130. Of course, the crew opened up the number-one hatch, raided all the beer, like mad. In any event, we headed for where we were supposed to go, to the middle of the Indian Ocean and then headed direct for the islands, and did make it through.

We were almost directly south of what was then called Ceylon. The Japanese war ended, but we didn't know it. We got a message. I'll never forget the message: "The United States, today, dropped an atom bomb on Japan." Period. Nobody on the ship knew what the hell an atom bomb was. That's all we heard. We were in the middle of the ocean, alone, not in combat, and then a couple of days later, I mean, intense speculation. Why is this? A couple of days later, another similar message: the second bomb [Nagasaki], and then an announcement that hostilities were over, turn on your lights, etc. Wow. Well, well. We didn't know anything. We were terrified of kamikazes or some Japanese sub guy figuring, this is the end, let's go out with style and take us out. And, we were almost exactly in the middle of the world from the United States. Then we got another message that said, in effect, turn about one hundred miles around, till you decide whether you're going back to the States, east or west. So here we are in the middle of the ocean, we're supposed to have our lights on. We're almost in revolt.

And then, finally, everybody in the ship went to a meeting as to whether or not to turn the lights on. This captain had no authority, morally or otherwise. He was, as I said, drunk all the time, and later on, about ten or fifteen years later, he wrecked a ship.

You were the third mate on the ship at the time?

Yes. Third mate. And that meant you really ran the ship for eight hours, because he was absent. There was a first mate, second mate, third mate, and captain.

So we had this astounding meeting, with a debate about whether to turn the lights on. And voted not to. That was that. Those lights were not turned on for some days. Then we suddenly got orders to go down under, to Melbourne, and we did. We sailed out of there, and went to Hawaii, went to Pearl Harbor, about a mile offshore. I'll never forget this one either, blinker light comes on, and it says: "Proceed forthwith to Seattle." So when we finally got up to Seattle, over eighty-six days at sea straight; it just was a bad scene. That ship was like *Mr. Roberts*. We were alone a lot of the time, in the middle of the Indian Ocean, underneath Australia, going across the Pacific. The war had ended, so everyone was in decompression, psychological and maybe other ways. And they were then beginning to wonder about their future.

They were erratic. The tension had started to come down, so instead of being disciplined, let's say, they used to be, they would be much more sloppy, or defiant, or resisting authority. They sort of let go. The crew and officers, too. And wacky things started to happen. For example, this ship had, before we got on, carried a cargo of grain, and it had a lot of rats in the bottom of the hold as a consequence. But this cargo had no grain. It was all bombs, steel. They were desperate. And they started eating each other, that was another thing, but they become a bit dangerous. They got so wild. They would come up around sunset; somehow they knew. Right after, we developed this crazy game. Everybody had a broom, and the winner was the guy who could knock the rat overboard, right over the rail. And you should have seen the officers on this ship, making the rounds, trying to compete with this. Everybody was that crazy.

Whatever it was, they were bored, and they cared nothing about the current circumstances. They wanted to get on with their lives. They didn't know what it was going to be.

We got to Seattle, and we sat there for four months while they tried to figure out what to do with the cargo of bombs coming back the other way. They finally unloaded the ship.

Rear Admiral Carl J. Seiberlich, Class of 1943

We arrived in Charleston, South Carolina, on December 7, 1945. On that day, 171 destroyers came into Charleston to go out of commission. "Lock up your daughter, Momma," you know. The Navy people were ordered to be in uniform. They brought a battalion of Marines into downtown Charleston, and if you were in uniform, the Marines took care of you. And if you weren't, the police did.

We had a lot of money in our recreation fund because we didn't have a chance to spend it. We were steaming all the time. So I went to the Knights of Columbus and said I would like to have a ship's party. I was a lieutenant jg. About eleven o'clock, the boys decided to take the place apart, and I said to the CO, "You had better get out of here." So he left. They were ripping commodes out by the roots and throwing them out the window. So I held the manager of the Knights of Columbus club up against the wall and said: "Don't call the police. We will pay for whatever damage we've done. We have plenty of money." I went back to the ship and told the captain what had happened. If my memory serves me, we paid the Knights of Columbus $23,000. I went down afterwards before we paid the bill to be sure all the work was done. I said to the manager: "Hey, you were a good guy by not calling the cops. We don't need to put our guys in jail after coming back from the war."

Captain Douglas F. Ponischil, Class of 1940

I stayed at the Moana Hotel because that was the big time on Waikiki [Hawaii], and I remember the newspaper headlines one morning: they had dropped the atomic bomb on Hiroshima. Harry Truman announced that they did it, so we knew the war was going to be over pretty soon. We didn't normally drink on board or anything, but we stocked up with some booze going back because we had a feeling the war was going to come to an end.

So you were saving it for the celebration?

For the celebration. As I say, we didn't normally drink at sea. This wasn't done. We had pretty good discipline. But, on the way back, we went from Pearl Harbor then to Peru, to load sugar. Halfway across, we got the word that the Japanese had completely surrendered, unconditionally, and we just went wild. The officers on watch, of course, still didn't drink, but everybody just got loaded and just had a great time, a celebration. Then we pulled into Peru and loaded sugar and went up, back through the canal, to Philadelphia.

After that, I made a couple more trips. We took a load of grain over to Messina, Sicily, because the war had ended over there, and they hadn't had any food or anything. It was really tough in Sicily. So we were there about a week, unloaded grain in Sicily, and back to the States. Then we took a load for UNRRA, United Nations Rehabilitation Association, I believe it was, into Trieste.

In Trieste, one of the secretaries at this place, when I took the ship's papers in, was a beautiful young lady who spoke seven languages, and I fell madly in love with her and decided this was the girl I was going to marry. It was great. I just thought she was great. So I had her aboard the ship, and we went out. We both happened to be Roman Catholic, and we went to the bishop there to try to get married. He said: "No way. You haven't known each other long enough. If you're still in love a year from now, I'll marry you by proxy. If you're back in the States, we'll work it out, but not now." So we decided that's what we'd do.

We had a big celebration; I was still captain. I had a big party on board on the ship for all our friends and all the crew. We had steak and champagne and big doings, and everybody was congratulating us for the idea that we were going to get married. We didn't actually get married. Engagement, I guess. I can still remember waving good-bye to them on the dock when we left Maria Christiana. But it didn't work. I got back to the States, and I called on the phone a couple of times. It was always hard to get through in those days. You didn't have the tremendous connections you have now, and it just kind of drifted away. We wrote a few letters, and I never saw her again. It was just one of those things.

And you subsequently married in the United States—someone else?

Yes, later. Someone else. The chief mate, Tom Walsh, was a good friend of mine, and he went over again on another trip, later. I saw him years later, and he told me that he had looked her up, and he found out that she was a spy now. This was just a romantic story, but I don't know. That is what he said. Trieste was a very international city, which I believe was being quarreled over between Italy and Yugoslavia, and I think it finally ended up being part of Italy.

This was in '45, and they were going to lay up the *George L. Baker*, from Philadelphia. It must have been Christmas of '45, and everybody wanted to go home for Christmas. There wasn't anybody left on the ship but me. I was the captain, and I think I had a mess boy, one other guy. There was just nobody, and you couldn't get anybody. We were at anchor, and somehow we managed the ship. I don't know how we did it, but we did. Finally, we were able to get off. They took it and laid it up, and I had decided I was going to go into the theater to be an actor. I wanted to be an actor. I loved the theater, and I actually signed a contract.

Then this shipping company called me and said: "We need you to make one more trip. We've got another ship here. The SS *Binger Hermann* has to take a load of grain to Germany. They're starving over there. They don't have any food, and we've got to do this, and we really need you." So I said, "Okay." This was a Weyerhaeuser ship. So I took that last trip on the *Binger Hermann*. We took a load of grain over to Germany, to Bremen and Hamburg. There was nothing there. Hamburg's a big city, but there was nothing left. Everything was flattened from the bombing. There was just not much there. We used to trade cigarettes for souvenirs to take back; there were no souvenirs! I ended up with an accordion, an old beaten-up accordion, and I think a German sword. I did get a huge pair of binoculars off a German tank, that I still have. I guess it was 15 power. Big buggers. I still have those. But there was just nothing there. The war was over, and nobody knew what to do. It was a strange situation. But we took our load and came back empty and then landed in Mobile, Alabama.

As captain, I had a little car, like a little Austin. It was a Crosley, a small car that would seat four. We used to take it off when we were in port. Like, we'd unload it in Trieste and different places. I took my car with me, and I had my friends, and the four of us would always go off with black market cigarettes. You could buy your way to anything with cigarettes. We could take a carton of cigarettes and get a full meal for four people, which we did lots of times, but we weren't supposed to do that. We found a way. We would wrap the cigarette cartons up with brown wrapping paper and tie them to the engine, because when they would search the car, they would look in the back, in the trunk, and they'd look all around, but they never thought of looking in the engine. We had these tied with the brown wrapping paper that would keep them just enough from catching on fire until we'd get away from the dock. Then we'd take them out and that was our money for having fun.

After that—and this was in April of 1946—we pulled into Mobile, and I decided that was it. I'd given ten years of my life to the merchant marine, to the sea, which I loved, but I wanted to go ashore and learn to live like a human being and stop drinking or whatever, and so I did. I got my car off, and I'd go to New Orleans and to Houston and stay with relatives, and that was the last of my sea duty [until Korea]. Because I'd been captain I had a Naval Reserve commission as a lieutenant, junior grade. The Navy called me to active duty in the Korean War. They rushed me out to Japan, so I was a public information officer for two years on the USS *Antietam*, CV-36; and, later, they transferred to the *Shangri-la*, which is CV-38. This was in '52 and '53. Then I went to New York; I got out of the service in August of '53. Met a beautiful young lady in New York that a friend from San Francisco had introduced me to, and married her six weeks later in Charlotte, North Carolina.

THE SIGNIFICANCE OF
THE MERCHANT MARINE

Invariably the merchant mariners interviewed have said that the war could not have been won without the American merchant marine. The merchant marine allowed the forces of the United States and its Allies to carry the war to the Axis powers in all theaters of operation. Indeed, the isolationist world of the 1930s was shattered not only by the advent of war on several continents, but also by the merchant ships endlessly crossing the oceans, using sea routes as never before. Final victory in 1945 ushered in a new world shaped not only by the force of arms, but also by the merchant mariners, who enabled the global endeavor to end in an Allied victory.

Captain George E. Kraemer, Class of 1944

I think that the American merchant marine was a really basic ingredient to the overall structure of our so-called war machine in those days. I think without that basic ingredient, they wouldn't have been able to do what they did, because we in the merchant marine really kept the British Isles from going under. If they hadn't been able to get the supplies into the British Isles, and of course the troops into the British Isles that they did, there couldn't have been an invasion, there couldn't have been a Second Front in Europe. God knows, you might not have even been able to have the African invasion. So I think that, basically, it was really an integral part of the overall war machine.

Douglas E. Wagner, Class of 1945

Douglas Wagner was the self-employed head of a packaging firm. After World War II, he had worked as a general plant manager for several companies, including Manville Forest Products, before managing his own business.

Well, the merchant marine served the military. We were such an integral part of their supplies, troops, logistics, and things like that. We wouldn't have a successful Navy. Nor would we have had a successful military, period, because we delivered the essentials that they needed to carry out their duties. In fact, they put gun crews on our ships. We all had gun crews, and part of our job was to handle 20-millimeters. We had two of us on the 20-millimeter, and you'd have a gun crew there with you, and they had usually about ten or eleven members, a gun crew with one officer.

So the merchant mariners were actually serving as part of the gun crew.

Oh, yes, sure. When they rang general alarm, you had to go up to your gun station. You'd look around, and you always startle when you're young. Hell, I could run, I could get out of anything. You look around, and there's no place to run. You're just sitting in the gun turret, and that's it. That's it. It's bye-bye.

Each ship carried roughly nine thousand tons of cargo, a Liberty ship. And when you're in the convoy and you have, say, 130, 140 ships, you could multiply roughly ten thousand tons times 140. That's what moves across at one time.

Captain Lewis J. Heroy, Class of 1944

Well, of course there were two sides. There was a fighting side, and there was a provision side, a logistics side. The merchant marine of course was not equipped to do this thing militarily. They were equipped to do it logistically. It was the merchant marine's job to get the equipment moving, get it to the right place at the right time, where it was needed so that they could use it militarily to fight the war. In all theaters of operation, whether it be the North Atlantic or the Pacific or the Mediterranean. I'm just awed at the people that pulled this thing together back in those days, to get all these

Liberty Ship John W. Brown, by Oswald Brett. Courtesy of Oswald Brett and Project Liberty Ship.

things moving at the same time and get them in one place at the right time where they were needed. I thought it was fantastic. I really did.

In fact, the whole world, the whole U.S. economy, was geared for the war effort, and we did it. We all did it. Everybody did it; everybody did their share, and nobody complained about it. They just went ahead and did their job. We were out there doing our part, driving the ships or running the ships to get them over there and get the cargoes to the right place at the right time. We were the "carrier," so-to-speak, of the provisions and supplies that were needed for the operation. It was a big, big job.

It was a big war, and everybody had to help out in their thing. A lot of us made sacrifices, and we sailed the ships from our end of it in the maritime industry. The training that we received here at Kings Point I think stood us in very well with the way we did the job, when we got out of here.

Donald G. Giesa, Class of 1944

Most of Don Giesa's career has been related to the Pacific Rim, although his World War II service included the Mediterranean theater as well as the Pacific. He was a representative for the National Shipping Authority during the Korean War in the Port of Pusan. Later, he headed his own insurance claims company.

From your vantage point of these two wars, what would you say would be the historical impact of significance of the merchant marine on military operations?

Without them, there wouldn't be any success. It's material. It is essential. It is extremely necessary. Without it, how are we going to get there? And, as my roommate said, "We did it without about a quarter of the complement of Navy personnel."

Charles M. Renick, Class of 1947

You hear it said that we wouldn't have won the war without the merchant marine. It is actually the truth. To have been there and seen the number of ships and the number of supplies—I mean, I guess we could have won the war without a lot of things. I mean the industrial or the military industrial complex in this country and the women and the men who were working in factories, and all, fine. But everything they made had to get overseas. Even today, this is true to a large extent. But then, they didn't have the big transport planes that could carry these things across. You couldn't put a tank on a plane back in those days. So everything had to get over there, and it was merchant ships. Although they had some armed men on them, they were really at the mercy of any attacking ship. They gave you a gun on the stern and a gun on the bow. A submarine was not likely to come up and just sit there and shell you as they sometimes did in the early days of the war, but there is nothing to stop them from torpedoing you. There is only one ship that I know of in World War II, a merchant ship, that was able to fight back, and that was the *Stephen Hopkins*.

On September 27, 1942, the German commerce raiders *Stier* and *Tannenfels* came upon the SS *Stephen Hopkins* and shelled the American ship. The crew of the outgunned *Hopkins* fought back and sank the *Stier* just prior to her own sinking. A Kings Point cadet-midshipman, Edwin O'Hara, chose to stay aboard the *Hopkins,* and he was observed firing the last shots at the enemy ship before he went down with the Liberty ship. A total of thirty-two crewmen and nine Navy men perished in the attack or on the rafts and lifeboats before reaching safety.[1]

Richard M. Larrabee, Class of 1944

When you stood, as we often did on many occasions, on the bridge of a cargo ship and saw to the left, to the right, and ahead a hundred ships, over 90 percent American built with American crews, you realized you were one of many, many, many participants. It was awe-inspiring. The Pacific was different because we ran alone. In the North Atlantic for the entire time except while on a faster passenger ship, we were always in convoy. I never was in a convoy where there were less than seventy to eighty ships. I was in one convoy with about 130. That is the one we made heading to Scotland, and eventually we wound up in Russia.

William H. Ford, Class of 1944

What would you say was the significance of the United States merchant marine effort in World War II?

I think it was very dramatic. We haven't been treated very fairly in that regard. I've been called a draft dodger because I was in a civilian service. That upset me terribly. I remember an incident when I was a seaman, working the forecastle in the West Indies somewhere. We were in a place that was approved with the PTA [Passenger Transport Authority], I'm sure. These soldiers came up, and one of them went to our boatswain mate, who was a strong, healthy, young man, and said, "You're a f—n young chap. Why aren't you in uniform?" Well, he got up and he beat him up. He really did. He mopped the deck with him because he was a little bit annoyed at that. And I could relate. Anyway, our man went to prison, and the soldier went to the hospital. I don't know what happened to the sailor.

We're the only government academy where our midshipmen went into the war zone. There was no Army cadet, no West Pointer. None of those went out in the war zone. None were lost. Yet, on my ship alone, we lost two good Kings Pointers, John Lambert and Richard M. Record.

Note: Cadet-Midshipmen John P. Lambert and Richard M. Record perished when the Liberty ship *James Oglethorpe* was torpedoed by the German submarine *U-758*, on March 16, 1943, and later, by *U-91* on March 19, 1943. They are among the 142 cadet-midshipmen who died during World War II.[2]

Paul L. Milligan Jr., Class of 1944

I've given it some thought. One of the biggest significances is that I, of course, doff my hat to the combat troops. They're the ones that ultimately had to do the job. But without the merchant marine, they just couldn't operate. The Navy was not prepared to deliver the goods, so to speak. I'm talking about strictly the seamen—merchant seamen, captains, and officers who hadn't been in the Academy. It was great to be associated with some of those fellows. They really took their jobs seriously. There wasn't a lot of kidding around, but there was a lot of friendly atmosphere. And the cadets were unmercifully put upon, but that was okay too because the end result of that was, after your work was done, they would sit down and wanted to hear about, "Well, what the heck do you do at the Academy," too. So, I think the merchant marine's importance was prime, not only the ongoing task during the war, but afterwards too. The merchant marine just had to be there afterwards in order to reinforce some of these cities, towns, islands, whatever, to bring them back to something normal. It was really with a great sense of pride that I say this.

James W. Gann, Class of 1944

What would you say was the historical significance of the merchant marine in World War II?

Well, the statistics showing the amount of cargo that was actually taken by the ships was very favorable. We were manning the ships with about fifty people, besides the Armed Guards, whereas the Navy ships of the same size had crews of about two hundred. So we did it with fewer men, and I'm sure less cost to the overall picture.

Captain Arthur E. Erb, Class of 1943

I think your major commanders of World War II attested to the fact that without the merchant marine, we would never have built up the supplies for the invasion of Europe or for the invasion of the Philippines. Eventually, if we had to have an invasion of Japan, the Navy would not have had the cargo ships to carry the tonnage that was required. Without the merchant marine, the war certainly would have been extended. Had we not the ship-building program and the cargo vessels and escort vessels, the German submarine efforts would have been successful, and initially they were successful. The war only turned when the shipbuilding and ship-manning of merchant vessels exceeded the tonnage that was being sunk.

Leslie Churchman, Class of 1944

You couldn't imagine the amount of equipment that was moved by the American merchant marine. I remember being in Africa and seeing acres and acres of airplanes, tanks, tank retrievers, and motor vehicles. Hundreds and hundreds of them that had been landed by merchant ships in North Africa, and just spread over acres. I don't think I ever saw the end of them. It was just phenomenal. I remember having locomotive engines on our deck, maybe three of them abreast, and airplanes. I don't think we could ever duplicate that effort again. It was indescribable. Probably we won't need it, with the technology that they have today. My feeling was always that it was a really difficult war, and I'm glad that I survived it. And knowing that I survived it, I would not have liked to have missed it because the effort was so great. I always think of it that way.

J. Richard Kelahan, Class of 1942

What would you say would be the contribution that people such as yourself had played from a historical point of view in World War II?

First of all, two ships that I served on were both requisitioned by the Navy for specific objectives. Those ships were initially staffed by MMR [Merchant Marine Reserve] officers. For example, on the USS *Hammondsport*, the acting CO, the navigator, the first lieutenant, the engineer officer, and the assistant engineer officer were all MMR officers called to active duty. The chief engineer of the USS *Hammondsport* had been the engineer on the *Sea Train Havana*. We took that ship on Christmas Day, 1941, from the Brooklyn Navy Yard, through the canal, over to San Diego, where we picked up the planes to take to Australia. It was in San Diego that the assigned skipper and executive officer came aboard to take command of the ship.

On the USS *Card* it was very similar. They'd take the ship right on the ways, then convert it into an escort carrier, aircraft carrier. We were manned like the sister ship there, the USS *Bogue*. The engineer officer that I sailed with on the *Mormacrey* was the engineer officer on the *Bogue*. In effect, the merchant marine officers were serving as Navy officers on these ships. Apparently these ships were to be auxiliaries, but we were actually engaged in combat.

I hope this convinces people that the secondary mission of the Academy was served by the activity and the various experiences that we had. It's proof that one mission of the Academy has been served.

Joseph H. Lion, Class of 1946

Without the merchant marine, I don't think they'd ever win a war. Britain would now have a nice swastika up on top of every building. I guess there was a lot of hard feeling between the merchant marine and the Navy because of the bonuses. But it was the merchant marine that did all the work. They didn't fire many guns and what have you, but they carried all the ammunition, they carried all the fuel, they carried it.

It worked like this, you can look back in your history, and T2 tankers transported more airplanes in the Pacific than all the aircraft carriers put together. Because you used to carry twelve aircraft on the royal deck. They had special framing built up on them. Now, we didn't because we were coming out of Panama, but all of them that came out of the east coast, on every trip they made they were carrying airplanes out to the Pacific. They actually transported more airplanes than the carriers ever carried, which is interesting, and that contributed a lot to the war effort.

It's kind of funny because anybody that had ever been near a World War II tanker would see that special superstructure. If you're familiar with a tanker, all the pipes run down the center and you have a catwalk, and then you just have tank tops there. Well, they had these structures all welded up even with the catwalk, and the airplanes were parked on that. I was several times where they were off-loading airplanes. They had special docks to do it.

Rear Admiral Carl J. Seiberlich, Class of 1943

The merchant marine was positively essential, and everybody would say that. I saw what equipment and people we took to the war in the convoys and the big battle to fend off the submarines. I think you can take a look at what happened at Murmansk and how important the cargo that got to Murmansk was keeping the Russians in the war. And look at the Pacific War. There was no question that the Army and Navy could not have sustained themselves without the U.S. merchant fleet. Admiral Land was just an outstanding person in my viewpoint.[3] He really had the Academy's interest at heart, and I was very fortunate to know him. For example, in the beginning, the Navy needed officers very badly. We started in 1940 with 9,800 officers. In February or March of 1944, there were 356,000. So the agreement with the Navy was that they would bring people on active duty. But then Admiral Land went to the secretary of the Navy and said: "Now the merchant ships are coming out. We would like to devote the graduates to the merchant marine." The Navy then said, "Fine, we will do that." So there was good cooperation.

I asked Admiral Land about how in the early part of the war the sink rate was quite high and the damage rate was low. And then later in the war, there was a very high damage rate and a low sink rate. He said in the early part of the war, the ships had been built by the bureaucrats and the budgeters. In the latter part of the war, they were built by the war fighters. In the early part of the war, the sailors didn't understand how to fight fire and flooding, and then in the latter part of the war, they did. I can certainly vouch for that because the first thing that they did to me when I came on active duty was put me through damage-control school in Philadelphia.

The thing that bothered me on the merchant ship is that you had an Armed Guard crew, but you really were not in the position to defend yourself. I told them, "You put me in a transporter or a supply ship, and I will stay in the merchant marine." I wanted to be on a ship that could defend itself from an attack.

And I will tell you, the Great Depression is what shaped the character of those who fought in World War II. You learned to hang in there in adversity, to stick together, and to have great religious faith. A lot of people don't realize that in the Great Depression every church was full on Sunday. And we took those lessons to the merchant ships that I have been on. We hung together.

William G. Holby, Class of 1944

From your vantage point and firsthand experience of World War II, both in the merchant marine and the U.S. Navy, how would you estimate the impact or significance of the merchant marine as part of our war effort?

Well, you know, this is something that when you're in the midst of it you don't see it, but you have to look back historically, and the impact is tremendous when you gather all the statistics and look at the event. That's the only way I'm able to look at it, outside of talking with other midshipmen who were survivors, and there are plenty of them. We organized a club at the Academy, which was a club for fun, I guess. It's called the Tin Fish Club. We had a big dinner at the Waldorf Astoria in New York.

"Tin Fish" being a torpedo.

Yes, that's right. Their ships were all sunk, but they survived. There were about probably thirty of us.

In other words, thirty midshipmen who, while still undergraduates, sustained torpedo attacks.

That's right. This happened on their sea duty. It was just about this time in 1943 that the United States or the Allied forces began getting the upper hand on the sea war and my father was assigned to work for the War Production Board for securing materials for destroyer escorts. And it was this type ship, chiefly, that helped defeat the submarine menace. Convoys were then much better protected. The merchant marine was necessary, when you consider all the ships built, all the ships that had to be manned, and then they improved. The construction of Liberties gave way to the Victory ship, which was a faster ship, a more efficient vessel. The Liberty, with its simple reciprocating engine, could be produced quickly, and that's what was needed. Then the Victory came along with its steam turbine, which was a much more difficult engine to produce, but they did it, and much more efficient. And Victories were taken by the Navy and converted into many types of auxiliaries. The "APT" they called it, the "Attack Personnel Transport." Still, it was that hull and design that was used.

Karl J. Aarseth, Class of 1943

They would not have won without the merchant marine. England was starving to death. When I met a longshoreman in Barry Dock, he says: "I have a son that's two years old. He's never seen or eaten oranges." I said, "I'll see if I can get you one." There was terrible damage to the country. They never repaired any of the bomb damage. If a pipe was torn and leaking gas, they never put it back in the ditch. They left new pipes above ground.

How do you think the war formed your outlook for the rest of your career?

Well, the war to me was survival. Everything was survival. And right now, I'm still alive. The training you got was better than anything.

Rear Admiral Thomas A. King, Class of 1942

I'm simply a tremendous believer in the American merchant marine. I am distressed that it is not being recognized at the high policy level that it should be. I believe that economically, and certainly as a national security resource, the American merchant marine is absolutely of great value. After the very fine performance of the American merchant marine, the breakout of all of the Ready Reserve Fleet, the answering of the call by hundreds of our own graduates, and by other merchant mariners manning the ships that made a tremendous sealift possible, with logistical support for our forces in the Persian Gulf under Desert Storm/Desert Shield, I find it shocking that there is not recognition of the value, and immediately stepping in to remedy what I think is the lack of an adequate promotional program on the part of the national policy, the national agenda.

Captain George M. Marshall, Class of 1942

You need more than just ships in a lay-up fleet. You need to have the men and women who can function and operate them. You must have a training program to keep their skills up-to-date so they can be deployed on very short notice.

I've served on ships where only three or four of us really knew how to operate that ship. That's the price you pay, and they are the conditions you have to live with in a real emergency. I don't think it's as critical today as it has been in the past, but I still think there ought to be some kind of reserve training program, particularly for younger people who go to sea for awhile and come ashore, just keep them up-to-date.

William E. Hooper, Ph.D., Class of 1945

What was the role of the merchant marine in World War II?

I feel it was a vital role then, and always will be. There's no other way to move massive pieces of machinery and supplies. There is talk about flying things over there, but it would take forever, and they can't do what the merchant marine can do. We operated the Army's Navy, and the Air Force's Navy, and the Navy's Navy. We were the supply corps for all. I don't want to say we would not have won the war without the merchant marine, but it was so vital.

Rear Admiral Thomas J. Patterson, USMS, Class of 1944

It's more real today than it was when the country was founded. We've always had a requirement because we are a maritime nation. We're surrounded by the sea except on our northern and southern boundaries. Everything that we need to survive has to come in from overseas in strategic materials.

Glenn Ohanesian, Class of 1945

I think it was most clearly brought home to me, the importance of a merchant marine during the time I was in, because when you stood out on the deck, and you saw all of these ships and you realized how much your one ship carried, and you multiplied it by the number of ships, tankers, whatever, there's just no way that they had any kind of carrying capacity by air, or any other way, that they could have carried this stuff.

Captain Thomas F. Hannigan, Class of 1945

Now retired, Tom Hannigan's lifetime "voyage" included sailing on several historic ships after the Second World War. As a ship's officer for twenty years with United States Lines, Hannigan served on the *America*, the *Washington*, and for thirteen years aboard the SS *United States* as chief officer. Subsequently, he returned to Kings Point to serve in various positions, including director of shipboard training. His pleasant demeanor and optimistic outlook are evident.

What would you say was the significance of the merchant marine?

We served a purpose. We got the cargo up from point *A* to point *B*. Of course, at that time we didn't have super cargo planes, but we did the job. We carried a lot of cargo, and certainly we lost a lot of cargo, ships, and lives.

Do you think the outcome of the war would have been different if the merchant marine had been less effective than it was?

I would say so. The same as for the Army, Navy, and the Marines, I suppose. We served our purpose and we did it well.

PERSONAL THOUGHTS

—————

The Kings Point training and sea year experience left their stamp on those who went through the school. The various views expressed below were, no doubt, harbored by other Kings Pointers as well.

Eliot H. Lumbard, Class of 1945

I switched ships [as a cadet at sea]. That was the system at that time, didn't stay too much on one ship. I would have liked to have stayed on that [first] ship, because the officer corps, by and large, was very receptive. And that was a big problem back in those days, because the cadets were not accepted by a lot of people. The second mate on that ship had come up through the "hawsepipe," so to speak, and hated cadets. Two things he did to me I'll just use as an illustration.

One day we were in heavy weather, storms. He ordered me go down to the foredeck, the very foredeck [at the bow], and see if the telephone worked, which was of course a complete sham, and stand between the windlasses with the green seas coming over. Unbelievable experience.

This ship had a tremendous long stick, as they called it, mast 150 feet high. Extraordinary. That was the style when the ship was built, back then in the late 1920s, '28, '29, something like that. When the ship rolled, the top of the mast would make an arc that was like a whip, and you would be way over the water, as you went there. He made me go up the mast, as we were rolling very heavily one day, and call him from the lookout station that was up there, again to see if the telephone worked, which it didn't.

But those two experiences were among my most terrifying ones. They really came out, though, out of the tremendous hostility that a lot of people felt in the old merchant marine for the new cadets in the new merchant marine. On the other hand, I had some spectacular good things. On that ship, there was an old seaman who was a professional gambler. And he rode that ship and those ships to clean out whoever played. As they got closer to Europe, they would play gigantic poker games, and they didn't care about money anymore, and they'd lose it all.

He'd clean it up. He'd wake me up every morning, because he took a kind of shine to me (he never had any kids) by flicking a roll of hundred-dollar bills across my nose. Time to get up, cadet. Rise and shine with the maritime. He was a great fellow, and I learned a lot from him.

This is by way of saying that these and a thousand other experiences were an unparalleled education, of a type not known to educators. You had to be able to function, as a kid literally who didn't know anything, with people older than your father. Sometimes with hostility, you were often treated as a silly joke, and that's very hard when you're alone.

There was another deck cadet, and there were two engine cadets. We had our sea projects. I worked very hard on my sea project. I found it a way to sort of ground myself, psychologically, and just get in there and do it.

And this was all during your war experience.

Oh, yeah. I'll say, having to balance all that, keep the captain happy, meet your duties, with the drills, the firing, the naval drills so to speak, control yourself psychologically, when you're really a kid. I was eighteen years old, and I'd come from a small town in Massachusetts, and nothing in my life had ever prepared me for anything like this. Zero.

So, then you had to do the academics, for which there was no course. You had to get along with the crew, because if you didn't, you were dead; you were nonfunctional. You couldn't get the information to do your sea project, you couldn't function on the ship, you wouldn't have any respect. A lot of the union delegates hated your guts, and they saw the people coming out of Kings Point as a threat to unionism. They didn't know whether the graduates at Kings Point would be receptive to the union.

And so you were halfway between being an officer and a seaman; you're a fink, you're a this, you're a that. It was psychologically very difficult to adapt, and you either adapted or you didn't, and that's the way it was.

Glenn Ohanesian, Class of 1945

Looking back on the war, how do you feel this early experience, early in your lifetime, affected you in terms of your subsequent outlook on things?

Well, I think for one thing, it was a stabilizing influence, in a sense that you had a more mature outlook on life. When you came back to the Academy, you were a different person, completely different, because you had seen something. You'd been personally involved in it, and you understood it a lot more than people who had never been there.

Douglas E. Wagner, Class of 1945

I think it was a very maturing experience, one that more or less set your goals, whether you stayed in the merchant marine or whether you were on the shore. There was something that you learned that made you strike for a goal and attain it, and, as far as hard work is concerned, you learned how to do that because you were on watch eight hours a day, four and four. You had to be there on time. You had to do this at a proper time, and so it gave you a good evaluation of how you would have to margin yourself when you got home.

James F. Tomeny, Class of 1945

Surviving the dangers of war, James Tomeny concluded he was fortunate. He had achieved the rank of shipmaster. After the war, he was employed as a stevedore superintendent. He now has his own consulting business in New Orleans.

I often thought at times, well, hell. You know, it can't get any worse, so go and just live day by day. So that, more or less, was the attitude that I kind of had. You were young, you were healthy, and you'd say hey, I'm still ahead of the game. I'm still alive.

Rear Admiral Thomas J. Patterson, USMS, Class of 1944

Let me ask you a question, if I may, and this is a personal question emanating from your experience during World War II. World War II was an extraordinary experience. From your description of your career, it was certainly very eventful. Looking back at that period, how, in general terms, do you believe it prepared you for the rest of your career? I'm not speaking now specifically of the maritime part of it, which is clear, but in the way you approach your work from the war experience.

Oh, I think it molded my life. I think I learned discipline both at the U.S. Merchant Marine Academy and on the early ships I sailed on and the masters I sailed with. I think I was held accountable. I always wanted to be prepared so that when I was held accountable, I wouldn't be criticized or chewed out or whatever you want to call it. Around Kings Point, you just made one step out of line and zap! You were on report. So your bunk was made up, and you had to flip a quarter and see it bounce off the bunk. You had to wear paper collars, and your uniform had to be immaculate. I mean, I still polish my shoes every morning before I leave the house. I learned that at Kings Point. There are the basics that people have to understand.

I always saw as marvelous that Kings Point prepared you for both peace and war. I mean you learned how to load ship, you knew how to operate ship's business. You could go in the Navy and feel comfortable, and you could compete with a Naval Academy graduate; in fact, you could beat him every time because you had the hands-on experience.

Karl J. Aarseth, Class of 1943

I recall Joseph Conrad. If you want to learn about the sea in English prose, read Conrad's *Mirror of the Sea*. He said, "Whatever craft he handles with skill, the seaman of the future shall not be our descendent, but only our successor."[1]

It is hoped that the present volume of interviews will help preserve the merchant mariner experience of World War II.

Appendix A

Ships of the U.S. Merchant Marine

This appendix provides a select listing of ships of the U.S. Merchant Marine cited in this volume.

Alfred Moore. Type: Liberty ship (freighter), Hull no. 892. Builder: North Carolina Shipbuilding Co. Built: 1943. Length: 441'6". Weight: 7,191 gross tons. Operator: Prudential Steamship Corp.

America (West Point). Type: passenger/troop ship. Builder: Newport News Shipbuilding & Dry Dock Co. Built: 1939. Length: 723'. Weight: 33,961 gross tons. Operator: U.S. Navy as USS *West Point* (Previously United States Lines Co.).

America Sun. Type: tanker. Builder: Sun Shipbuilding & Dry Dock Co. Built: 1940. Length: 524'6". Weight: 11,355 gross tons. Operator: Sun Oil Co.

American Packer. Type: general cargo. Builder: Western Pipe & Steel Co. Built: 1941. Length: 395'. Weight 6,778 gross tons. Operator: American Pioneer Line.

Andrea F. Luckenbach. Type: general cargo (freighter). Builder: Bethlehem Steel Co. (Bethlehem Shipbuilding Corp.). Built: 1919. Length: 496'. Weight: 10,652 gross tons. Operator: Luckenbach Steamship Co., Inc.

Argentina. Type: general cargo/passenger. Builder: Newport News Shipbuilding & Dry Dock Co. Built: 1929. Length: 614'1". Weight: 20,614 gross tons. Operator: Mooremack South American Line, Inc.

Atenas. Type: fruit carrier/passenger. Builder: Workman, Clark & Co., Belfast. Built: 1909. Length: 394'. Weight: 4,639 gross tons. Operator: United Fruit Steamship Corp.

Athelduchess (British). Type: tanker. Builder: Wm. Hamilton & Co., Ltd. Built: 1929. Length: 492'. Weight: 8,940 gross tons. Operator: Athel Line.

Benjamin Hawkins. Type: Liberty ship (freighter), Hull no. 913. Builder: Bethlehem Fairfield Shipyard, Inc. Built: 1942. Length: 441'6". Weight: 7,191 gross tons. Operator: War Shipping Administration.

Binger Hermann. Type: general cargo. Builder: Oregon Shipbuilding Corp. Built: 1943. Length: 417'8¾". Weight: 7,176 gross tons. Operator: Weyerhauser Steamship Co.

Boundbrook. Type: tanker. Builder: Sun Shipbuilding & Dry Dock Co. Built: 1944. Length: 503'. Weight, 10,317 gross tons. Operator: Marine Transport Lines, Inc.

Brazil. Type: passenger/troop carrier. Builder: Newport News Shipbuilding & Dry Dock Co. Built: 1928. Length: 613'1". Weight: 20,614 gross tons. Operator: American Republics Line.

Bucyrus Victory. Type: Victory ship (general cargo). Builder: Permanente Metals Corp. Built: 1944. Length: 436'6". Weight: 7,607 gross tons. Operator: U.S. Navy.

Cantigny. Type: tanker. Builder: Sun Shipbuilding & Dry Dock Co. Built: 1945. Length: 503'. Weight: 10,296 gross tons. Operator: Keystone Shipping Co.

Cape Alava. Type: general cargo. Builder: Seattle Tacoma Shipbuilding Corp. (Todd Pacific Shipyard, Inc.). Built: 1941. Length: 395'. Weight: 6,751 gross tons. Operator: U.S. Maritime Commission.

Cape Cod. Type: general cargo. Builder: Bethlehem Steel Co. (Bethlehem Shipbuilding Co.). Built: 1941. Length: 395'. Weight: 6,797 gross tons. Operator: United Mail Steamship Co.

Cape May. Type: general cargo. Builder: Consolidated Steel Corp. Built: 1943. Length: 395'. Weight: 6,711 gross tons. Operator: United States Lines Co.

Cape San Martin. Type: general cargo/passenger. Builder: Bethlehem Steel Co. (Bethlehem Shipbuilding Co.). Built: 1941. Length: 417'9". Weight: 6,250 gross tons. Operator: U.S. Maritime Commission; later, War Shipping Administration Transport Board.

Capillo. Type: general cargo. Builder: American International Shipbuilding Corp. Built: 1920. Length: 401'. Weight: 5,135 gross tons. Operator: Pacific Northwest Oriental Line, operator of Puget Sound Orient Line.

Cardinal Gibbons. Type: Liberty ship (freighter), Hull no. 920. Builder: Bethlehem-Fairfield Shipyard. Built: 1942. Length: 441'6". Weight: 7,191 gross tons. Operator: Sword Steamship Line, Inc.

Cardonia. Type: general cargo. Builder: American International Shipbuilding Corp. Built: 1920. Length: 400'4". Weight: 5,104 gross tons. Operator: Lykes Bros. Steamship Co., Inc.

Charles Carroll. Type: Liberty ship (freighter), Hull no. 15. Builder: Bethlehem-Fairfield Shipyard. Built: 1941. Length: 441'6". Weight: 7,191 gross tons. Operator: American Export Lines.

City of Omaha. Type: general cargo. Builder: George A. Fuller Co. Built: 1920. Length: 395'6". Weight: 6,124 gross tons. Operator: Lykes Bros. Steamship Co., Inc.

City of San Francisco. Type: general cargo/passenger. Builder: Bethlehem Steel Co. (Bethlehem Shipbuilding Co.). Built: 1919. Length: 506'. Weight: 8,378 gross tons. Operator: Baltimore Mail Steamship Co.

David G. Farragut. Type: Liberty ship (freighter, limited troop carrier), Hull no. 317. Builder: Delta Shipbuilding Co. Built: 1942. Length: 441'6". Weight: 7,191 gross tons. Operator: United Fruit Co.

Delaires. Type: freighter. Builder: Federal Shipbuilding & Dry Dock Co. Built: 1942. Length: 435'. Weight: 6,509 gross tons. Operator: Mississippi Shipping Co., Inc.

Delrio. Type: general cargo. Builder: American International Shipbuilding Corp. Built: 1919. Length: 400'4". Weight: 5,052 gross tons. Operator: Mississippi Shipping Co., Inc. (Delta Line).

Dorchester. Type: passenger. Builder: Newport News Shipbuilding & Dry Dock Co. Built: 1926. Length: 350'. Weight: 5,649 gross tons. Operator: Merchants & Miners Co., Inc.

Eagle Wing. Type: general cargo. Builder: Moore Dry Dock Co. Built: 1944. Length: 435'. Weight: 6,214 gross tons. Operator: Waterman Steamship Corp.

Edmond B. Alexander (formerly *Amerika*). Type: troop carrier. Builder: Harland & Wolff, Belfast. Built: 1905. Length: 700'. Weight: 22,225 gross tons. Operator: U.S. Maritime Commission.

Edmund Fanning. Type: Liberty ship (freighter), Hull no. 710. Builder: California Shipbuilding Corp. Built: 1943. Length: 441'6". Weight: 7,191 gross tons. Operator: Isthmian Steamship Co.

Edward B. Dudley. Type: Liberty ship (freighter), Hull no. 889. Builder: North Carolina Shipbuilding Co. Built: 1943. Length: 441'6". Weight: 7,191 gross tons. Operator: Bulk Carriers Corp.

Eli Whitney. Type: Liberty ship (freighter), Hull no. 264. Builder: Permanente Metals Corp. Built: 1942. Length: 441'6". Weight: 7,191 gross tons. Operator: Grace Line, Inc.

Elwood Mead. Type: Liberty ship (freighter), Hull no. 2579. Builder: Oregon Ship Building Corp. Built: 1944. Length: 441'6". Weight: 7,191 gross tons. Operator: Interocean Steamship Corp.

Emery Rice (formerly the USS *Ranger*). Type: steam-powered iron-hulled school ship with barque-rigged auxiliary sails. Builder: Harlan and Hollingsworth. Built: 1876. Length: 177'4". Displacement: 1,020 tons. Operator: U.S. Merchant Marine Academy.

Ethan Allen. Type: Liberty ship (freighter/limited troop carrier), Hull no. 204. Builder: New England Shipbuilding Corp. Built: 1942. Length: 441'6". Weight: 7,191 gross tons. Operator: United States Lines.

Exceller. Type: general cargo. Builder: Bath Iron Works. Built: 1941. Length: 400'. Weight: 6,535 gross tons. Operator: American Export Lines, Inc.

Exchange. Type: general cargo/passenger. Builder: Bethlehem Steel Co. (Bethlehem Shipbuilding Co.). Built: 1940. Length: 450'. Weight: 6,736 gross tons. Operator: American Export Lines, Inc.

Exmoor. Type: general cargo/passenger. Builder: American International Shipbuilding Corp. Built: 1919. Length: 401'. Weight: 4,999 gross tons. Operator: American Export Lines, Inc.

Fairland. Type: general cargo. Builder: Gulf Shipbuilding Co. Built: 1942. Length: 445'4". Weight, 6,165 gross tons. Operator: Waterman Steamship Lines.

Fort Cumberland. Type: tanker. Builder: Sun Shipbuilding & Dry Dock Co. Built: 1944. Length: 503'. Weight: 10,296 gross tons. Operator: Marine Transport Lines.

George Dewey. Type: Liberty ship (freighter), Hull no. 1202. Builder: St. Johns River Shipbuilding Co. Built: 1943. Length: 441'6". Weight: 7,191 gross tons. Operator: American Export Lines.

George L. Baker. Type: Liberty ship (freighter), Hull no. 1614. Builder: Oregon Ship Building Corp. Built: 1943. Length: 441'6". Weight: 7,191 gross tons. Operator: Weyerhauser Steamship Co.

George Washington. Type: passenger. Builder: Stettiner Maschinebau AG "Vulcan," Stettin, Germany. Built: 1908. Length: 722'. Weight: 23,788 gross tons. Operator: U.S. Maritime Commission.

Hoosier. Type: freighter. Builder: American International Shipbuilding Corp. Built: 1920. Length: 392'. Weight: 5,060 gross tons. Operator: Federal Marine Corp.

James King. Type: general cargo. Builder: Permanente Metals Corp. Built: 1943. Length: 417'8¾". Weight: 7,176 gross tons. Operator: Mississippi Shipping Co. Inc.

James Lykes. Type: general cargo. Builder: Bethlehem Steel Co. (Bethlehem Shipbuilding Co.). Built: 1940. Length: 395'. Weight: 6,760 gross tons. Operator: Lykes Bros. Steamship Co., Inc.

James McKay. Type: general cargo. Builder: Bethlehem Steel Co. (Bethlehem Shipbuilding Co.). Built: 1940. Length: 417'9". Weight: 6,760 gross tons. Operator: Lykes Bros. Steamship Co., Inc.

James Oglethorpe. Type: Liberty ship (freighter), Hull no. 341. Builder: Southeastern Shipbuilding Corp. Built: 1942. Length: 411'6". Weight: 7,191 gross tons. Operator: South Atlantic Steamship Line.

James Sprunt. Type: Liberty ship, Hull no. 886. Builder: North Carolina Shipbuilding Co. Built: 1943. Length: 441'6". Weight: 7,191 gross tons. Operator: Black Diamond Steamship Corp.

James Turner. Type: Liberty ship (freighter, limited troop carrier), Hull no. 166. Builder: North Carolina Shipbuilding Co. Built: 1942. Length: 441'6". Weight: 7,191 gross tons. Operator: International Freighting Corp., Inc.

Jean Lykes. Type: general cargo. Builder: Consolidated Steel Corp. Built: 1943. Length: 345'. Weight: 6,711 gross tons. Operator: Lykes Bros. Steamship Co., Inc.

Jeremiah O'Brien. Type: Liberty ship (freighter), Hull no. 806. Builder: New England Shipbuilding Corp. Built: 1943. Length: 441'6". Weight: 7,191 gross tons. Operator: Grace Line, Inc.

Jeremiah Van Rensselaer. Type: Liberty ship (freighter), Hull no. 155. Builder: North Carolina Shipbuilding Co. Built: 1942. Length: 441'6". Weight: 7,191 gross tons. Operator: Agwilines, Inc.

Jim Bridger. Type: Liberty ship (freighter), Hull no. 610. Builder: Oregon Ship Building Corp. Built: 1942. Length: 441'6". Weight: 7,191 gross tons. Operator: James Griffiths & Sons, Inc.

John Bell. Type: Liberty ship (freighter), Hull no. 834. Builder: Todd Houston Shipbuilding Corp. Built: 1943. Length: 441'6". Weight: 7,191 gross tons. Operator: J. H. Winchester & Co., Inc.

John Carroll. Type: Liberty ship (freighter), Hull no. 1557. Builder: Permanente Metals Corp., Yard no. 1. Built: 1943. Length: 441'6". Weight: 7,191 gross tons. Operator: American-Hawaiian Steamship Co.

John H. Couch. Type: Liberty ship (freighter), Hull no. 1618. Builder: Oregon Ship Building Corp. Built: 1943. Length: 441'6". Weight: 7,191 gross tons. Operator: Weyerhauser Steamship Co.

John W. Brown. Type: Liberty ship (freighter/limited troop carrier), Hull no. 312. Builder: Bethlehem-Fairfield Shipyard. Built: 1942. Length: 441'6". Weight: 7,191 gross tons. Operator: States Marine Corp.

John Witherspoon. Type: Liberty ship (freighter), Hull no. 31. Builder: Bethlehem-Fairfield Shipyard. Built: 1942. Length: 441'6". Weight: 7,191 gross tons. Operator: Seas Shipping Co., Inc.

Joshua Thomas. Type: Liberty ship (freighter), Hull no. 1760. Builder: Bethlehem-Fairfield Shipyard. Built: 1943. Length: 441'6". Weight: 7,191 gross tons. Operator: American Export Lines, Inc.

Lakewood Victory. Type: Victory ship (general cargo). Builder: Permanente Metals Corp. Built: 1944. Length: 436'6". Weight: 7,607 gross tons. Operator: U.S. Navy.

Markay. Type: tanker. Builder: Federal Shipbuilding & Dry Dock Co. Built: 1939. Length: 553'. Weight: 11,355 gross tons. Operator: Keystone Tankship Corp.

Mary Bickerdyke. Type: Liberty ship (freighter), Hull no. 2116. Builder: Permanente Metals Corp. Built: 1943. Length: 441'6". Weight: 7,191 gross tons. Operator: Seas Shipping Co.

Matsonia. Type: passenger/troop transport. Builder: Wm. Cramp & Sons Ship & Engine Building Co. Built: 1927. Length: 582'. Weight: 17,226 gross tons. Operator: Matson Navigation Co.

Mendoza (French/British). Type: passenger/general cargo. Builder: Swan, Hunter & Wigham Richardson, Ltd., Wallsend. Built: 1920. Length: 450'5". Weight: 8,199 gross tons. Operator: Societe Generale de Transports Maritimes a Vapeur Sa.; later, Royal Navy.

Meriwether Lewis. Type: Liberty ship (freighter), Hull no. 170. Builder: Oregon Ship Building Corp. Built: 1941. Length: 441'6". Weight: 7,191 gross tons. Operator: American Mail Line, Ltd.

Michael J. Stone. Type: Liberty ship (freighter), Hull no. 99. Builder: Todd Houston Shipbuilding Corp. Built: 1942. Length: 441'6". Weight: 7,191 gross tons. Operator: Lykes Bros. Steamship Co., Inc.

Mission San Gabriel. Type: tanker. Builder: Marinship Corp. Built: 1944. Length: 503'. Weight: 10,461 gross tons. Operator: Deaconhill Shipping Co.

Monterrey. Type: passenger/troop carrier. Builder: Bethlehem Steel Co. (Bethlehem Shipbuilding Co.). Built: 1932. Length: 638'. Weight: 18,017 gross tons. Operator: Oceanic Steamship Co./War Shipping Administration Transport (Dec. 1941–Sept. 1946).

Mormacrey. Type: general cargo. Builder: Los Angeles Shipbuilding & Drydock Corp. Built: 1919. Length: 423'. Weight: 5,946 gross tons. Operator: American Republics Line (Mooremack South American Line, Inc.).

Mormacswan. Type: general cargo. Builder: Federal Shipbuilding & Dry Dock Co. Built: 1940. Length: 435'. Weight: 7,194 gross tons. Operator: Moore-McCormack Lines.

Morro Castle. Type: passenger ship. Builder: Newport News Shipbuilding & Dry Dock Co. Built: 1930. Length: 508'. Weight: 11,520 gross tons. Operator: Atlantic Gulf & West Indies Steamship Lines.

Nashaba. Type: general cargo. Builder: Pacific Coast Shipbuilding Co. Built: 1921. Length: 416'. Weight: 6,062 gross tons. Operator: Lykes Bros. Steamship Co., Inc.

Norlantic. Type: general cargo. Builder: Detroit Shipbuilding Co. Built: 1920. Length: 251'. Weight: 2,606 gross tons. Operator: Norlasco Steamship Corp.

Pacific Sun. Type: tanker. Builder: Sun Shipbuilding & Dry Dock Co. Built: 1929. Length: 497'10". Weight: 9,097 gross tons. Operator: Motor Tankship Corp.

Patrick Henry. Type: Liberty ship (freighter), Hull no. 14. Builder: Bethlehem-Fairfield Shipyard. Built: 1941. Length: 441'6". Weight: 7,191 gross tons. Operator: Lykes Bros. Steamship Co., Inc.

President Cleveland. Type: passenger/general cargo. Builder: Newport News Shipbuilding & Dry Dock Co. Built: 1921. Length: 535'2". Weight: 12,568 gross tons. Operator: American President Lines, Ltd.

Rachel Jackson. Type: Liberty ship (freighter), Hull no. 721. Builder: California Shipbuilding Corp. Built: 1943. Length: 441'6". Weight: 7,191 gross tons. Operator: Black Diamond Steamship Corp.

Roger Moore. Type: Liberty ship (freighter), Hull no. 903. Builder: North Carolina Shipbuilding Co. Built: 1943. Length: 441'6". Weight: 7,191 gross tons. Operator: Merchants & Miners Transportation Co.

Sabine Sun. Type: tanker. Builder: Sun Shipbuilding & Dry Dock Co. Built: 142. Length: 521'. Weight: 11,359 gross tons. Operator: Sun Oil Co.; War Emergency Tankers Corp.

Salvation Lass. Type: general cargo. Builder: American International Ship Building Corp. Built: 1919. Length: 390'. Weight: 5,753 gross tons. Operator: Mississippi Shipping Co.

Sam Jackson. Type: Liberty ship (freighter), Hull no. 1591. Builder: Oregon Ship Building Corp. Built: 1943. Length: 441'6". Weight: 7,191 gross tons. Operator: American Mail Lines, Ltd.

Santa Elena. Type: passenger. Builder: Federal Shipbuilding & Dry Dock Co. Built: 1933. Length: 484'. Weight: 9,135 gross tons. Operator: Grace Line, Inc.

Sea Train Havana. Type: railway car carrier. Builder: Sun Shipbuilding & Dry Dock Co. Built: 1932. Length: 478'. Weight: 8,061 gross tons. Operator: Seatrain Lines, Inc.

Seakay. Type: tanker. Builder: Sun Shipbuilding & Dry Dock Co. Built: 1939. Length: 553'. Weight: 11,355 gross tons. Operator: Keystone Tankship Corp.

Snug Hitch. Type: general cargo. Builder: Consolidated Steel Corp. Built: 1945. Length: 321'4". Weight: 3,805 gross tons. Operator: United States Lines.

Spottsylvania. Type: tanker. Builder: Sun Shipbuilding & Dry Dock Co. Built: 1943. Length: 503'. Weight: 10,195 gross tons. Operator: Gulf Oil Corp.

Star of Oregon. Type: Liberty ship (freighter), Hull no. 171. Builder: Oregon Ship Building Corp. Built: 1941. Length: 441'6". Weight: 7,191 gross tons. Operator: States Steamship Co.

Steel Traveler. Type: general cargo/passenger. Builder: Federal Shipbuilding Co. Built: 1922. Length: 442'. Weight: 7,056 gross tons. Operator: Isthmian Steamship Co.

Stephen Hopkins. Type: Liberty ship (freighter), Hull no. 2283. Builder: Permanente Metals Corp., Yard no. 2. Built: 1942. Length: 441'6". Weight: 7,191 gross tons. Operator: Oliver J. Olson & Co.

Thomas H. Barry. Type: passenger/troop ship. Builder: Newport News Shipbuilding & Dry Dock Co. Built: 1930. Length: 482'. Weight: 11,520 gross tons. Operator: U.S. War Department.

United States. Type: passenger ship. Builder: Newport News Shipbuilding & Dry Dock Co. Built: 1952. Length: 990'. Weight: 53,529 gross tons. Operator: United States Lines.

Villanova Victory. Type: Victory ship (general cargo). Builder: California Shipbuilding Corp. Built: 1945. Length: 436'6". Weight: 7,607 gross tons. Operator: Coastwise Line.

Wade Hampton. Type: Liberty ship (freighter), Hull no. 315. Builder: Delta Shipbuilding Co. Built: 1942. Length: 441'6". Weight: 7,191 gross tons. Operator: Mississippi Shipping Co., Inc.

Washington. Type: passenger ship. Builder: New York Shipbuilding Co. Built: 1933. Length: 705'. Weight: 24,289 gross tons. Operator: United States Lines Co.

William C. Clairborne. Type: Liberty ship (freighter), Hull no. 120. Builder: Delta Shipbuilding Co. Built: 1942. Length: 441'6". Weight: 7,191 gross tons. Operator: Mississippi Shipping Co., Inc.

William D. Pender. Type: Liberty ship (freighter, limited troop carrier), Hull no. 894. Builder: North Carolina Shipbuilding Co. Built: 1943. Length: 441'6". Weight: 7,191 gross tons. Operator: American South African Line.

William H. Crawford. Type: Liberty ship (freighter), Hull no. 830. Builder: Todd Houston Shipbuilding Corp. Built: 1943. Length: 441'6". Weight: 7,191 gross tons. Operator: Lykes Bros. Steamship Co., Inc.

William Tyler Page. Type: Liberty ship (freighter), Hull no. 993. Builder: Bethlehem-Fairfield Shipyard. Built: 1943. Length: 441'6". Weight: 7,191 gross tons. Operator: Polarus Steamship Co., Inc.

SOURCES OF DATA

American Bureau of Shipping. *Record of the American Bureau of Shipping.*
Bunker, *Liberty Ships.*
Jaffee, *The Liberty Ships.*
Jordan, *The World's Merchant Fleets, 1939.*
Kludas, *Great Passenger Ships of the World.*
Lloyd's Register of Shipping.
Sawyer and Mitchell, *The Liberty Ships.*

APPENDIX B

Ships of the U.S. Navy

This appendix provides a select listing of ships of the U.S. Navy cited in this volume.

Antietam, CV-36. Type: aircraft carrier. Builder: Philadelphia Navy Yard. Built: 1944. Length: 888'. Displacement: 27,100 tons.

Arcturus, AK-18. Type: cargo ship. Builder: Sun Shipbuilding & Dry Dock Co. Built: 1939. Length: 459'1". Displacement: 14,225 tons.

Arkansas, BB-33. Type: battleship. Builder: New York Shipbuilding Co. Built: 1911. Length: 562'. Displacement: 26,000 tons.

Barbero, SS-317. Type: submarine. Builder: Electric Boat Co. Built: 1943. Length 311'9". Displacement: 1,526 tons.

Benson, DD-421. Type: destroyer. Builder: Bethlehem Steel Co. Built: 1939. Length: 348'2". Displacement: 1,620 tons.

Block Island, ACV-21. Type: auxiliary aircraft carrier. Builder: Seattle-Tacoma Shipbuilding Corp. Built: 1942. Length: 465'8". Displacement: 7,800 tons.

Bogue, ACV-8 (later CVE-9). Type: auxiliary aircraft carrier. Builder: Seattle-Tacoma Shipbuilding Corp. Built: 1942. Length: 495'8". Displacement: 9,800 tons.

Card, AVG-11 (later CVE-11). Type: auxiliary aircraft carrier. Builder: Seattle-Tacoma Shipbuilding Corp. Built: 1942. Length 495'2". Displacement: 9,800 tons.

Cimarron, AO-22. Type: oiler. Builder: Sun Shipbuilding and Dry Dock Co. Built: 1939. Length: 553'. Displacement: 7,470 tons.

Clay, APA-39. Type: attack transport. Builder: Western Pipe and Steel Co. Built: 1943. Length: 492'. Displacement: 8,100 tons.

Cutlass, SS-478. Type: submarine. Builder: Portsmouth Navy Yard. Built: 1944. Length: 311'8". Displacement: 1,570 tons.

Cuttlefish, SS-171. Type: submarine. Builder: Electric Boat Co. Built: 1933. Length: 274'. Displacement: 1,130 tons.

Freestone, APA-167. Type: attack transport. Builder: Oregon Shipbuilding Corp. Built: 1944. Length: 455'. Displacement: 6,720 tons.

Guadalcanal, CVE-60. Type: escort aircraft carrier. Builder: Kaiser Co. Built: 1943. Length: 512'. Displacement: 7,800 tons.

Haddo, SS-255. Type: submarine. Builder: Electric Boat Co. Built: 1942. Length: 311'9". Displacement: 1,526 tons.

Hammondsport, APV-2 (later AKV-2). Type: transport/cargo ship. Builder: Sun Shipbuilding & Dry Dock Co. Built: 1932. Length: 478'. Displacement: 4,000 tons.

Harris, AP-8. Type: transport. Builder: Bethlehem Shipbuilding Corp. Built: 1921. Length: 535'2". Displacement: 13,529 tons.

Hornet, CV-12 (later CVS-12). Type: aircraft carrier. Builder: Newport News Shipbuilding & Dry Dock Co. Built: 1943. Length: 872'. Displacement: 27,000 tons.

Indianapolis, CA-35. Type: heavy cruiser. Builder: New York Shipbuilding Corp. Built: 1931. Length: 610'. Displacement: 9,800 tons.

Lakehurst, APV-3. Type: transport. Builder: Sun Shipbuilding Co. Built: 1940. Length: 483'. Displacement: 7,450 tons.

Marblehead, CL-12. Type: light cruiser. Builder: William Cramp & Son. Built: 1923. Length: 555'6". Displacement: 7,050 tons.

Mayo, DD-422. Type: destroyer. Builder: Bethlehem Shipbuilding Co. Built: 1940. Length: 374'4". Displacement: 1,620 tons.

Mercy, AH-8. Type: hospital ship. Builder: Consolidated Steel Corp. Built: 1943. Length: 416'. Displacement: 11,250 tons.

Milwaukee, CL-5. Type: light cruiser. Builder: Seattle Construction & Dry Dock Co. Built: 1921. Length: 555'6". Displacement: 7,050 tons.

Missouri, BB-63. Type: battleship. Builder: New York Naval Shipyard. Built: 1944. Length: 887'3". Displacement: 45,000 tons.

Monrovia, APA-31. Type: attack transport. Builder: Bethlehem-Sparrows Point Shipyard, Inc. Built: 1942. Length: 491'. Displacement: 8,889 tons.

Mulberry, AN-27. Type: net laying ship. Builder: American Shipbuilding Co. Built: 1941. Length: 163'2". Displacement: 805 tons.

Nevada, BB-36. Type: battleship. Builder: Fore River Shipbuilding Co. Built: 1914. Length: 583'. Displacement: 27,500 tons.

Pennsylvania, BB-38. Type: battleship. Builder: Newport News Shipbuilding & Dry Dock Co. Built: 1915. Length: 608'. Displacement: 31,400 tons.

Ranger. Type: steam-powered iron-hulled vessel with auxiliary sails. Builder: Harlem and Hollingsworth. Built: 1876. Length: 177'4". Displacement: 1,020 tons.

Redfin, SS-272. Type: submarine. Builder: Manitowoc Shipbuilding Co. Built: 1943. Length: 311'9". Displacement: 1,526 tons.

Shangri-la, CV-38. Type: aircraft carrier. Builder: Norfolk Navy Yard. Built: 1944. Length: 888'. Displacement: 27,100 tons.

Taconic, ABC-17. Type: amphibious force flagship. Builder: North Carolina Shipbuilding Co. Built: 1945. Length: 459'2". Displacement: 13,910 tons.

Texas, BB-35. Type: battleship. Builder: Newport News Shipbuilding Co. Built: 1912. Length: 573'. Displacement: 27,000 tons.

Tuscaloosa, CA-37. Type: heavy cruiser. Builder: New York Shipbuilding Co. Built: 1933. Length: 588'2". Displacement: 9,950 tons.

Vulcan, AR-5. Type: repair ship. Builder: New York Shipbuilding Co. Built: 1940. Length: 530'. Displacement: 12,911 tons.

Wichita, CA-45. Type: heavy cruiser. Builder: Philadelphia Navy Yard. Built: 1939. Length: 608'4". Displacement: 10,000 tons.

William P. Biddoe, AP-15 (later APA-8). Type: transport. Builder: Bethlehem Shipbuilding Corp. Built: 1919. Length: 507'. Displacement: 14,450 tons.

SOURCES OF DATA

Jane's Fighting Ships.
U.S. Naval History Division, *Dictionary of American Naval Fighting Ships.*

Acknowledgments

Many individuals deserve thanks for helping with this book. First and foremost, we thank the Kings Point graduates of the war years who told their stories as participants in the Mariners at War Project. They were truly part of the "greatest generation." For many of these veterans, the interviews dredged up memories that had long lain dormant.

The volume was greatly enhanced by the unique artwork of Robert Glenn Smith, himself a Kings Point veteran, class of 1944. During World War II, Mr. Smith drew the sketches that appear in this volume while he was a cadet-midshipman and after graduation. In addition, we sincerely thank Donald W. Patterson for permission to reproduce his watercolor of the Liberty ship *Jeremiah O'Brien*. We also offer sincere thanks to Oswald Brett and Michael J. Schneider of Project Liberty Ship for permission to reproduce two of Mr. Brett's illustrations of the Liberty ship *John W. Brown*. We also sincerely thank the U.S. Naval Institute and the U.S. Merchant Marine Academy for permission to use photographs from their holdings. Martin P. Skrocki, Public Information Officer, deserves our special thanks for providing the historical photographs concerning the cadet-midshipmen at Kings Point.

Very special thanks go to RADM Thomas A. King, who suggested the project of interviewing Kings Point veterans and for his steadfast encouragement. This volume was made possible through generous grants of funds provided by Kings Point alumni James Ackerman, Virgil Allen, Kenneth DeGhetto, Eugene McCormick, and Carroll J. O'Brien, as well as by the USMMA Alumni Foundation. In addition, at Kings Point we thank VADM Joseph D. Stewart, RADM Christopher McMahon, Shashi Kumar, Charles Hubert, Warren F. Mazek, Peter Rackett, and Frank Todesco for their advice and encouragement.

Sincere thanks go to Alfreda E. Dunham, Lee Funken, and Jon Helmick for helping to conduct interviews that appear in this volume. In addition, we thank Robert M. Browning Jr., Jose Femenia, Robert P. Gardella, Jon S. Helmick, Dave Rosen, Martin P. Skrocki, Gene Allen Smith, Joshua Smith, and Marilyn Stern for reading the manuscript and for making helpful suggestions. David Kahn, Patrick J. Kelly, Robert Richardson, Elly Shodell, and Norman I. Silber deserve thanks for their helpful advice concerning the manuscript.

A very special thank-you goes to Laura Cody for her invaluable suggestions, her expertise in working on key technical aspects of the manuscript, and her untiring enthusiasm for the project. Creating typescripts from audiotapes was an arduous task, and deep gratitude is extended to Norma Walby for her helpful suggestions and dedicated service in the early days of the project and to Norma Panico of Arlington Typing and Mailing for preparing numerous transcripts. In addition, we thank Catherine Graham and Diane Martin for preparing several other transcripts.

Special thanks are also owed to Meredith Morris-Babb, Director of the University Press of Florida, and to her staff for their unfailing kindness and technical expertise in this endeavor.

Finally, we thank two members of our family, Valerie McGreevy Billy and Margaret M. Billy, for their very helpful suggestions and strong support during the many years that this project evolved. Any flaws and errors are, of course, entirely our own.

Notes

INTRODUCTION

1. U.S. Merchant Marine Academy, *Superintendent's Notice 2007–06*, 1.

2. Carse, *The Long Haul*, 15.

3. Ibid., 75, 78–80; Lane, *Ships for Victory*, 1, 754, 764.

4. Bunker, *Liberty Ships*, 19–28, 33, 269; see also Jaffee, *The Liberty Ships*.

5. Mitchell, *We'll Deliver*, 19–21, 69–79.

6. Ibid., 69–79.

7. Ibid.

8. U.S. War Shipping Administration, Division of Training, *U.S. Merchant Marine Cadet Corps Circular No. 41–40*.

9. Mitchell, *We'll Deliver*, 105.

10. Ibid., 129.

11. Ibid., 69–70, 73–74; U.S. War Shipping Administration, *United States Maritime Service, Information Booklet*, 54.

12. Morison, *Strategy and Compromise*, 18–23; Reynolds, *Command of the Sea*, 519.

13. Reynolds, *Command of the Sea*, 519.

14. Ibid., 520.

15. Morison, *Strategy and Compromise*, 39–40.

16. Bunker, *Heroes in Dungarees*, 103; see also Herbert, *The Forgotten Heroes*, 90–100.

17. Reynolds, *Command of the Sea*, 521; Spector, *At War at Sea*, 286; Parillo, *The Japanese Merchant Marine in World War II*, 207.

18. Reynolds, *Command of the Sea*, 539–40.

19. Ibid., 521.

20. The exact number of merchant mariner deaths is unknown. Herbert sets the figure at 8,380. See Herbert, *The Forgotten Heroes*, 101, 265–66. On the other hand, Bruce L. Felknor cites the number of deaths at 6,845. See *The U.S. Merchant Marine at War, 1775–1945*, 331.

CHAPTER 1. AROUND THE WORLD

1. The "roaring forties" is a name that mariners apply to the latitudes between 40° and 50° south latitude where prevailing westerly winds blow strongly, unimpeded by any major land mass.

2. Jordan, *The World's Merchant Fleets, 1939*, 460.

3. Paddy Brennan had the reputation of being a hard-knuckled disciplinarian. See McCready, *The Men and Ships of the War Years*, 28.

CHAPTER 2. TRAINING FOR WAR

1. King, "The Merchant Marine Cadet Corps," 273–81; see also Mitchell, *We'll Deliver*, 106, 132–34.

2. The Plimsoll mark is a figure painted on the side of cargo carriers. Different horizontal lines indicate the depth limits to which a ship can be loaded in different seas or conditions.

3. Aarseth never received protective gear.

4. See Browning, *U.S. Merchant Vessel War Casualties*, 256; and Moore, "A Careless Word," 143.

5. The term "degaussing" describes an anti-mine measure performed by arranging a cable around the hull of a ship and feeding electricity through it to neutralize the magnetic effect of the metal hull.

6. The former residence of Walter P. Chrysler, automobile manufacturer, and since 1943 the central administration building of the U.S. Merchant Marine Academy.

7. The Rules of the Road are international ship handling rules and procedures designed to avoid ship collisions.

8. Browning, *U.S. Merchant Vessel War Casualties*, 179–80; Moore, "A Careless Word," 131.

CHAPTER 3. THE BATTLE OF THE ATLANTIC

1. Valle, "United States Merchant Marine Casualties," 263. For an authoritative description of the role of Kings Pointers in World War II, see King, "The Merchant Marine Cadet Corps, 273–81. See also Browning, *U.S. Merchant Vessel War Casualties*; and Moore, "A Careless Word," for detailed descriptions of the losses of individual merchant ships. For the story of breaking the German secret codes, see Kahn, *Seizing the Enigma*.

2. Browning, *U.S. Merchant Vessel War Casualties*, 40–41; Moore, "A Careless Word," 41.

3. The German submarine *U-69* shelled and torpedoed the *Norlantic* on May 12, 1942, ninety miles east of Bonaire Island. Seven crewmen were lost. See Browning, *U.S. Merchant Vessel War Casualties*, 100–101; Moore, "A Careless Word," 203.

4. The *James Oglethorpe* was torpedoed on her maiden voyage by *U-758* on March 16, 1943 at 2324 hours. The Liberty ship survived until the next day, when the German submarine *U-91* sank her with three torpedoes. See Browning, *U.S. Merchant Vessel War Casualties*, 301; Moore, "A Careless Word," 143.

5. On February 3, 1943 the German submarine *U-223* attacked ships in Convoy SG-19, including the troopship SS *Dorchester*, causing an explosion and the subsequent sinking of the ship with heavy loss of life. See Browning, *U.S. Merchant Vessel War Casualties*, 270–71.

6. The German submarine *U-456* torpedoed and sank the SS *Jeremiah Van Rensselaer*, carrying nine thousand tons of general Army cargo, at 0032 hours on February 2, 1943. Traveling as part of Convoy HX-224, her complement was forty-two crewmen and twenty-eight Naval Armed Guardsmen. Crewmen lost numbered thirty-five, and an additional eleven Navy gunners were lost. See Browning, *U.S. Merchant Vessel War Casualties*, 269–70; Moore, "A Careless Word," 47.

7. Browning, *U.S. Merchant Vessel War Casualties,* 284; Moore, *"A Careless Word,"* 289.

8. The term "fiddley" refers to casting or grating above the engine room or boiler room, or to the upper part of a boiler room below the funnel.

9. The German submarine *U-221* torpedoed and sank the *Andrea F. Luckenbach* on March 10, 1943. The *Luckenbach* had a crew of fifty-eight, an additional twenty-six Naval Armed Guard personnel and one U.S. Army officer. A total of eleven crewmen and eleven Naval Armed Guardsmen were lost. See Moore, *"A Careless Word,"* 16–17; see also Browning, *U.S. Merchant Vessel War Casualties,* 296–97.

10. Cadet-Midshipmen Lee T. Byrd and Francis R. Miller were aboard the *Harry Luckenbach* when a German submarine, the *U-91,* sank the ship on March 17, 1943. No one survived. See Browning, *U.S. Merchant Vessel War Casualties,* 302; Moore, *"A Careless Word,"* 123.

11. Browning, *U.S. Merchant Vessel War Casualties,* 491; Moore, *"A Careless Word,"* 199.

CHAPTER 4. CONVOYS

1. A convoy diagram for Convoy HX-2333 notes that the *Pender* was listed as carrying explosives and general cargo on this voyage. See Haskell, *Shadow on the Horizon,* 22.

2. For details of the *Spencer*'s destruction of *U-175,* see Willoughby, *The U.S. Coast Guard in World War II,* 201.

3. A versatile "amphibian," DUKW was General Motors' letter code for their amphibious vehicle: D = 1942 (year of design); U = utility truck amphibious; K = front-wheel drive; W = dual rear-drive axles. They were called "ducks."

4. Browning, *U.S. Merchant Vessel War Casualties,* 408; Moore, *"A Careless Word,"* 256–57.

5. Browning, *U.S. Merchant Vessel War Casualties,* 374–75; Moore, *"A Careless Word,"* 253–54.

6. On April 20, 1944, the *Milwaukee* was transferred to the Soviet Union under a lend-lease agreement; after performing convoy and patrol duty, it was transferred back to the United States on March 16, 1949. U.S. Naval History Division, *Dictionary of American Naval Fighting Ships,* 4: 363.

7. The *U-505* was captured intact, revealing a German secret codebook for disguising grid positions. See Kahn, *Seizing the Enigma,* 264.

8. U.S. Naval History Division, *Dictionary of American Naval Fighting Ships,* 1: 132.

CHAPTER 5. LIBERTY SHIPS

1. Bunker, *Liberty Ships,* 19–28, 33, 269. Details for the Liberty ships vary in different accounts. See Sawyer and Mitchell, *The Liberty Ships,* 1–4, 30–31. See also Jaffee, *The Liberty Ships,* which is quite comprehensive and handy to use. Lane, *Ships for Victory;* Sawyer and Mitchell, *Victory Ships and Tankers.*

2. Jaffee, *The Liberty Ships,* 121.

3. For various historical accounts of the battle, see Browning, *U.S. Merchant Vessel War Casualties of World War II,* 221–22; Moore, *"A Careless Word,"* 269–70; Reminick,

Action in the South Atlantic, 246. For further information, see Bunker, *Heroes in Dungarees*, 154–55; Gleichauf, *Unsung Heroes*, 110, 125, 136–37, 165.

4. A variation of *gunwale*, the upper edge of a boat's side.

CHAPTER 6. THE MURMANSK RUN

1. For more information on the convoys to Russia, see Carse, *A Cold Corner of Hell*; Irving, *The Destruction of Convoy PQ.17*; Merrill, *The Winter Winds of Hell*; Ruegg and Hague, *Convoys to Russia, 1941–1945*.

2. Irving, *The Destruction of Convoy PQ.17*.

3. The SS *John Witherspoon* was sunk by the German submarine *U-255* on July 6, 1942. Two torpedoes struck the Liberty ship on the starboard side between holds four and five. After the crew had abandoned ship, the U-boat sent two more torpedoes into the port side of the *Witherspoon* amidships, causing the ship to break in two and sink. See Browning, *U.S. Merchant Vessel War Casualties*, 175–76; Moore, "A Careless Word," 158–59.

4. The phrase "dropped the stick" means dropped the bomb.

5. At 0600 hours on July 10, 1942, German aircraft bombed and sank the SS *El Capitan*. The ship contained a crew of thirty-seven merchant seamen, eleven members of the U.S. Naval Armed Guard, and nineteen survivors from the SS *John Witherspoon*. The HMS *Lord Austin* picked up the entire group. See Browning, *U.S. Merchant Vessel War Casualties*, 176; Moore, "A Careless Word," 638.

6. When it left Iceland, Convoy PQ-17 comprised thirty-three merchant ships, from which a total of twenty-three ships were sunk. See Bunker, *Heroes in Dungarees*, 103; see also Gleichauf, *Unsung Heroes*, 205–6.

CHAPTER 7. THE MEDITERRANEAN

1. For more information on Mediterranean operations, see Bunker, *Liberty Ships*, 111–25.

2. The term "General Quarters" refers to a general alarm sounded in time of danger.

3. The bulwark is the plating around the outboard edge of the upper deck of a ship to prevent entry of the sea.

4. The military unit fought in Italy under the name Hermann Goering Division.

5. The Nisei troops were second-generation Japanese Americans, and many were from the West Coast.

CHAPTER 8. D-DAY

1. SS *George Dewey*, Bridge Log Book No. 2.

CHAPTER 9. THE VAST PACIFIC

1. Lighters are barges used for carrying cargo to and from larger ships.

2. Browning, *U.S. Merchant Vessel War Casualties*, 371; Moore, "A Careless Word," 154.

3. The abbreviation LST stands for landing ship tank, a cargo ship with large doors in the bow that permitted military vehicles to roll off onto beachheads.

4. Kludas, *Great Passenger Ships of the World*, 3: 170–71; Gibson and Donovan, *The Abandoned Ocean*, 137–38, 148–49.

5. The term "marks" refers to Plimsoll line marks on the hull of a ship, which indicate how much cargo can be loaded safely under various conditions.

6. U.S. Naval History Division, *Dictionary of American Naval Fighting Ships*, 3: 435.

CHAPTER 10. WEATHER

1. Jaffee, *The Last Liberty*, 10–12.

2. The gunwale is the upper edge of a vessel's or boat's side.

CHAPTER 12. PRISONERS OF WAR

1. Browning, *U.S. Merchant Vessel War Casualties*, 5; Moore, *"A Careless Word,"* 40–41.

CHAPTER 13. INDIAN OCEAN

1. Browning, *U.S. Merchant Vessel War Casualties*, 451; Moore, *"A Careless Word,"* 98–99.

CHAPTER 14. NAVY

1. The abbreviation IFF stands for Identification, Friend or Foe, an electronic system used to determine the friend-or-foe status of a radar target.

2. Blair, *Silent Victory*, 962; U.S. Naval History Division, *Dictionary of American Naval Fighting Ships*, 1: 94.

3. For an informative biography of Rear Admiral Seiberlich, see U.S.S. Hornet Museum, "Splash Down 2004," July 16–25, www.uss-hornet.org/splash/bio-seiberlich.html, 1–2.

CHAPTER 16. THE SIGNIFICANCE OF THE MERCHANT MARINE

1. Browning, *U.S. Merchant Vessel War Casualties*, 221–22; Moore, *"A Careless Word,"* 269–70; Bunker, *Heroes in Dungarees*, 154–55; Reminick, *Action in the South Atlantic*, 46.

2. Browning, *U.S. Merchant Vessel War Casualties*, 301; Moore, *"A Careless Word,"* 143.

3. Rear Admiral Emory S. Land, former Maritime Commission chairman.

CHAPTER 17. PERSONAL THOUGHTS

1. Conrad, *Mirror of the Sea*, 73.

BIBLIOGRAPHY

Primary Sources

Bland Memorial Library (U.S. Merchant Marine Academy Library)

CORRESPONDENCE

Moore, Arthur R., to G. J. Billy, June 29, 2004.
Nottingham, Milton G., to G. J. Billy, March 28, 2002.
Smith, Robert Glenn, to G. J. Billy, October 15, 2004, and January 28, 2005.

INTERVIEWS

Unless noted otherwise, George J. Billy conducted the following interviews, which
   were recorded at the U.S. Merchant Marine Academy:
Aarseth, Karl J. October 19, 1995.
Ackerman, James H. October 15, 1994.
Anderson, Taylor A. October 16, 1992.
Antos, Steve. October 15, 1994.
Bark, George H. October 15, 1994.
Bartlett, Francis. October 20, 1997.
Beltran, Pedro N. October 23, 1995.
Botto, Walter J. October 15, 1994. By Lee Funken.
Burke, John J. October 14, 1994.
Cahill, Richard A. December 7, 1995.
Churchman, Leslie. October 14, 1994.
Davis, Robert H. October 20, 1990.
DeGhetto, Kenneth A. October 14, 1995.
Erb, Arthur E. October 15, 1992.
Evans, Henry H. October 15, 1994.
Ford, Francis J., Jr. October 16, 1992.
Ford, William H. October 15, 1994.
Gann, James W. October 14, 1992.
Giesa, Donald G. October 14, 1994.
Hannigan, Thomas F. October 14, 1995.
Harrower, Eugene. October 16, 1992.
Heroy, Lewis J. October 15, 1994. By Lee Funken.
Holby, William G. October 15, 1994.
Hooper, William E. October 14, 1995. By Jon Helmick.
Jacobs, Perry. November 15, 1994.
Kaminski, Edwin C. October 20, 1990.
Kelahan, J. Richard. October 16, 1992.

Kersh, Jack R. October 15, 1994.

King, Thomas A. October 17, 1992.

Koury, George F. October 23, 1993.

Kraemer, George E. November 15, 1994.

Krause, Richard H., Jr. October 15, 1994.

Larrabee, Richard M. October 15, 1994.

Lion, Joseph H. October 26, 1996.

Lumbard, Eliot H. May 11, 1991, and October 13, 1995.

Marshall, George M. October 17, 1992. By Alfreda Dunham.

Milligan, Paul L., Jr. October 14, 1994.

Mitchell, William T. October 20, 1997.

Murray, Lee Roy, Jr. October 20, 1994.

O'Brien, Carroll J. October 13, 1994.

Ohanesian, Glenn. October 13, 1995.

Patterson, Thomas J. October 16 and 17, 1994.

Ponischil, Douglas F. October 17, 1992.

Renick, Charles M. December 5, 1990.

Risk, James L. October 17, 1992. By Lee Funken.

Scott, Edward Lewis, Jr. October 15, 1994.

Seiberlich, Carl J. March 26, 2002.

Slayton, Wendell D. October 20, 1990.

Smith, Stanley D. October 14, 1994.

Sweeney, John K. (Jack). October 16, 1994.

Tomeny, James F. October 13, 1995.

Torf, Phillip M. October 15, 1994.

Van der Linde, Peter. October 19, 1991.

Wagner, Douglas E. October 13, 1995.

Weir, Ralph J. October 13, 1995.

Wells, Robert B. October 19, 1991.

SHIP LOG BOOK

SS *George Dewey*. Bridge Log Book No. 2, Voyage No. 3, May 18, 1944–July 13, 1944. American Export Lines.

U.S. Government Documents

U.S. Merchant Marine Academy. *Superintendent's Notice 2007–06*. March 28, 2007. Kings Point, N.Y.: U.S. Merchant Marine Academy, March 28, 2007.

U.S. Naval History Division. *Dictionary of American Naval Fighting Ships*. 9 vols. Washington, D.C.: Government Printing Office, 1969.

U.S. War Shipping Administration. *United States Maritime Service, Information Booklet*. Washington, D.C.: War Shipping Administration, Training Organization, 1944.

———. Division of Training. *U.S. Merchant Marine Cadet Corps Circular No. 41–40*. Washington, D.C.: November 1, 1942.

Secondary Sources

Blair, Clay, Jr. *Silent Victory: The U.S. Submarine War against Japan.* Philadelphia: Lippincott, 1975.

Browning, Robert M., Jr. *U.S. Merchant Vessel War Casualties of World War II.* Annapolis, Md.: Naval Institute Press, 1996.

Bunker, John Gorley. *Heroes in Dungarees: The Story of the American Merchant Marine in World War II.* Annapolis, Md.: Naval Institute Press, 1995.

———. *Liberty Ships: The Ugly Ducklings of World War II.* Annapolis, Md.: Naval Institute Press, 1972.

Cahill, Richard A. *Collisions and Their Causes.* London: Fairplay, 1983.

———. *Disasters at Sea,* Titanic *to* Exxon Valdez. London: Century, 1990.

———. *Strandings and Their Causes.* London: Fairplay, 1985.

Carse, Robert. *A Cold Corner of Hell: The Story of the Murmansk Convoys, 1941–45.* Garden City, N.Y.: Doubleday, 1969.

———. *The Long Haul: The United States Merchant Service in World War II.* New York: Norton, 1965.

Conrad, Joseph. "The Mirror of the Sea." In *The Mirror of the Sea and a Personal Record.* Oxford, England, and New York: Oxford University Press, 1988.

Cooper, Sherod. *Liberty Ship: The Voyages of the* John W. Brown, *1942–1946.* Annapolis, Md.: Naval Institute Press, 1997.

Gibson, Andrew, and Arthur Donovan. *The Abandoned Ocean: A History of United States Maritime Policy.* Columbia: University of South Carolina Press, 2000.

Gleichauf, Justin F. *Unsung Heroes: The Naval Armed Guard in World War II.* Annapolis, Md.: Naval Institute Press, 1990.

Haskell, Winthrop A. *Shadows on the Horizon: The Battle of Convoy HX-233.* Annapolis, Md.: Naval Institute Press, 1998.

Herbert, Brian. *The Forgotten Heroes: The Heroic Story of the United States Merchant Marine.* New York: Tom Doherty Associates, 2004.

Irving, David John Caldwell. *The Destruction of Convoy PQ.17.* New York: Simon and Schuster, 1968.

Jaffee, Walter W. *The Lane Victory: The Last Victory Ship in War and in Peace.* Palo Alto, Calif.: Glencannon Press, 1997.

———. *The Last Liberty: The Biography of the S.S.* Jeremiah O'Brien. Palo Alto, Calif.: Glencannon Press, 1993.

———. *The Liberty Ships from A* (A. B. Hammond) *to Z* (Zona Gale). Palo Alto, Calif.: Glencannon Press, 2004.

Jane's Fighting Ships. Edited by Frank E. McMurtrie. New York: Macmillan, 1941–46.

Jordan, Roger W. *The World's Merchant Fleets, 1939: The Particulars and Wartime Fates of 6,000 Ships.* Annapolis, Md.: Naval Institute Press, 1999.

Kahn, David. *Seizing the Enigma: The Race to Break the German U-Boat Codes, 1939–1943.* Boston: Houghton Mifflin, 1991.

King, Thomas A. "The Merchant Marine Cadet Corps." In *To Die Gallantly: The Battle of the Atlantic,* edited by Timothy J. Runyan and Jan M. Copes, 273–81. Boulder, Colo.: Westview Press, 1994.

Kludas, Arnold. *Great Passenger Ships of the World*. 5 vols. Cambridge, England: Patrick Stephens, 1972–74.

Lane, Frederic C. *Ships for Victory: A History of Shipbuilding under the U.S. Maritime Commission in World War II*. Baltimore: Johns Hopkins University Press, 1951.

Lloyd's Register of Shipping. London: Lloyd's Register of Shipping, 1939–45.

McCready, Lauren S. *The Men and the Ships of the War Years, 1942–1945*. Kings Point, N.Y.: U.S. Merchant Marine Academy Alumni Association, 1993.

Merrill, Zed. *The Winter Winds of Hell: The Nightmare Run to Murmansk*. Videorecording. Portland, Ore.: Zed Merrill, 1997.

Mitchell, C. Bradford. *We'll Deliver: Early History of the United States Merchant Marine Academy, 1938–1956*. Kings Point, N.Y.: U.S. Merchant Marine Academy Alumni Association, 1977.

Moore, Arthur R. *"A Careless Word . . . a Needless Sinking": A History of the Staggering Losses Suffered by the U.S. Merchant Marine, Both in Ship and Personnel during World War II*. Kings Point, N.Y.: American Merchant Marine Museum, 1998.

Morison, Samuel Eliot. *Strategy and Compromise: A Reappraisal of the Crucial Decisions Confronting the Allies in the Hazardous Years, 1940–1945*. Boston: Atlantic Monthly Press, 1958.

Parillo, Mark P. *The Japanese Merchant Marine in World War II*. Annapolis, Md.: Naval Institute Press, 1993.

Reminick, Gerald. *Action in the South Atlantic: The Sinking of the German Raider* Stier *by the Liberty Ship* Stephen Hopkins. Palo Alto, Calif.: Glencannon Press, 2006.

Reynolds, Clark G. *Command of the Sea: The History and Strategy of Maritime Empires*. New York: William Morrow, 1974.

Ruegg, Bob, and Arnold Hague. *Convoys to Russia, 1941–1945: Allied Convoys and Naval Surface Operations in Arctic Waters 1941–1945*. Kendal, England: World Ship Society, 1992.

Sawyer, L. A., and W. H. Mitchell. *The Liberty Ships: The History of the "Emergency" Type Cargo Ships Constructed in the United States during the Second World War*. London: Lloyd's of London Press, 1985.

———. *Victory Ships and Tankers: The History of the "Victory" Type Cargo Ships and of the Tankers Built in the United States of America During World War II*. Cambridge, Md.: Cornell Maritime Press, 1974.

Spector, Ronald H. *At War at Sea: Sailors and Naval Combat in the Twentieth Century*. New York: Viking, 2001.

To Die Gallantly: The Battle of the Atlantic. Edited by Timothy J. Runyan and Jan M. Copes. Boulder, Colo.: Westview Press, 1994.

The U.S. Merchant Marine at War, 1775–1945. Edited by Bruce L. Felknor. Annapolis, Md.: Naval Institute Press, 1998.

U.S.S. Hornet Museum. "Splash Down 2004, July 16–25," www.uss-hornet.org/splash/bio-seiberlich.html.

Valle, James E. "United States Merchant Marine Casualties." In *To Die Gallantly: The Battle of the Atlantic*, edited by Timothy J. Runyan and Jan M. Copes, 259–72. Boulder, Colo.: Westview Press, 1994.

Willoughby, Malcolm. *The U.S. Coast Guard in World War II*. Annapolis, Md.: Naval Institute Press, 1957.

Index

George J. Billy is chief librarian at the United States Merchant Marine Academy. He has a Ph.D. in history and is keenly interested in World War II.

Christine M. Billy was assistant to the public information officer at the United States Merchant Marine Academy. She holds degrees from Yale University; University of Dublin, Trinity College; and Harvard Law School.

Maritime Heritage of the Cayman Islands, by Roger C. Smith (1999; first paperback edition, 2000)

The Three German Navies: Dissolution, Transition, and New Beginnings, 1945–1960, by Douglas C. Peifer (2002)

The Rescue of the Gale Runner: *Death, Heroism, and the U.S. Coast Guard*, by Dennis L. Noble (2002)

Brown Water Warfare: The U.S. Navy in Riverine Warfare and the Emergence of a Tactical Doctrine, 1775–1970, by R. Blake Dunnavent (2003)

Sea Power in the Medieval Mediterranean: The Catalan-Aragonese Fleet in the War of the Sicilian Vespers, by Lawrence V. Mott (2003)

An Admiral for America: Sir Peter Warren, Vice-Admiral of the Red, 1703–1752, by Julian Gwyn (2004)

Maritime History as World History, edited by Daniel Finamore (2004)

Counterpoint to Trafalgar: The Anglo-Russian Invasion of Naples, 1805–1806, by William Henry Flayhart III (first paperback edition, 2004)

Life and Death on the Greenland Patrol, 1942, by Thaddeus D. Novak, edited by P. J. Capelotti (2005)

X Marks the Spot: The Archaeology of Piracy, edited by Russell K. Skowronek and Charles R. Ewen (2006, first paperback edition 2007)

Industrializing American Shipbuilding: The Transformation of Ship Design and Construction, 1820–1920, by William H. Thiesen (2006)

Admiral Lord Keith and the Naval War Against Napoleon, by Kevin D. McCranie (2006)

Commodore John Rodgers: Paragon of the Early American Navy, by John H. Schroeder (2006)

Borderland Smuggling: Patriots, Loyalists, and Illicit Trade in the Northeast, 1783–1820, by Joshua M. Smith (2006)

Brutality on Trial: "Hellfire" Pedersen, "Fighting" Hansen, and The Seamen's Act of 1915, by E. Kay Gibson (2006)

Uriah Levy: Reformer of the Antebellum Navy, by Ira Dye (2006)

Crisis at Sea: The United States Navy in European Waters in World War I, by William N. Still Jr. (2006)

Chinese Junks on the Pacific: Views from a Different Deck, by Hans K. Van Tilburg (2007)

Eight Thousand Years of Maltese Maritime History: Trade, Piracy, and Naval Warfare in the Central Mediterranean, by Ayşe Devrim Atauz (2008)

Merchant Mariners at War: An Oral History of World War II, by George J. Billy and Christine M. Billy (2008)